Programmed Learning Aid for

BASIC PRINCIPLES OF THE SOCIAL SCIENCES

Programmed Learning Aid for

BASIC PRINCIPLES OF THE
SOCIAL SCIENCES

PAUL B. HORTON
Western Michigan University

ROBERT L. HORTON
Idaho State University

and

JOSEPH OLSON
KEITH FABIAN
GERALD SICARD
LARRY WINEBRENNER
All of Miami-Dade Community College

Programming Editor:
ROGER H. HERMANSON
Georgia State University

LEARNING SYSTEMS COMPANY

A division of
RICHARD D. IRWIN, INC. Homewood, Illinois   60430

Also available through
IRWIN-DORSEY INTERNATIONAL London, England   WC2H 9NJ
IRWIN-DORSEY LIMITED Georgetown, Ontario   L7G 4B3

ISBN 0-256-01474-4
Printed in the United States of America

1 2 3 4 5 6 7 8 9 0 K 3 2 1 0 9 8 7 6 5 4

FOREWORD

This text for the PLAID Social Science Series is in programmed learning format to provide the reader with a quick, efficient, and effective means of grasping the essential subject matter.

The specific benefits of the programmed method of presentation are as follows:

1. It keeps the reader *active* in the learning process and increases his comprehension level.
2. Incorrect responses are *corrected immediately*.
3. Correct responses are *reinforced immediately*.
4. The method is *flexible*. Those who need more "tutoring" receive it because they are encouraged to reread frames in which they have missed any of the questions asked.
5. The method makes learning seem like a game.

The method of programming used in this PLAID is unique and simple to use. The reader begins by reading Frame 1^1 in Chapter 1. At the end of that frame he will answer the True-False questions given. To determine the correctness of his responses he merely turns the page and examines the answers given in Answer Frame 1^1. He is told *why* each statement is true or false. He should use his performance on the questions given as a measure of his understanding of all the materials in Frame 1^1. If he misses any of the questions asked, he is encouraged to reread Frame 1^1 before continuing on to Frame 2^1. This same procedure should be used throughout the book. Specific instructions are given throughout as to where to turn next to continue working the program.

The reader may desire to go through the PLAID a second time, leaving out the programming questions and answers. Or he may desire to further test his understanding by going through it a second time, answering all of the questions once again and rereading only those frames in which his comprehension is unsatisfactory.

PAUL B. HORTON
Senior Editor

JOSEPH L. OLSON
Project Coordinator

ROGER H. HERMANSON
Programming Editor

PREFACE

This *Programmed Learning Aid for Basic Principles of the Social Sciences* contains the basic material that most general social science courses cover. It is an integrated approach to the social sciences and gives a general introduction to the entire field of social science. It should be useful to:

1. Students enrolled in a general social science course, as a self-study aid in helping them satisfactorily complete their course work.
2. Students taking a general social science course which uses a different text, as a self-study supplement in helping them do better work in their course.
3. Students who missed the introductory course, and are enrolled in an advanced course in the social sciences.
4. Graduate students who have never taken an undergraduate social science course and now wish to enroll in graduate social science courses.
5. Any others who wish a "capsule" summary of introductory social science.

As noted on the inside of both the front and back cover, this Programmed Learning Aid is a component of Learning Systems Company's Introduction to Social Science Package. Descriptions of each specific component are as follows:

1. *Basic Principles of the Social Sciences* (basic text): This *basic programmed text* is predicated on the assumption that a student of the social sciences must master specific seminal concepts in order to intelligently analyze contemporary social problems.
2. *Selected Readings in the Social Sciences:* The purpose of this book of readings is predicated on the need for the student to recognize:
    a. All social issues are subject to multiple interpretations.
    b. All social issues are complex and do not avail themselves to simple solutions.
    c. All social issues are subject to rational analysis on the basis of selected behavioral principles drawn from disciplines comprising the social sciences.

    The book of readings *Selected Readings in the Social Sciences,* through the presentation of conflicting points of view, should encourage the student to examine his own philosophic stance.
3. *Problems Modules* (programmed):
    a. *Basic Facts on Drug Abuse.*
    b. *Basic Facts on Technology: Its Impact on Social and Cultural Change.*
    c. *Basic Facts on Ecology and the Social Sciences.*
    d. *Basic Facts on Poverty: As a Social Problem in America.*
    e. *Basic Facts on the Generation Gap.*
        (In preparation)
    f. *Basic Facts on the Energy Crisis.*
    g. *Basic Facts on the Relationship of the Individual to the State (Civil Rights).*
        Other subject area modules are to come.

4. In summary, the *basic text* provides the student with the basic tools of analysis. The *modules* provide him with the essential background material. The *book of readings* completes the learning package by providing the student with conflicting opinions.

This PLAID may be used as a basic textbook, but it also may be used as a supplement to aid the student's understanding through systematic, programmed self-study. In some courses where the instructor assigns no basic text, using instead a syllabus of reading or a series of paperbacks, this PLAID will provide a minimum framework of principles and concepts.

The unique feature of this PLAID is its programmed sequence, explained more fully in the Editor's Foreword. We offer a few suggestions to the student when it is used with a different text:

1. Since no two textbooks follow the same chapter sequence, you should first check the Contents and select those topics in the PLAID that parallel the assigned chapter in your textbook.
2. Carefully answer the questions at the end of each frame. Then check your answers and restudy that frame if you had any of them wrong.
3. Check the meaning of any unfamiliar concepts in the Glossary—Index before reading any further.
4. Do not be frustrated if the definition of a term differs somewhat from the one in other textbooks.

Very often the same idea will have been put in different words. But since there is no complete standardization of definitions in the social sciences, it is also possible that two definitions may actually differ in meaning. If you are ever confused, ask your instructor for an explanation.

This PLAID was thoroughly tested in prepublication format. We hope you will find the PLAID as helpful as did the students who tested its effectiveness for us.

PAUL B. HORTON
ROBERT L. HORTON
JOSEPH L. OLSON
KEITH FABIAN
GERALD SICARD
L. M. WINEBRENNER

CONTENTS

Section IV. SOCIAL CONCERNS

chapter 1

PRESCIENTIFIC ORIGINS

Frame 1[1]

The most important things in our lives are our ties with other people. Our relationships to others and our interaction within groups are what make our lives meaningful. So important are these relationships and interactions that they have been made the subject of intensive study. This study is the focus of the social sciences. The specific areas of study in which man seeks to discover more about his relationships in order to understand his behavior are called the *disciplines* of social science. Generally included among the social science disciplines are sociology, psychology, anthropology, economics, political science, and cultural geography. History (although often classified among the humanities) is sometimes added to the list.

Anyone who tries to trace the origins of the scientific study of man's social relationships finds his inquiry delving farther and farther into the past. Clearly, foundations were laid for today's social sciences in the 17th, 18th, and 19th centuries, and the early years of the 20th, by such pioneers, among others, as Adam Smith in economics, Auguste Comte in sociology, Sigmund Freud in psychology, and Sir Edward Burnett Tylor in anthropology. But Comte, Freud, and the others did not arrive full-blown on the scene. Like Newton, each would have to admit, "If I have seen further . . . it is by standing upon the shoulders of giants."

Social thinkers in the period of the Industrial Revolution in Europe drew heavily upon those of the Middle Ages—notably the great theologian and philosopher Saint Thomas Aquinas in 13th-century Europe and the Arab historian Ibn Khaldoun in the 14th-century Moslem world. The sages of the Middle Ages, in turn, drew upon thinkers of the classical Greek and Roman era—Plato, Herodotus, and others. These thinkers, in turn, were indebted to the Egyptian, Babylonian, Hebrew, and other ancient civilizations.

In spite of the difficulty of tracing origins, some landmarks stand out along the way. It is evident from the most ancient writings that man has from the very earliest times attempted to come to some understanding of his group life and to control it. No doubt, as the first wandering family groups began to settle down to a more permanent homesite and practice agriculture, they also began to ponder the difficulty of getting along with several different families living in the same area. There may have been no question as to how a man was to treat his own sister, but how should he treat his neighbor's sister? There may have been little question as to his responsibility to his own family member who became ill, but how did he treat a sick neighbor? So, while it is likely that the earliest control of human behavior was familial, it became necessary for settled groups to turn to a different, wider authority for controls.

Indicate whether each of the following statements is true or false by writing "T" or "F" in the space provided.

_____ 1. There is general agreement that history is not a social science.

_____ 2. The social sciences began in the middle of the 19th century.

_____ 3. The attempt to understand and control group life is a recent phenomenon.

_____ 4. The social sciences probably have their origins in the attempts to solve intergroup problems.

Now turn to Answer frame 1[1] on page 4 to check your responses.

Frame 2[1]

Religious and Political Roots

Indications are that these earliest attempts at control and understanding were in the religious and political fields. In many cases the political organization was set up around the religious authority. More than 1,900 years before the birth of Christ, the *Code of Hammurabi* (also spelled *Hammurapi*) was graven on rock in Babylonia. It was laced with religious references and proscriptions. This ancient code was so extensive and covered human behavior so completely that its impact has been felt on practically every civilization of the Middle Eastern and Western worlds ever since, including the *Mosaic Code* found in the Old Testament.

Further east, in India, probably between 200 B.C. and A.D. 200, the same kind of religio-political unity was evidenced in the *Laws of Manu*. The Hindu caste system, growing out of this compilation of laws from even more ancient sources, has exercised a great deal of control over millions of people in India for a period of more than 2,000 years.

Foundations from Philosophy and History

In addition to the religious and political sources of understanding and control, other areas of intellectual development contributed to the origins of social science. Its earliest points of view, for example, were taken from philosophy, and much of its initial material was provided by the historians. This is not to say that the early philosophers, such as the Greeks, ever achieved a social science. There is no question that Plato

felt that he had found much of the answer to the question of how to understand and control society and had embodied it in *The Republic*. But when he tried to apply these principles under Dionysius II at Syracuse, the results were less than satisfactory.

The Greek philosophers did, however, lay the foundations for Western rationalism, a basic factor in the development of science in the Western world. And they did influence later thinkers, such as Francis Bacon and Auguste Comte, who had a great deal to do with the development of social science. The philosophers, from the Greeks through those of the Age of Reason (to be discussed later), prepared the ground and tilled the soil in which the seeds of social science were eventually planted.

In the same way that philosophy provided the point of view, history provided the materials. It is very hard to break away from "common-sense" explanations of why men act the way they do. Some things seem "right" and "natural," as if endowed with these qualities by some divine power. Historians as far back as Herodotus in the fifth century, B.C., and even earlier, began to discover that different people considered different behavior "natural." In *History of the Persian Wars* (1.140) Herodotus, as a Greek observer, says this about the Persians:

This much can I declare of the Persians with entire certainty, from my own actual knowledge. There is another custom which is spoken of with reserve, and not openly, concerning their dead. It is said that the body of a male Persian is never buried, until it has been torn either by a dog or a bird of prey. . . .

The Magi are a very peculiar race, differing entirely from the Egyptian priests, and indeed from all other men whatsoever. The Egyptian priests make it a point of religion not to kill any live animals except those which they offer in sacrifice. The Magi, on the contrary, kill animals of all kinds with their own hands, excepting dogs and men. They even seem to take a delight in the employment, and kill as readily as they do other animals, ants and snakes, and such like flying or creeping things. However, since this has always been their custom, let them keep to it.

We see here not only that he recognizes different kinds of behavior among different peoples but also (1) that he tells others about this difference in his writing of history, and (2) he makes comparisons which indicate what behavior he considers more "natural." This enables readers from different times and countries to also make comparisons with their own "human nature." Such writings, not only by Herodotus but by other historians became the materials for the first faltering steps of social science.

Label each of the following statements as true or false.

_____ 1. The oldest attempt at codification of human behavior was the *Mosaic Law.*

_____ 2. Western rationalism was a basic factor in the development of social science.

_____ 3. Early historians helped Western man break away from his narrow provincialism.

_____ 4. History provided a point of view for social science, but philosophy provided the materials.

Now turn to Answer frame 2[1] on page 4 to check your answers.

Frame 3[1]

Attempts at Social Theory

These philosophical and historical roots were not formulated into a coherent social science at an earlier date, however, for a very good reason. In order to have a tenable theory, you have to have some method of testing your conclusions, and the lack of a verifiable method became a barrier to the development of an acceptable social theory.

Probably the best-known attempt at putting social theory into practice was the one made by Plato at Syracuse, mentioned earlier in the chapter. Dionysius II became ruler of Syracuse under the regency of his uncle, Dion, upon the death of his father, Dionysius I in 367 B.C. The second Dionysius was really unprepared for the task of ruling and he thought it fortunate that his regent, Dion, was a friend and pupil of the famous teacher-philosopher, Plato. Uncle Dion had studied for many years at Plato's Academy, where many political leaders had studied the art of government. Dion, in turn, invited Plato to

come to Syracuse as the royal tutor, and Plato accepted. He began to put into practice his theories for the ideal state, but the project was unpopular with others in the ruler's court and eventually it backfired. In the end, Plato was dismissed, Dion banished, and Dionysius driven out. Thus, Plato's dream of a government ruled by a philosopher-king was shattered.

Another early attempt to develop a systematic theory of how society works was made by the Arab philosopher and historian, Ibn Khaldoun (1332–1406). Probably his most basic contribution was the assertion that society worked as a result of natural laws which could be discovered if a person searched and observed diligently enough. These natural laws described *how* society worked, he claimed, not *why* it should work in a particular way. And they were not laws that imposed patterns, but laws that could be descriptive if patterns were carefully observed. He promoted and practiced the idea of searching history in particular to discover uniform patterns in society. He believed that human affairs

Answer frame 1[1]

1. False. Some consider that the social sciences are composed only of psychology, sociology, anthropology, economics, and political science, but others include history as one of the social sciences.
2. False. Although Auguste Comte is the "father of sociology," the study of human behavior goes back at least as far as Plato.
3. False. It is evident from our most ancient writings that man has from the very earliest times attempted to come to some understanding of his group life and to control it.
4. True. While it is likely that the earliest control of human behavior was familial, the larger the settlement, the more it became necessary to turn to other authorities for controls.

An attempt has been made in each frame to test the reader on the most important concepts within that frame. It is unlikely that this has been accomplished in every instance. Therefore, you should use your performance on the questions asked at the end of each frame as an indication of your comprehension of *all* of the concepts in that frame. If you missed *any* of the above questions you should go back and reread Frame 1[1] before turning to Frame 2[1] on page 2. You should use this same procedure throughout the PLAID.

Answer frame 2[1]

1. False. The *Code of Hammurabi* predated the Mosaic and other codes.
2. True. Philosophers from the Greeks through the Age of Reason laid the foundations for social science.
3. True. The early historians from Herodotus on discovered that different people considered different behavior "natural."
4. False. In the same way that philosophy provided the point of view, history provided the materials. It was very hard to break away from "commonsense" explanations.

If you missed any of the above, you should reread Frame 2[1] before turning to Frame 3[1] on page 3.

Frame 3[1] continued

could eventually be understood in terms of natural laws that could be found by studying these uniformities. This emphasis set the stage for the social philosophers of the Age of Reason to develop their ideas.

Beginnings of Scientific Study in the Age of Reason

The scientific study of the natural order based on reason, experimentation, and careful direct observation was the great contribution of the social philosophers in the Age of Reason. Thinkers built a new approach on the model for scientific study presented by the Italian astronomer and physicist Galileo Galilei (1564–1642); the theoretical knowledge of calculus and physics developed by Sir Isaac Newton (1642–1727); the systematic analysis of knowledge provided by Francis Bacon (1561–1626); and the contributions of René Descartes (1596–1650) to mathematics and to the modernization of philosophy by freeing it from the bonds of the scholastics. In doing so, these men proceeded to popularize the scientific attitude until it became a common way of thinking. Francis Bacon, himself, was extremely effective in pursuing this way of thinking. Political and social philosophers of the era tried to use a rational approach to explain human conduct as a result of natural laws. Thomas Hobbes (1588–1679) developed a social contract theory in his *Leviathan*. John Locke (1632–1704) like Descartes turned away from the scholastics toward experimental science and laid the foundation of modern empiricism. In his *Émile,* Jean Jacques Rousseau (1712–78) pointed the way toward modern elementary educational methods, and in *Le Contrat Social* explored the principles upon which political authority rests. The rational emphasis of all these thinkers provided the groundwork for the scientific approach to the study of society developed initially in the 19th century.

True or false?

_____ 1. A method of verification is important for the social sciences.

_____ 2. Ibn Khaldoun believed that the natural laws of society were observable.

_____ 3. The scientific study of the natural order was the great contribution of the social philosophers of the Age of Reason.

_____ 4. Philosophers in the Age of Reason popularized the scientific attitude as a way of thinking.

Now turn to Answer frame 3[1] on page 6 to check your answers.

Answer frame 3[1]

1. True.   In order to have a tenable theory you have to have some method of testing your conclusions.
2. True. He believed that society worked as a result of natural laws which could be discovered if a person observed diligently enough.
3. True. Building on the work of Galileo, Newton, Bacon, and Descartes, thinkers like Hobbes, Locke, and Rousseau tried to explain human conduct as a result of natural laws.
4. True. Francis Bacon, for example, was extremely effective in moving from natural science to social science.

If you missed any of the above, you should restudy Frame 3[1] before beginning Chapter 2 below.

chapter 2

FOCUS OF THE SOCIAL SCIENCES

Frame 1[2]

Social science shares with other sciences the basic assumption that regularity—order—exists in nature and that this order can be discovered, described, and understood. We shall explore this point further in Chapter 4. In Chapter 1, we noted that the social sciences are traditionally listed as including sociology, psychology, anthropology, economics, political science, cultural geography, and sometimes history. But it is important to keep in mind that any and all forms of study that deal with man and his social behavior come within the scope of social science. In this chapter, we shall be emphasizing the main disciplines but will also have something to say about the extensions of social science in other branches of study. The interrelationships of the disciplines will also be discussed, as will the practical applications of the social sciences.

The Disciplines Invade
One Another's Boundaries

The borders of the social science disciplines are open. In pursuit of a particular interest, a researcher in one of the social sciences will give little regard to invading another's area of study. It is impossible, and would not be sensible, to keep the disciplines entirely separated. A study of the community, for example, will bring together anthropologists, social psychologists, sociologists, and political scientists. The economists' study of consumer behavior or marketing draws freely from insights provided by psychologists, anthropologists, and sociologists.

The interrelationships of psychology, anthropology, and sociology are so intensive and their common interest in exploring social behavior so great that they have been joined in what is termed *behavioral science.*

Social science draws within its orbit parts of philology (linguistics), sections of biology (human ecology), and ethics, philosophy, and education insofar as these branches of learning deal with social behavior. As mentioned in Chapter 1, history can be viewed as one of the humanities or as a part of social science.

Invasion of other disciplines by the social science disciplines necessarily includes borrowing from the natural and physical sciences because the life of society takes place in a biological and physical context. Man is a biological entity, and he exists in a physical world, subject to its natural cycles and laws. His tendency to forget this accounts for some of the most troublesome of his present environmental and social problems—air and water pollution, overpopulation, and violence.

This brings us to the science of geography, which overlaps with social science in human or cultural geography. This branch of geography functions to explain how man's physical setting influences his social behavior. Historically, man has concentrated on mastering nature through science and technology. It is ironic that his technological success is rapidly destroying his habitat. Pollution and the population explosion have forced him to rediscover the physical world and to develop a new discipline—environmental science.

Practical Application of the Social Sciences

It might be useful to note that application of the social sciences does take practical forms, leading to separate professions, as in the physical sciences. Social workers bring the social sciences, especially sociology, to bear on the problems of maladjusted people and families to help them find a place in the community, while at the same time alerting society to their needs. Psy-

chology is practically applied by the psychiatrist and clinical psychologist and by doctors versed in psychosomatic medical practice. The Freudian psychologist practices psychoanalysis, and the post-Freudians have broadened the role of psychoanalysis to include contributions to child rearing and education.

The findings of the social sciences permeate many fields of practical endeavor. It is inconceivable that one could train a teacher without knowledge of learning theory and its applications, that is, psychology. Businessmen profit from an understanding of what economics has revealed about the operation of the economic, marketing, and monetary systems as a whole and of the individual firm in particular. And the behavioral sciences have, as mentioned, contributed to the businessman's understanding of the consumer.

The social sciences provide a framework for our attempts to achieve a safe and an orderly society through law, jurisprudence, and criminology.

The Central Disciplines

Having indicated and emphasized how fuzzy are the boundaries between the social sciences—and indeed between social and other forms of science—we will now focus more closely on the scope of the central disciplines—psychology, sociology, economics, political science, and anthropology, with an added note on history. In Chapter 4, the historical background and the emergence of these disciplines in modern thought will be discussed in detail, but here we will be examining their scope and what differentiates them from one another.

Psychology. Defined traditionally as the science of mind or of the mental processes, psychology today also concerns itself with the way the living organism adjusts to its total environment. Psychology's goal is to explain how man's body, including his brain and his nervous system, affects his social behavior; it shows how his social life stems from his psychological processes. In studying such processes as cognition, emotion, perception, and learning, psychologists focus on personality and emphasize the uniqueness of the individual. They explore the nature of personality, study intelligence, effects of the emotions on behavior, and such aspects as motivation, drives, and attitudes. When it investigates the physical nature of the brain and nervous system, psychology merges into biology.

Psychology and sociology have shared so many aspects of analysis and application that a discipline labeled *social psychology* has emerged. This discipline attempts to show how individuals relate to one another and to the group, as well as how groups interact. Obviously, both psychology and sociology are involved in accomplishing this. (And one should note that social psychology also draws on economics and anthropology.)

An interesting example of how conformity to the group (a sociological concept) and perception (a psychological process) are related is provided by experiments reported by Solomon Asch in his book *Social Psychology*. To help answer the question, "To what extent is the indi-

vidual's judgment distorted by the influence of others' incorrect judgments?" Asch resorted to a hoax. He instructed members of a group to judge which of three lines on one card was the same length as a line on a second card used as a standard of comparison. One member of the group remained in the dark about the hoax, while the rest were instructed to make obviously wrong judgments. Thus, the uninstructed group member was caught in a conflict between what he saw and the unanimous answers of the others. In the majority of instances, as the experiment was repeated, the individual would go along with the group, even though his senses told him otherwise. This shows how a psychic process (perception) can be influenced by a social situation (minority status), producing perceptual distortion.

What, then, mainly differentiates psychology from sociology? We shall try to answer this question in the next section.

Indicate whether each of the following statements is true or false by writing "T" or "F" in the space provided.

_____ 1. A basic assumption of the social sciences is that human behavior is predictable.

_____ 2. Unlike the physical sciences, the social sciences have no related applied fields.

_____ 3. The borders of the social sciences are rigorously and precisely defined.

_____ 4. Conformity to group pressure can produce perceptual distortion.

Now turn to Answer frame 1[2] on page 10 to check your responses.

Frame 2[2]

Sociology. Sociology is commonly defined as the scientific study of society.

Sociology as a science studies human interaction—that is relations among humans—through controlled observation and interpretation of the patterns observed. If psychology is the science of the individual, then sociology is concerned with the regularized relations among people. An example of the difference between sociology and psychology lies in watching a baseball game. With no batters out or on base, the lead-off man hits a grounder to third base. A knowledge of sociology—more particularly the

role of third baseman—allows us to predict that over 90 times out of 100 he will throw the ball toward the first baseman. (Maybe this is why it is called the "science of the obvious.") However, if we were to explain how Brooks Robinson performs this act better than others, a knowledge of psychology, involving analysis of his unique perceptual skills and motivation, is necessary. Sociology, in studying the interaction of individuals, tends, then, to focus on the collectivity or group, whereas psychology focuses on the individual.

Economics. Mainly concerned with the production, distribution, and consumption of scarce goods and services, economics also develops theories, and studies how to make the economic system more effectively serve the goals of society (economic policy). Reality tells us that this is related to man's group life (sociology), his psychological drives, and his geographical location. However, the variables traditionally studied in economics—price, demand and supply, input-output ratios, money flows, supply of labor, and so on—have kept the analysis very specialized. Economics shares a concern for systems analysis and mathematical models with sociology.

Political Science. While the unit of analysis in economics may be said to be the *exchange value* of a good or service, the unit which political science deals with is *power*. It concerns itself with the ways in which a society allocates the right to use legitimate power—power being expressed usually as the probability that *A* can get *B* to do something. In other words, power is the extent to which a person or group can control the behavior of another person or group, along with the possession of the means to enforce this control. Legitimate power is that which is approved by the society. Political science analyzes ideas concerning authority and attempts to analyze the actual distribution of public power and the institutions through which it is exercised. Sociology intersects with political science in its analysis of the distribution of power, not only in the public sphere, but in other areas such as small groups, families, and large-scale organizations in general.

C. Wright Mills' book, *The Power Elite*, illustrates the convergence of public and private power structures and their influence on U.S. foreign affairs. In the profitable business of developing weaponry, his term "the Military-Industrial Complex" has become part of the concern today not only of the New Left but of the "populists" in politics as well. Political science in its applied form has led to specialized degree programs in foreign service, city management, and other areas. Ironically the political process is manipulated primarily by attorneys, who usually have a limited background in political science but a great deal of practical political experience.

By way of summary, then, political science is

the specialized study of power and influence as expressed in "government." It has two main interests: political theory and governmental administration. Recently it has become more concerned with political behavior and as such has intersected with sociology in the use of opinion polls to determine probable voting outcomes and in studies of how bureaucracies affect the political process.

Anthropology. A unifying science, anthropology may be defined as the all-embracing study of man and society. It incorporates archaeology, the study of prehistoric and extinct cultures; ethnology, the comparative analysis of the various cultures; physical anthropology, which focuses on man's bodily and physiological attributes, deals with problems of human evolution, and studies race and body build; linguistics, the comparative study of languages; and social or cultural anthropology. The latter is very close to sociology, the main difference being that traditionally anthropologists have studied preliterate and preindustrial societies while sociologists have focused on contemporary, complex, industrialized ones. However, the gap has been narrowing, and these two social sciences are the closest of those reviewed in this PLAID. There is even today an applied branch of anthropology, extending anthropological techniques to administration, industrial relations, and minority-group problems.

In studying the cultures of preliterate and preindustrial peoples, the anthropologist selects a particular culture and tries to learn everything he can about it. If the culture is a surviving one, he collects his observations by living with the group, applying a method called *participant observation*. Thus, the anthropologist—or in this case, the ethnographer—surveying an African tribe, studies its language, economic system, sexual and marital practices, kinship system, religion, child rearing, and daily routines. He views the society as a whole and compares it with other cultures.

The terms *preliterate* and *preindustrial* are used advisedly by modern anthropologists to avoid any label such as *primitive* which might indicate an attitude that the culture involved is inferior to their own, thereby justifying its exploitation. Such a biased attitude is called *ethno-*

Answer frame 1²

1. True. The basic assumption, shared with the other sciences, is that there is a regularity in nature and that this regularity can be described and understood.
2. False. The application of the social sciences takes practical forms and often leads to separate professions, for example, clinical psychology and social work.
3. False. In pursuit of a particular interest a researcher often gives little regard to invading the area of another discipline.
4. True. The fact that the uninformed subject tends to conform to the group illustrates how perception can be influenced by a social situation.

If you missed any of the above, you should restudy Frame 1² before turning to Frame 2² on page 8.

Frame 2² continued

centrism, the conviction that one's own culture is automatically the best and that all others are barbarous and in some way inferior.

History.   History is the record, as interpreted by scholars, of man's past. Because of the wide range that historical interpretation can encompass, some universities list it as one of the humanities. However, in establishing the sequence of events—that is, the arrangement of man's behavior in time and place—history is basic to all social science. Without history, social scientists are hard put to explain change and continuity, be it in the areas of intellectual thought, political process, economics, or family relations.

Therefore, it is important to consider the social sciences as a group: psychology, history, anthropology, geography, economics, and political science. Social science, then, is a label to categorize them collectively. They relate to one another, but more often differ in theoretical premises, analytical focuses, and methods employed.

Label each of the following statements as true or false.

_____ 1. Psychologists are interested in individual behavior, whereas sociologists are interested in interaction.

_____ 2. Political science is concerned with the distribution of legitimate power.

_____ 3. The recent concern of political scientists with political behavior blurs the distinction between political science and sociology.

_____ 4. Most anthropologists use sophisticated ethnocentric research techniques.

Now turn to Answer frame 2² on page 12 to check your answers.

chapter 3

EMERGENCE OF MODERN SOCIAL SCIENCE

Frame 1[3]

Knowing the historical roots of social science does help a person to understand where social science is today: why it deals with some aspects of life in a particular way and why it seems to ignore, or "play down" some other aspects of life. The social scientists' attempt to be "scientific" explains, for example, why they shy away from nonscientific or pseudoscientific studies such as astrology and why there is reluctance to do original research in hitherto scientifically questionable areas such as parapsychology. An examination of historical roots gives some insight into why social scientists strive to be considered scientific.

Social Science Disciplines Are Integrated

There are limitations, however, as to how much historical background can be included in an introductory text. In this text we shall limit ourselves to the first chapter, which dealt with nonscientific roots, and this chapter, which will deal specifically with some of the pioneers in social science.

As mentioned in Chapter 1, many discussions of early social scientists begin with Auguste Comte because of his pioneering work in establishing a scientific approach in the field of sociology, and perhaps because sociology claimed in the early 19th century to embrace all of social science.

There is a real sense in which you can say that each of the disciplines embraces all of so-

cial science. We noted in Chapter 2 that the social science disciplines overlap—merge into one another. People's lives are not divided into distinct little compartments so that at one moment a man says, "I am making a political decision. This has nothing to do with my family life, or my economic life, or my religious life, or any of my other discrete lives." No, our lives are all of a piece, and to that extent economics cannot exclude sociology and anthropology and political science, nor can sociology exclude the others, nor can any discipline exclude all the disciplines. Each discipline, however, does focus on one aspect of our lives. To that extent we might examine the pioneers of particular disciplines, but we do so with the recognition that social science is all one piece of cloth woven from the various threads of life that make up the disciplines. Thus, let us talk about persons rather than disciplines, for the pioneers contributed to all the disciplines, even when they focused on just one.

Pioneers in Economics

Some comment on economic life can be found as far back as in the writings of Plato and Aristotle and even earlier. However, not until the 18th century was economics really identified as a separate field of research and study. In 1776, the Scottish philosopher Adam Smith laid the foundations for a science of "political economy" in his book *An Inquiry into the Nature and*

Answer frame 2² ———————————————————————————

1. True. If psychology is the science of the individual, then sociology is concerned with the regularized relation between or among people.
2. True. It is concerned with the ways in which a society allocates the power to legitimately control the behavior of another person or group.
3. True. Political sociology and sociology of politics are virtually indistinguishable. Both use sample survey research techniques to study political behavior.
4. False. Anthropologists try to avoid ethnocentrism by maintaining that no culture should be evaluated by the values of some other culture.

If you missed any of the above, you should reread Frame 2² before beginning Chapter 3 on page 11.

Frame 1³ continued

Causes of the Wealth of Nations. This classical work exerted a profound influence on all subsequent thinking in politics and economics. Smith sought to reveal in economic life principles of order comparable to the principles Newton and other thinkers of the Age of Reason had found in the natural universe a century earlier.

Some of the giants who followed after Adam Smith and refined and further developed the study of economics were David Ricardo (1722–1834), Thomas Malthus (1766–1834), John Stuart Mill (1806–73), and Karl Marx (1818–83).

Ricardo decided to become an economist after reading *The Wealth of Nations.* He is regarded as the founder of the classical school of economics. In his *Principles of Political Economy and Taxation* (1817), he developed a theory of rent, profits, and wages and made the classical statement of the quantity theory of money.

In his *Essay on the Principle of Population* (1798), Thomas Malthus demonstrated how population tended to increase in geometric ratio while the means of subsistence lagged far behind in arithmetic ratio, thus dooming the bulk of mankind to life at the subsistence level. This gloomy prognosis—later modified by advances Malthus could not have foreseen—caused economics to be dubbed "the dismal science." Today's concern with the so-called population explosion has revived interest in Malthus' ideas. We shall explore them further in Chapter 20.

The influence of John Stuart Mill has been strong not only in economics but also in politics and philosophy. He developed a system of logic, wrote on ethics, and advocated political and social reforms verging on socialism. In his *Principles of Political Economy* (1848), he made an important contribution to classical economics, though it was not quite the complete and final exposition of economic theory that he thought it to be. It is interesting to note that Mills did point out, however, that there is no objective law of distribution that applies to every society but that, rather, each society has its own laws and customs that determine distribution of goods in each society.

Nourished at first on the ideas of the Utopian Socialists in the period of the Industrial Revolution in Western Europe, Karl Marx became the chief theorist of modern socialism. His influence has shaped the political and economic institutions of a large part of the human race. We shall have more to say about him at a later point in the book. But here we should note that Marx is regarded by many not only as a political influence but as a great contributor to economic theory and history as well. In developing, with his life-long associate Friedrich Engels, a theory of "dialectical materialism," Marx charted the inevitable course of history as leading to the eventual breakdown of the capitalistic system and to the triumph of the "proletariat" or working class. His book *Das Kapital* (published in several volumes and translations from 1867 to 1909) has been the bible of international socialism.

Indicate whether each of the following statements is true or false.

_____ 1. An examination of the historical roots of social science helps us to understand contemporary social science.

_____ 2. Each of the pioneers in the social sciences contributed only to his own discipline.

_____ 3. The *Origin of Species* was the classical statement of economics.

_____ 4. According to J. S. Mill, there is no universal law of distribution.

Now turn to Answer frame 1³ on page 14 to check your responses.

Frame 2³

Alexis De Tocqueville

Political science is one of the oldest of the social sciences, going back to Aristotle and to Plato's *Republic* and following a long course through the contributions to theory of such thinkers as Thomas Aquinas, Machiavelli, Locke, Hobbes, Hegel, and Rousseau, down to Karl Marx and the contemporary theorists of government. In addition, Alexis de Tocqueville (1805–59) may be singled out as of special interest because he presented a picture of the political situation in America within the social context which gave rise to political phenomena. His *Democracy in America* was a classic contribution to social history. Along with other writings it demonstrated the value of an empirical examination of the social and political factors in a country.

Auguste Comte and Herbert Spencer

Two giants stand out in the scientific development of sociology; indeed, their presence is felt across the spectrum of disciplines in social science. These two men are Auguste Comte (1798–1857) and Herbert Spencer (1820–1903). Comte is often called "the father of sociology" because of the way in which he systematized the study of society. He took his point of view from philosophy and his subject matter largely from history. He wed them in what he at first called a philosophy of positivism, later named "sociology." Comte did not divide the study into subsciences; rather he looked upon society as an organic whole and upon the study of society as a single discipline.

Herbert Spencer built upon the work of Comte. He followed the objective and systematic approach of Comte, but he recognized that while society is an organic whole, even the whole is composed of parts—institutions, for example. His work with particular social subsystems and institutions, and his speculation about the evolutionary nature of society sometimes causes him to be considered a pioneer in the field of biology as well as sociology. He became identified as the philosopher of evolution. He saw himself as a positive influence on the thought of Charles Darwin. Darwin agreed with him.

Others besides the two giants made significant contributions to the early development of the field of sociology. The French sociologist Émile Durkheim (1858–1917) was influenced by Comte's positivism but went beyond it to study the origins of religion and morality in group life and to draw heavily on anthropological materials. His classic study, *Suicide* (1897), marked an advance in the use of the scientific method in sociology. The German, Max Weber (1864–1920), developed a methodology for the social sciences, first formulated the concept of bureaucracy in the sociological sense, and in his *Protestant Ethic and the Spirit of Capitalism* (1920) directed attention to the connection between the puritanical tenets of Calvinism and the rise of the capitalistic system.

In America, William Graham Sumner (1840–1910) was a contributor both to economics and to sociology. In economics, he advocated laissez-faire and opposed any form of government interference with the operation of the economic system. As a sociologist, he focused on human customs—folkways and more—particularly in his classic study *Folkways*, published in 1907.

Answer frame 1³

1. True. For example, an examination of historical roots gives some insight into why social scientists strive to be considered scientific.
2. False. The pioneers contributed to all the disciplines, even when they focused on just one.
3. False. Adam Smith's *The Wealth of Nations* (1776) was the first statement of classical economics. The *Origin of Species* by Darwin was written nearly 100 years later and was concerned with evolution.
4. True. Mill held that each society has its own laws and customs that determine distribution of goods in that society.

If you missed any of the above, you should restudy Frame 1³ before turning to Frame 2³ on page 13.

Frame 2³ continued

Charles Darwin and E. B. Tylor

It was the work of Charles Darwin (1809–1882) that sparked widespread interest and reaction to the study of primitive man and, subsequently, existing preliterate groups. Darwin, influenced by Spencer and others, presented a consistent picture of biological evolution of man in his now famous *Origin of Species* (1859). It is interesting to note that Darwin's theory was worked out and lay dormant for 14 years until Alfred Wallace spurred him to publish his findings by sketching the same idea in an independent work. Thus, Darwin and Wallace shared the honor of developing the theory that later became attributed solely to Darwin.

As valuable as his contributions were, Darwin is not generally regarded as the founder of the discipline of anthropology. The man who generally holds that honor is Sir Edward Burnett Tylor (1832–1917). He began his work as an archaeologist trying to reconstruct the prehistory of Mexico. In 1861, he published a book about his work on this expedition; but he is best remembered for a book published ten years later entitled *Primitive Culture*. This classic in anthropology initiated the scientific study of culture. Tylor observed a kind of cultural relativity that was virtually unknown in his time. The great anthropologists who followed Tylor—Sir James Frazer, Franz Boas, Bronislaw Malinowski, Alfred Kroeber, and Ruth Benedict—were greatly influenced by the man, his method, and his work.

Label each of the following statements as true or false.

_____ 1. Political and social factors can be understood best in isolation from each other.

_____ 2. Herbert Spencer is known as the "father of sociology."

_____ 3. Comte wed philosophy (organicism) and the results of observation to produce the "positive" philosophy.

_____ 4. Charles Darwin is the person most responsible for the development of the discipline of anthropology.

Now turn to Answer frame 2³ on page 16 to check your answers.

Frame 3³

The Geographers

Just as E. B. Tylor began his career in anthropology by studying the prehistory of Mexico, Baron Alexander von Humboldt (1769–1859) also turned to Latin America to make observations based on expeditions to South America, Cuba, and Mexico. His conscious attempt to establish scientifically the bases for geography influenced Karl Ritter (1779–1859), who generally is considered the real founder of geography as a scientific study. Ritter demonstrated the influence of geography upon history. His scientific approach, however, was marred by his concept of Divine providence in the establishment of specific habitats for particular types of men. Friedrich Ratzel (1844–1904) tried to avoid this nonscientific avenue by theorizing that environment determines the conditions of culture. He showed the connection between geography, anthropology, and politics. While this was a more empirical and methodological approach, it did not satisfy many of the men who followed. Frederic Le Play (1806–82), for example, also attempted to establish a more empirical approach, but he did so by establishing the observational case-history method. The success of this method modified Ratzel's determinism, and cultural geography as a social science was initiated.

Pioneers in the Field of Psychology

Psychology—once thought of as the science or study of the mind—is today broadened to include concern with the interactions of the living organism and its environment, with behavior as well as mental processes. The origins of psychology go back at least to Aristotle, but modern psychology began with Hobbes, Spinosa, and Leibniz in the 17th century. Empirical psychology owes its beginnings to Locke, Berkeley, and Hume in England. In the 19th century, the experimental method, on the one hand, and the applications of the evolutionary principle giving rise to "dynamic psychology," on the other, became the main avenues of development of the discipline. The latter was represented by the American, William James (1842–1910), in his *Principles of Psychology* (1890) and the former by the German, Wilhelm Wundt (1832–1920). Wundt founded the first laboratory for experimental psychology, conducted experiments in controlled introspection, and reduced the content of consciousness to a quantity of items that could be listed specifically.

The early experimenters in psychology attempted to find their explanations of human behavior in a study of physiology of the individual, focusing on the brain and nerves. Laboratory experiments were modeled on those done in physics. This seemed to extend to the experimental laboratory method in psychology the prestige and scientific precision of the physical sciences, and it became widely accepted as the most scientific approach.

Another experimenter who observed physiological behavior in his study of behavior was a Russian animal biologist, Ivan Petrovich Pavlov (1849–1936). In a classical experiment with dogs, Pavlov developed the concept of conditioned responses as a factor in behavior. The experiment centered on the salivary glands, as Pavlov attempted to discover what stimuli would cause the glands of a dog to secrete saliva. The ringing of a bell did not cause salivation, but the presence of food did. Then, with brilliant insight, Pavlov decided to ring the bell and present the food at the same time. After several presentations of this sort, he then rang the bell without presenting the food. The dog salivated at the stimulus of the bell, and from this Pavlov proposed a mechanistic theory of human behavior which became the foundation for the entire field of psychology known as behaviorism.

Associated with behaviorism is the name of John B. Watson (1878–1958). Watson attempted to explain human behavior as solely the result of physiological activity of the nervous system —of physiological response to stimuli. He rejected any concept involving consciousness or unconscious mental activity. This view, too, had the virtue of fostering the development of laboratory techniques, and it became popular; but it did not remain dominant in psychology.

Answer frame 2³

1. False. De Tocqueville's *Democracy in America* demonstrated the value of an empirical examination of the social and political factors in a country.
2. False. Spencer built upon the work of Auguste Comte—the real "father of sociology."
3. True. He wed philosophy to the subject matter of history to produce what he called "sociology."
4. False. The one who holds that honor is Edward B. Tylor. His *Primitive Culture* initiated the scientific study of culture.

If you missed any of the above, you should reread Frame 2³ before turning to Frame 3³ on page 15.

Frame 3³ continued

Other methods of empirical study were developed, particularly clinical studies based on the analysis of actual cases. Sigmund Freud (1856–1939) opened an entirely new approach to the study of personality when he began to observe that the process of "talking through" a problem often was sufficient to alleviate the pain and fears that were associated with it. From this observation he went on to develop an entire approach to studying and understanding personality which is known as psychoanalysis. Freud delved into the unconscious, and his greatest contribution to psychology was the understanding he gave us about the unconscious. In addition, Freud popularized the field of psychology by his extensive writings, possibly having had greater influence in the field than any other person.

While the number of new names with which you were confronted in this chapter may seem like a great many, the fact is that they are all too few. There were many, many pioneers who made significant contributions to the development of social science, but not all could be recognized, for the field is too extensive. Nor could all the emphases of those who were mentioned be examined. Perhaps this discussion has shed a little light on the roots of social science from the past which give character to the field of social sciences today.

The next chapter will turn to the basic focus of the social sciences.

True or false?

_____ 1. Karl Ritter is considered the real founder of geography as a scientific study.

_____ 2. Frederic Le Play established the observational case-history method.

_____ 3. One of the "fathers" of modern psychology was an animal biologist.

_____ 4. The father of behaviorism is Sigmund Freud.

Now turn to Answer frame 3³ on page 18 to check your answers.

chapter 4

SOCIAL SCIENCE AND
THE SCIENTIFIC METHOD

Frame 1[4]

The goal of any science is to accumulate and systematize knowledge and to increase understanding of natural phenomena. Scientific inquiry is based on the assumption of regularities in nature. By revealing these regularities, science enables us to predict what will happen under certain circumstances and to some extent to control what happens. The great contributions science has made to human life have largely been made possible by the consistent use of the scientific method, guided by the scientific attitude or approach.

The Scientific Method

The scientific method advances through a series of steps. Let us examine them.

First, the Facts. The beginning step in any scientific inquiry is to gather data and examine experience through direct observation. All the facts and experience relevant to the problem are recorded. Science demands that the methods of collecting data be rigorous. To the extent that science relies on such observation of data and experience, rather than upon theory, it is said to be empirical.

Then the Hypothesis. Having assembled a set of facts, the scientist immediately begins to try to account for them, to look for cause and effect relationships, for regularities that can form the basis for prediction. Through inductive reasoning he forms hypotheses, tentative generaliza- tions, which, though speculative and unverified, can form the basis for further investigation and research.

Then the Testing and Verification. Now further observation and repeated experiment are brought to bear on the hypothesis to test its validity. It may fall by the wayside, or it may become established as a scientific law or theory. A law is a relatively low-level generalization, a verified regularity in the facts observed. A theory is a broader generalization stating regularities extracted from a number of laws.

Laws and Theories Must Stand the Test of Time. From a strictly scientific point of view, as new facts are discovered that contradict or cast doubt on laws and theories, these laws and theories must be modified to accommodate the new facts or be discarded.

The Scientific Attitude

To be scientific is to act in a scientific way. This means to devise and use rigorous methods for gathering the facts and to use logical reasoning in drawing conclusions from them. Above all, science demands an unbiased and objective approach. Closely related to objectivity is the attitude that science should be value-free.

Especially important to the scientific approach is its emphasis on controlled observation and experiment and a strict regard for accuracy.

Answer frame 3[3]

1. True. His approach was marred, unfortunately, by his concept of Divine providence in the establishment of specific habitats for particular types of men.
2. True. His intention was to establish a more empirical method for geography. Le Play is considered by many to be an early sociologist.
3. True. Ivan Pavlov was able to condition a dog to salivate at the ringing of a bell. His real interest was in discovering the controlling stimuli of salivary glands.
4. False. Pavlov and Watson are the "fathers" of behaviorism. Freud developed an alternative approach known as the psychoanalytic theory of personality.

If you missed any of the above, you should restudy Frame 3[3] before beginning Chapter 4 on page 17.

Frame 1[4] continued

The Social Sciences as Science

To the extent that the social sciences share in the scientific method and the scientific attitude as described in the foregoing paragraphs, they may logically be included among the sciences. They do so participate. Like other sciences, social science attempts to discover regularities in phenomena—in this case, social phenomena. Social scientists collect data through direct observation, set up hypotheses, test them for validity, and establish laws and theories. Social science, too, relies on controlled observation, and to the extent possible when dealing with human beings, controlled experiment.

Social science values objectivity. It, too, holds that insofar as it is to be scientific, it must remain value-free. In social science, the behaviors observed are not judged to be "good" or "bad." Such judgments are reserved for ethics and religion.

Concepts, Laws, and Theories

Admittedly, because social science deals with human behavior, it cannot reduce everything to formula and simply stated laws, even though it does go far beyond the raw empirical data. Theory is, in the social sciences, an intellectual creation, imaginative and creative but disciplined. Thus, the social sciences attempt to organize their fields of knowledge into concepts, laws, and theories—approximations that are constantly criticized and revised. Concepts are the key terms of theory—words or symbols that stand for the phenomena being studied. They are labels given to specific events, objects, or situations of concern to the scientist. Examples are such concepts as motives, drives, status, roles, norms, and cultures.

Just as physical science deals with variables in temperature, weight, pressure, mass, and so on, social science also studies variables, developing scales or indexes for their quantitative measurement and relating them to one another. One of the recurring problems in social science is that many concepts are treated qualitatively when they could more profitably be measured quantitatively.

Social science laws set forth relationships among variables, noting that as one variable changes in a regular fashion, predictable changes will take place in others. An example would be: The birthrate of a society tends to decline as the degree of industrialization increases. The two variables involved here are *birthrate* and *degree of industrialization;* the relationship expressed is an inverse or negative one. This law is based on a number of studies in Western society. It has been modified but generally holds good. The facts concerning the births and the extent of industrialization provided the raw data. The generalization stating the relationship is an empirical law—one based on observed realities.

The Encyclopedia of the Social Sciences points out that laws or generalizations are so essential to social science that they do not have to operate perfectly to be valued and retained. They are kept as long as they describe regularities or cause and effect relationships over a reasonable range of circumstances.

Indicate whether each of the following statements is true or false by writing "T" or "F" in the space provided.

_____ 1. All sciences assume that there is regularity in nature.

_____ 2. The social scientist is qualified by his method to tell people how they ought to behave.

_____ 3. A theory is a low-order generalization setting forth the observed relationships among variables.

_____ 4. A hypothesis is an unverified prediction.

Now turn to Answer frame 1^4 on page 20 to check your responses.

Frame 2^4

Criticisms of Social Science Theory

As ideal standards of conduct or value, norms serve a purpose. They provide guidance to the members of a group as to proper and acceptable behavior; they set up values against which existing actions and achievements may be measured. But normative theories in the social sciences—those based on the way the theorist wishes the world to be—are open to criticism. Such theories may result from selecting only such facts as support the theorist's ethical position and ignoring those that do not. But to be scientific, theory must be value-free or objective.

Theories based upon goals or objectives held as norms by the theorist usually are used to give a pseudoscientific basis to an ideology. An example would be the development of a social psychology in Germany based upon the assumption that complex behaviors are genetically transmitted. German folklore then was studied in order to justify national superiority and to unify the German people. Pseudoscience, then, was used to further the development of Bismarck's political goals for a unified nation-state. Theory such as this is normative rather than scientific—concerned with the way the formulators of the theory want their world to be rather than with a scientific approach to reality.

One of the recurrent criticisms of social science theory is that too often it is normative, not scientific. Critics maintain that the concepts formulated by the social science researcher are never value-free, that is, unbiased by personal prejudice. They maintain that we are all products of cultures that slant the questions we ask, which in turn determine our answers or color the analysis of the data being observed. For example, most early research on urban life in America tended to be biased by the rural or small-town preferences of the social scientists involved.

Other criticisms of social science research are based upon the interrelated nature of the variables being studied. How can one analyze the relationship between the birthrate and degree of industrialization without considering the cultural motivations to have children? In India a son is considered a necessity for religious reasons. Would industrialization necessarily affect such a consideration? Obviously, in zeroing in on one or two variables, other factors are ignored in the observation process.

How Criticism Is Met

Hopefully, adherence to the value of objectivity and relying upon tests of reliability and validity in properly following the methods of science will minimize the above criticisms.

Objectivity is a basic value—the researcher should not let his personal bias influence his efforts. Even the symbol used for labeling a concept can reflect one's bias—note the present confusion over the terms nonwhite, black, Negro, Afro-American, et al.

Reliability and validity are two necessary components of scientific technique. Reliability is the ability of the technique chosen to give the same result each time it is used. Validity means that the scientific technique should measure what it is supposed to measure. In defining the variable

Answer frame 1⁴

1. True. The task of science is to discover these regularities through observation and to explain them.
2. False. In social science, the behaviors observed are not judged good or bad by the scientist. The task of making normative judgments is reserved for ethicists.
3. False. That is a law. A theory is a high-level exploration that states regularities abstracted from a number of laws.
4. True. A generalization that has not been verified by repeated observations is called a hypothesis.

If you missed any of the above, you should restudy Frame 1⁴ before turning to Frame 2⁴ on page 19.

Frame 2⁴ continued

in operational terms—that is, terms that allow us to quantify, for example, measure, the variable—some of the meaning may be lost. For instance, if we were to define *dating* as the ability of young couples to be alone together, then we would find that we have oversimplified a complex set of behaviors. A classic example involving definitions is the development of the I.Q. score. Does it really measure native mental ability or is its measurement really that of the cultural environment? Most studies show that the score reflects *both* native intelligence and the effects of the social environment; and as recent studies demonstrate, diet deficiencies can also affect these scores. Of course, the scientist must take into account any changes that have occurred in the environment in the intervals between successive uses of the technique.

Social scientists are *multiple-factor determinists*. They acknowledge that a number of causes and effects are necessary for adequate understanding. Intellectual *monism*, single-factor determinism, is taboo for modern-day social scientists.

Label each of the following statements as true or false.

_____ 1. Normative theory has to be value-free.
_____ 2. Critics of social science say that it cannot be value-free.
_____ 3. Reliability means that the scientific technique should measure what it is supposed to measure.
_____ 4. Most contemporary social scientists are monocausal theorists.

Now turn to Answer frame 2⁴ on page 22 to check your answers.

Frame 3⁴

Another Look at the Scientific Method in the Social Sciences

One may think of formal scientific method as following this order:

1. *Defining the problem and formulating a testable hypothesis.* To repeat—a hypothesis is an expected relationship between variables. These may be formed inductively from the researcher's observations or experience. Common sense has in the past been a useful source of hypotheses. Induction is a process of looking at a set of effects and trying to reason backwards to determine causes. Most modern social scientists tend to deduce their hypotheses from existing theories. In setting up hypotheses, it is prudent to make a careful review of the accumulated knowledge in the area under question. One stu-

dent of family relations, without reviewing existing studies, obtained his hypotheses from observing his relatives' behavior. Actually, he duplicated earlier studies. Even so, this was not a complete waste of time, since many studies are replications done in order to measure reliability or the effects of change. But the researcher should know what he is doing.

2. *Establishing a research design.* What are the variables and how can they be measured? Obviously a thermometer is the tool for measuring temperature. A questionnaire would be an instrument for the measurement of attitudes— at least for folks that can read. Since the procedure has to be verifiable, observations should be as rigidly controlled as possible to eliminate extraneous factors. Experimentation in a laboratory is conducted under ideal conditions because there the variables may be rigidly controlled; however, other strategies for collecting data are in use today.

Since funds are rarely available to gather data on all the population being examined, the research design usually involves selection of a sample. The concern here is to have enough cases to be representative of the population being studied. Since the conclusions will be expressed in terms of a probability statement, the sample should be collected in a random manner. This involves establishing rules of selection which insure that there is an equal probability that the cases examined represent the population being studied.

Having hypothesized a relationship between particular variables, the research designer is allowed to change an *independent* variable in some regular manner so that he can observe change in a second variable (the *dependent* variable). All extraneous variables have to be controlled so that their effects can be ruled out.

3. *Summarizing the results.* After collecting the data, the researcher summarizes results, usually statistically. Based on probability theory, statistical tests will tell the researcher how far he can trust his conclusions and *possibly the extent to which extraneous factors may have influenced them.* At this point, the hypothesis is accepted or rejected. If verified, it becomes the basis for a generalization which can furnish the framework for further research.

Generalizations in the social sciences rarely are capable of predicting what a specific individual will do—even as a biologist won't predict the number of fruit a specific tree will bear. However, we can make probability statements that different categories of people in a given setting will tend to perform in certain predictable ways.

The methods of collecting data in the social sciences are the following: autobiographies, case histories, documents concerning past events, direct observations, interviews, questionnaires, and controlled experiments. No one technique is better than the other for all purposes—all have advantages and disadvantages and are related to the behavior being measured.

In conclusion, social science is scientific when it acts in a scientific way. That involves using rigorous controls to maintain objectivity, following the scientific method, and remaining unbiased in explanation of conclusions. Remember, this summary represents scientific ideals never completely realized. But the scientific method and approach offer our best guide in the acquisition of knowledge and understanding of natural phenomena.

True or false?

_____ 1. Most hypotheses are formed by common sense.

_____ 2. The best research design is an experimental design.

_____ 3. In social science the object is to prove hypotheses.

_____ 4. Generalizations in the social sciences rarely reach a stage where they attempt to predict what a specific individual will do.

Now turn to Answer frame 3⁴ on page 22 to check your answers.

Answer frame 2⁴

1. False. By its very character normative theory cannot be value-free. Normative theories ultimately are based upon goals (values) of the theorist and tend to give pseudoscientific support to an ideology.
2. True. These critics say that sociologists cannot avoid personal bias and the pressures of the culture of which they are a part.
3. False. *Validity* means that it should measure what it is supposed to measure. Reliability is the ability of the technique chosen to give the same result each time it is used.
4. False. Social scientists tend to be multiple-factor determinists. Single-factor determinism is a taboo for modern-day social scientists.

If you missed any of the above, you should reread Frame 2⁴ before turning to Frame 3⁴ on page 20.

Answer frame 3⁴

1. False. Most social scientists deduce their hypotheses from their current theory. This means a careful review of the accumulated knowledge in the area under question.
2. True. In an experimental design, variables may be carefully measured, and extraneous variables may be controlled.
3. False. It is impossible to prove hypotheses. The best you can do is to disprove false hypotheses (null hypotheses).
4. True. However, social scientists can make probability statements concerning different categories of people in a given setting tending to perform in certain predictable ways.

If you missed any of the above, you should restudy Frame 3⁴ before beginning Chapter 5.

chapter 5

PERSONALITY ORGANIZATION

Frame 1[5]

"Personality" is a term which everyone uses, but without agreement upon its exact meaning. Generally it refers to the organization of attitudes, emotions, expressions, and temperament of a person. Some authors include the habits, beliefs, and values of a person as well. We judge subjectively and react emotionally to the personalities of other people. Thus, the same man may be described as friendly, considerate, and attentive, or as egoistic, manipulative, and deceitful. Personality is highly complex; we have many faces which we reveal to different persons or in different situations. Thus, many a bride discovers that her long sought ideal is in fact an irresponsible child who cannot hang up his own clothes, and many a bridegroom comes to the disheartening realization that his wife's expensive tastes will keep him perpetually insolvent. Probably no one ever fully understands anyone's personality—least of all his own.

Factors in the Development of Personality

Personality is generally defined today as including all of a person's behavior characteristics. Each person's personality develops through the interaction of physical environment, heredity, culture, group, and unique experience.

Physical Environment. There have been many attempts to explain personality and behavior by climatic, geographic, or topographical factors. These doubtless are factors in behavior; on a humid, muggy day, people act and feel different than on a bracing day; mountain valleys isolate people while broad river valleys throw them into ready contact with one another. But such factors do not *determine* behavior, for when a factor is determining, its controlling effects are predictable and invariable. No single-factor explanation of behavior proves to be sound, for there are too many exceptions. Thus, the mountain pockets of Greece which supposedly kept the ancient Greeks from unity did not prevent the unification of Peru under the Incas. The convivial Eskimo and the stern Northern Canadian Indians inhabited a similar locale. We can find many examples of similar cultures in differing environments, and of differing cultures in similar environments. If physical environment is determining, why didn't the American Indians develop an industrial society, or, conversely, why didn't the Pilgrims "turn Indian"? Physical environment does not force any specific responses upon man; it merely sets the limits within which the culture may develop. Eskimos cannot grow oranges and desert peoples cannot fish! We are learning today that man can destroy his environment to the point where it cannot support human life. But the influence of physical environment upon man's personality is minor compared with other factors. All attempts to link any particular personality characteristics with a particular physical environment can promptly be demolished by any competent anthropologist, who can easily rattle off a string of contradictions.

Heredity. By *heredity,* we mean *everything one receives through his parents' genes as a human being.* Each person inherits certain characteristics which are shared with all other physically normal human beings—a physical body

23

with two hands, two feet, five senses, and a set of organic drives (for food, sleep, sex, etc.), and learning capacities. These organic human characteristics provide the raw material for personality. If the human animal were designed to eat once a week and mate once a year, personality and social life would be different in ways we can only guess.

Heredity also includes individual differences in genetic inheritance—coloring, facial features, size potentialities, probably some differences in learning capacities, and possibly in neurochemical systems. Only identical twins have identical heredity, and studies of identical twins raised separately are too few and too small to be conclusive. We simply do not know to what extent personality differences may be rooted in differences in heredity. Each person's personality develops through the interaction of several factors operating upon his unique heredity. It is widely believed by behavioral scientists, however, that most individual and group differences in personality are far more greatly due to experience than to differences in heredity.

Culture and Personality. A man five feet six inches tall is a giant among pygmies but a runt in Scandinavia, and the fat girl is a doll in some societies but a wallflower in others. The *meaning* of a physical characteristic is a matter of cultural definition. Attempts to link a physical characteristic with a particular personality trait are necessarily culture-bound; a different culture, defining that trait differently, would encourage different personality outcomes. In a society where redheads are expected to be scrappy and fatties to be jolly, they often are. This gives rise to the mistaken notion that the physical trait has produced the personality outcome, whereas the society has provided many subtle encouragements for the redhead to scrap and the fattie to act jolly. It is this cultural definition of physical traits, and the social treatment given to a person with a particular physical trait, that largely determine the effects of a physical trait upon personality.

Each culture includes certain experiences which are common to practically everyone who lives in the society. American children are encouraged to be individualistic, competitive, and self-assertive; Hopi children are encouraged to

be group-conscious, cooperative, and soft-spoken. A comparison of personality development in two very different cultures—those of the Dobuans on a small island off New Guinea, and of the Zuñi of New Mexico—reveals how personality is shaped by the culture.

The Dobuans, described by R. F. Fortune in *The Sorcerers of Dobu,* live in a world ruled by magic. Nothing happens naturally; every event is believed to have been caused by someone's witchcraft. If one succeeds in love or if his yams grow well, this attests to his powerful magic. If he falls ill or his wife betrays him, this shows the power of the malevolent magic of other persons. All success is secured at the expense of others, and all failure has been produced by others. Ill will and treachery are necessary for survival. Married couples alternate between the villages of husband and wife, so that at all times one of them is a feared and distrusted outsider who lives in daily fear of being poisoned. Social relations are polite and correct, but never genial or relaxed, for it is dangerous to give offense and one must always be on guard.

What kind of personality develops in such a cultural atmosphere? The Dobuan is suspicious, hostile, deceitful, distrustful, secretive, jealous, fearful, and anxious. In our society, such a person would be called *paranoid;* but where a paranoid person *imagines* that other people are threatening him, this is *real* and not a delusion in Dobu. These personality characteristics are rational reactions to a world filled with demons and witches where no one can be trusted. Thus the Dobuan culture shapes a personality which is normal and is functionally useful for survival amid such hazards.

The Zuñi of New Mexico are a calm people, living in an emotionally placid world. Magic is never malevolent, and supernatural beings are not feared. The Zuñi have no sense of sin, no image of a world contest between good and evil, and no feelings of guilt or unworthiness. Children are welcomed with warm affection and are never disciplined or punished; yet people of all ages are well-behaved and serious misconduct is rare. The dominant features of Zuñi behavior are cooperation, moderation, and lack of individualism. They reject alcohol and drugs because they view immoderate behavior as undignified. In sharp contrast to the anxious, suspicious Dobuans, the Zuñi are serene, secure, confident, trusting, cooperative, and habitually conformist. Thus the child develops a personality which fits him to function comfortably in Zuñi society.

As this contrast illustrates, the common experiences of those who are raised in a particular culture will create in most of them a *modal personality* which is characteristic of most members of that society. (Note that the word is not mode*l* it is mod*a*l; it is pronounced to rhyme with "yodel" and comes from the word *mode*.) Although many persons may imperfectly reflect the modal personality for their society, average differences in modal personality are obvious to the world traveler—the somber Swede, the talkative, gesticulating Italian, the grave, reserved American Indian. Common cultural experience (meaning those experiences common to most people in a particular culture) accounts for similarities in personality *within* a society and for differences in modal personality *between* societies.

Indicate whether each of the following statements is true or false by writing "T" or "F" in the space provided.

_____ 1. Physical environment is the sole determinant of a person's personality.

_____ 2. Behavior scientists concede that most individual personality differences are far more greatly due to differences in heredity than to experience.

_____ 3. Cultural definition of physical traits largely determines the effects of a particular physical trait on personality.

_____ 4. Differing cultural experience accounts for personality differences among Swedes, Italians, and so on.

Now turn to Answer frame 1[5] on page 26 to check your responses.

Frame 2[5]

Group and Personality. The group is the medium whereby the person experiences the culture. One becomes aware of customs, perceives taboos, and receives rewards and punishments through the group. It is the group, therefore, which is the direct instrument for transmittting the culture to the individual.

Without group experience, normal personality does not develop. There are mythical and pseudoscientific accounts of so-called "feral" children, supposedly raised by animals, but social scientists doubt their authenticity. Instead, these are believed to be "autistic" children, raised by humans but denied human responses—ignored, neglected, unloved, and mistreated. Denied normal group experience, they failed to develop a characteristic human personality.

Unique Experience and Personality. No two persons have exactly the same set of personal experiences, not even two children in the same family. Every person's experience is unique in that no one else duplicates his experience. Furthermore, experiences do not just add up; they *integrate*. By this, we mean that today's incidents get their meaning from all those which have preceded them. Today's victory or defeat or argument or insult affects one in a manner determined by a long succession of past victories or defeats or arguments or insults. This explains why people seldom show dramatic changes of personality throughout life. They perceive new incidents in the light of past experience, and thus define new incidents in such a way as to confirm and reinforce their established personality characteristics. Thus the pupil with a long succession of happy school experiences and pleasant teacher contacts behind him will perceive the teacher today as being helpful to him; the pupil with a long succession of unhappy school experiences and abrasive teacher contacts will perceive the teacher today as nagging and pestering him. New experiences and new contacts seldom change

Answer frame 1⁵

1. False. Each person's personality develops through the interaction of physical environment, heredity, culture, group, and unique experience.
2. False. Just the opposite is true. They are of the opinion that experience is far more important than differences in heredity in explaining individual personality differences.
3. True. A fat person may be thought of as attractive in one society and repulsive in another, depending on the cultural definition given the trait in the society.
4. True. Those experiences common to most people in a society account for similarities in personality *within* a society (i.e., Italian society) and for differences in modal personality *between* societies (i.e., Italian vs. Swedish societies). Rather extreme differences can be seen when contrasting the Dobuans (near New Guinea) with the Zuñi of New Mexico.

If you missed any of the above, you should restudy Frame 1⁵ before turning to Frame 2⁵ on page 25.

Frame 2⁵ continued

one's personality greatly because these new experiences are defined and interpreted in terms of one's established attitudes, hostilities, and reaction patterns. The aggressive child therefore usually continues throughout life the pattern of meeting situations with a blunt directness, while another child follows a lifelong pattern of conciliation and circumvention. The outward expression of basic personality traits may change, but the basic characteristics themselves rarely change. Behavior therapy most often consists of helping people to find socially acceptable ways of expressing their basic personality traits, not of trying to change the basic personality traits themselves.

Socialization

An infant is born into this world with no language, no culture, and no concern for anything beyond his own organic drives. He is incapable of caring for himself and could not survive without the loving attention of adults. He must learn all the skills necessary for his survival. *Socialization is the process by which we develop a personality by internalizing the culture of our society.*

Origin of the Self. As a person is socialized to become a functioning human being, he must develop a separate identity and personality. This identity is termed his social *self*. The self is *the individual's awareness of and attitudes toward his own person*, the person's perception of himself as an individual. Whenever one uses the words "I" or "me," he is referring to his self.

The child is not born with a self; this must be developed through socialization. In the early months of infancy, the child gradually becomes aware of his physical limits—his ears, toes, fingers—where he leaves off and the rest of the world begins. His behavior is very "selfish." The infant cares not that his parents wish to eat, or sleep, or talk, or make love; his stomach is sending hunger pangs and he howls until his discomfort is eased. Parents expect such behavior from the infant and are not alarmed at his heedless demands for attention.

Living with people, however, requires that the child learn to control his desires and become responsive to the wishes of others. The small child is taught to take his turn in play and share his playthings with others. He begins to become a socialized human being when he develops an awareness of others and begins to modify his behavior in response to their expectations.

The child must also incorporate the norms and values of his culture, and learn the proper roles for him to play. He learns these through his group experience, in which the family is his first and most important teacher. It is not surprising that most children reflect the behavior and attitudes of their parents. Next comes the play group, the first of many "peer groups" (groups of equals) which influence him throughout life.

In this fashion the child is socialized to live in the culture of the society into which he is born.

Is each of the following true or false?
_____ 1. The group is the medium by which one becomes aware of customs, perceives taboos, and receives rewards and punishments.
_____ 2. Since experiences integrate, people often show dramatic changes of personality during their lives.
_____ 3. Behavior therapy consists mainly of trying to change people's basic personality traits.
_____ 4. Socialization involves changing one's behavior and internalizing the norms and values of his culture.

Now turn to Answer frame 2⁵ on page 28 to check your answers.

Frame 3⁵

Cooley and the "Looking-Glass Self." An early sociologist, Charles Horton Cooley, formulated the concept of the "looking-glass self" to explain how a person develops his picture of the kind of person he is. He suggests that we derive our image of self through (1) imagining how we appear to others, (2) our perception of their judgments of how we appear, and (3) our feelings about these judgments. We form our image of self through our perception of the reactions of others to us. A pretty girl first learns that she is pretty by being told how pretty she looks. If this is repeated often enough, and consistently enough, these responses become incorporated into her personality so that she eventually feels and acts as a beautiful person. Even a pretty girl, however, will believe that she is plain if, early in life, her parents act disappointed in and apologetic for her appearance, and treat her as unattractive and unworthy. One's self-image need bear no relation to the real facts about one's qualities. A very ordinary child will develop feelings of competence and self-confidence if his efforts are defined as successful, while a brilliant child can become obsessed with feelings of incompetence and unworthiness if his efforts are regularly defined as failures. It is mainly through early family experiences that one concludes whether he is bright or stupid, handsome or repulsive, worthwhile or worthless.

Mead and Role Theory. George Herbert Mead expanded upon Cooley's theory in emphasizing the function of role taking and role playing in socialization. ("Role taking" is an effort to assume the behavior of a status one does not actually hold, as when children "play house," while "role playing" is acting out the behavior of a status which one genuinely holds.) Mead proposed a three-stage mechanism through which the child learns to perform roles—the preparatory, play, and game stages. The preparatory stage (1–3 years) consists of meaningless imitation of adult roles. The child imitates the roles of adults through his play activities, but fails to understand the meaning and purpose of the role he is performing. Thus the small girl "mothers" her doll, then uses it as a club to strike her older brother. The play stage (3–4 years) is characterized by proper but inconsistent role behavior. The child may understand the meaning and purpose of the role, but may switch roles inconsistently and purposelessly in his play behavior. One moment the small boy may be a truck driver; ten seconds later he is an astronaut. This stage represents his first capability to act out adult roles, but the child does not relate these to any goals or purposes of his own. The game stage (4 or 5 years and thereafter) is characterized by consistent and proper role behavior and the ability to take the role of the other into consideration. For the child to play the game of baseball, he not only has to internalize and perform his own role in the game, but also the roles of the other members of the teams.

Answer frame 2⁵

1. True. The group is the direct instrument for transmitting the culture to the individual.
2. False. Experiences do integrate, that is, today's incidents get their meaning from all those which have preceded them. But this explains why people *seldom* show dramatic changes of personality throughout their lives.
3. False. Behavior therapy does not try to change people's basic personality traits (for example, to change an aggressive person into a nonaggressive person); instead, it tries to help people find socially acceptable ways of expressing their basic personality traits.
4. True. A socialized human being has developed an awareness of others and begins to change his behavior in response to their expectations. He also takes as his own the norms and values of his culture, thus enabling him to live harmoniously in the culture of the society into which he is born.

If you missed any of the above, you should review Frame 2⁵ before continuing with Frame 3⁵ on page 27.

Frame 3⁵ continued

Mead termed this awareness of others' roles as the *generalized other*. It could also be described as the internalized standards of the community. In our social behavior, we not only act in reference to our own identity or self, but we also take into consideration the expectations of other people in our behavior. We restrain our behavior in public because "people will talk," and we do not wish to appear crude or odd. The generalized other might be crudely viewed as the conscience, the internal "voice" telling us the right thing to say.

Other sociologists have added the concept of the *significant other*. Our significant others are those persons whose advice and direction we accept. These might be parents, ministers, teachers, athletic coaches, or perhaps a somewhat older child whom one idolizes. We respect these significant others and try to behave as they wish since we crave their approval and acceptance. Today, possibly our popular celebrities such as actors and pop singers might also be included.

The process of socialization is continuous and never-ending. We are constantly being resocialized to new situations in life—from childhood to adolescence, to marriage, to parenthood, to new occupations, finally to retirement. Each life stage requires some retraining to new roles and life patterns.

The Freudian Approach to Socialization.

Whereas Mead viewed self and society as harmonious, Sigmund Freud saw the self and society as in conflict. The society represses and denies the self the pleasure of desired indulgences. From the beginning of childhood, society imposes its restraints upon the child and punishes severely for nonconformity. Those who cannot handle the stress of this conflict between self and society develop neuroses and psychoses.

Freud is perhaps best known for his concepts of the *id, ego,* and *superego*. The *id* is the impulsive self, the unsocialized desires. When a young child sees a toy he likes, he wants it; when he is restrained, he strikes out and screams in rage. The id is the basic biological core of the self—the basic drives, needs, and desires in expression.

The *superego* is the ideal self, the internalized values and restraints of parents and others. Freud would contend that the child is socialized through internalizing the goals, values, and norms of the parents, and these serve as reference points for future behavior. Thus the middle-aged man may hide his cigars and liquor when his parents visit because he does not want to damage his image of his ideal self. The superego could also be broadly viewed as one's conscience, the internalized social standards of right and wrong.

The *ego* is the rational control mechanism

which mediates the conflict between the id and the superego. The ego finds a tolerable balance between what one wants to do (id) and what one believes it to be right to do (superego). The person with an adequate ego will not use temper tantrums to get his way or lose control of himself in stress situations.

The validity of Freud's psychoanalytic concepts is much debated, and his scholarly reputation is currently declining. Yet psychoanalysis still remains at the base of a great deal of our behavior therapy today.

Theories of the development of the self may not fully agree, but the importance of the self and self-image is beyond question. Self-image undeniably affects behavior! Experimental data show that those who feel self-confident will perform better; those who lack self-confidence are all the more likely to fail. The "good" child typically perceives himself as worthwhile, loved, appreciated, and competent; the "bad" child sees himself as incompetent, unworthy, unloved. A series of psychological labels—compensation, repression, projection, rationalization, reaction-formation—describe various efforts one makes to correct or improve an unsatisfactory image of self. They are called "defense mechanisms," because they are one's defenses against an unendurable picture of self, and are ways of trying to improve one's self-image.

Indicate whether each of the following statements is true or false by writing "T" or "F" in the space provided.

_____ 1. The concept of the "looking-glass self" says that we derive our image of self by examining the real facts about our qualities.

_____ 2. The "generalized other" is an awareness of others' roles.

_____ 3. The process of socialization starts at birth and is usually completed by age 18.

_____ 4. The superego mediates the conflict between the id and the ego.

Now turn to Answer frame 3^5 on page 30 to check your responses.

Answer frame 3⁵ ──────────────────────────────

1. False. The concept says that we form our image of self through our perception of the *reactions of others* to us. Specifically, we form our image through (1) imagining how we appear to others, (2) our perception of their judgments of how we appear, and (3) our feelings about these judgments.
2. True. It can also be described as the internalized standards of the community or could be crudely viewed as the conscience.
3. False. The process of socialization is continuous and never-ending.
4. False. The *ego* mediates the conflict between the id (what one wants to do) and the superego (what one believes it right to do).

If you missed any of the above, reread Frame 3⁵ before beginning Chapter 6 below.

chapter 6

SOCIAL PROCESSES

Frame 1⁶ ──────────────────────────────

The *social processes* are the *repetitive kinds of behavior through which people interact with one another.* The most common processes are cooperation, competition, conflict, and the two alternatives to conflict—accommodation and assimilation.

Cooperation

Cooperation is perhaps the most pervasive of the social processes. Even the most highly competitive society could not function without a great deal of cooperation. *Cooperation is a joint effort to attain a shared goal.* Most cooperation is covert, or without conscious recognition, as in a conversation where each alternately talks and listens. Driving a car on the highway depends upon the cooperation of a great many people—other drivers keeping in their lane, others who built and maintain the road, and still others who built and service the car, provide the gasoline, etc. Without the cooperation of a number of adults, infants would promptly die and the human race would long since have perished.

Societies vary in their emphasis upon cooperation. Some aboriginal tribes in Australia valued cooperation so highly and were so noncompetitive that researchers were unable to administer intelligence tests; no one would answer the questions for fear that their friends might not perform equally well. In simple societies, cooperation is mostly primary group in nature as small groups work together in fishing or repairing a hut. While such informal cooperation continues in industrial societies, such societies also require elaborate systems of secondary impersonal cooperation in large-scale organizations. An assembly line worker may cooperate with a thousand other workers in assembling a product, while countless thousands of others cooperated in preparing and transporting the various components of the finished product. Each such organization must be coordinated with many other organizations ranging from banks to street cleaners for modern society to function.

Each social process has its personality outcomes. Cooperation tends to encourage sensitivity to others, concern for others, emotional security, and a relatively calm, nonaggressive disposition. A society which is highly cooperative and minimizes competition and conflict is likely to be quiet and orderly, with relatively little individuality, little emotional stress or insecurity, and a relatively low rate of social change.

Competition

Competition is an effort to surpass others in attaining a goal. The goal may be tangible, such as money or property, or the intangible rewards of status, prestige, recognition, or affection. Competition is a culturally patterned process which varies in form and frequency among societies. The Kwakiutl of British Columbia compete ferociously in acquiring goods to enhance their family's social status, where a Zuñi would consider all such displays of wealth as exceedingly bad taste, and if asked to run a race, he would probably ask "Why?" Ours is a highly competitive society. While there is more cooperation than most people realize, we also compete for practically everything possible—for money, status, love, even for fun. All of our games are competitive, with score-keeping and designated winners and losers. Competition can even become an end in itself. The monarchs of the financial and industrial worlds continue to work twelve hours a day, even after they have more money than they could ever possibly spend, because making money and exercising power have become pleasurable games in themselves.

Competition may be personal, where one is competing directly against another person, or impersonal, such as in examinations where one is competing against each of a large number of persons. Competition can be individual, as illustrated above, or it can be group competition, with the members of a group cooperating with one another in order to compete with another group, as in a football game.

The personality outcomes of the competitive process are almost the opposite of those from cooperation. Competition encourages ruthlessness, selfishness, and insensitivity to others, creates insecurity and anxiety, promotes individuality, and develops independence, initiative, self-confidence, and ambition in those who compete successfully, while producing feelings of inadequacy, frustration, apathy, and withdrawal from those who consistently fail.

The social functions of competition include the allocation of scarce rewards. Whether competition is the ideal way to allocate income, prestige, and privilege may be argued, but it undeniably is one way of doing so.

Competition stimulates hostility between competitors, and individual competition threatens the unity and solidarity of the group to which the individuals belong. Group competition stimulates unity and loyalty within the group, and is often deliberately used for this purpose.

The effects of competition upon performance are variable. Research studies show that in routine, repetitive tasks, such as stuffing boxes, competition increases output, while in complex, intricate, or intellectual tasks, competition often reduces output. Furthermore, for competition to stimulate maximum effort, the conditions of competition must give all competitors a feeling that they have a fair chance of winning. When the conditions of competition are unequal or the competitors are unevenly matched, a maximum effort is unnecessary for the stronger and futile for the weaker. Countless numbers of people drop out from competition in sports, in academic studies, and in competition for good jobs and upward mobility because of repeated failures and no hope of ever winning. There is research evidence that repeated failures destroy not only the desire to compete, but even cripple the *ability* to perform at one's highest level.

Competition encourages innovation and social change. Its overall effect probably is to increase the productivity of a society, while increasing both its number of conspicuously successful people and its number of failures.

A final characteristic of competition is its tendency to escalate into conflict. Every competitive situation has its rules, and there is a constant temptation to violate the rules in pursuit of victory.

Indicate whether each of the following statements is true or false by writing "T" or "F" in the space provided.

_____ 1.   Conflict is the most pervasive of the social processes.

_____ 2.   Each social process has distinctive personality outcomes.

_____ 3.   Competition varies in form and frequency among societies.

_____ 4.   Competition between groups tends to create competition among the members of each of the competing groups.

_____ 5.   Competition has a tendency to escalate into conflict.

Now turn to Answer frame 1[6] on page 34 to check your responses.

Frame 2[6]

Conflict

Conflict is the process wherein a person or group *seeks to gain a reward by weakening or eliminating the competitors*, rather than by surpassing them in "fair" competition. Conflict may be overt and violent, including beating, shooting, terrorizing, bombing, and burning. Or conflict may be covert, using tariffs, price-fixing, import quotas, special legislation, and other contractual arrangements to prevent effective competition. Much of the time of legislators is absorbed in considering legislation whose unadvertised but true purpose is to provide a government subsidy to some interest group or to heave a brickbat at its competitors. To bankrupt a competing storekeeper by offering better service and better values is competition; to put him out of business by burning his store, bribing the building inspector to padlock it, or circulating false rumors about him is conflict. The "price war," wherein one sells below cost until a competitor with limited financial resources must give in, is a form of conflict.

Group conflict, like all interaction between groups, is impersonal. This means that one reacts aggressively to all members of an opposing group, regardless of any personal feelings or relationships they may have. Sometimes group conflicts divide old friends or separate families. Civil wars always do, providing the material for many romantic civil war novels. In group conflict, one must loyally support his group or face denunciation as a "scab" or "traitor." Those who try to remain neutral in a group conflict situation are likely to be clobbered by both sides.

The *cumulative nature of conflict* helps to explain the extremes which conflict reaches. Within each group, members reassure one another of the justice and rightness of their cause, and of the venality of the opposing group. The aggressions and injuries they inflict upon each other will serve to intensify their feelings of self-righteousness, of outrage, and of justification for the severe reprisals which each returns to the other. Thus the violence and bitterness of group conflict tends to escalate. Sometimes the conflict becomes so intense and the parties so emotionally involved that the goals become secondary and the conflict becomes an end in itself.

The conflict process has certain personality outcomes—hatred of enemies, bitterness, ruthlessness, and a callous unconcern for suffering, along with intensified group loyalties and willingness to sacrifice for the group.

One of the social functions of conflict is to define and resolve issues. It is not possible to hesitate in endless indecision or postpone action. Some kind of settlement of issues normally follows a decisive conflict.

Another function is to increase the unity, solidarity, and sacrificial dedication of groups in conflict, while conflict within a group has the opposite effect of creating disunity and inability to act. Many groups, ranging from a local labor union to a nation, have quieted internal conflicts by promoting conflict with another group or nation.

Conflict generally accelerates change, although many of the changes may be unforeseen and undesired. Conflict brings about new align-ments, new associational and administrative structures, and resolves old issues while creating new ones.

Conflict is too costly a process to be continued indefinitely. Unless conflict ends with the total extermination or expulsion of one of the parties—a rare event in history—it is replaced by some form of accommodation, and perhaps eventually by assimilation.

Label each of the following statements as true or false.

_____ 1. It is difficult to remain neutral in a group conflict situation.
_____ 2. Conflict is a cumulative process and easily reaches extremes.
_____ 3. Within-group solidarity is a function of between-group conflict.
_____ 4. Group conflict generally results in the total extermination or expulsion of one of the parties.

Now turn to Answer frame 2[6] on page 34 to check your answers.

Frame 3[6]

Accommodation

Accommodation is the process of *achieving temporary working agreements between parties who are in present or potential conflict.* An accommodation may be deliberately negotiated, as in a peace treaty following a war; or it may be arrived at through an unplanned and even unconscious process of mutual trial-and-error until two groups eventually come to an informal live-and-let-live understanding.

One form of accommodation is *displacement*, in which one conflict is resolved by replacing it with another conflict. The country which resolves internal conflicts by a threat of war against another country is encouraging its people to displace their conflicts upon the foreign enemy. The henpecked husband who "takes it out" on his employees, or in scraps with his neighbors or fellow church members, or in political arguments, has displaced his domestic conflicts. Conversely, the frustrated employee, instead of fighting it out at the office, may displace this conflict in marital combat. Displacement does not solve the original conflict; it diverts one's discontents and absorbs one's energies in a new conflict, so that one can allow the old conflict to lie dormant and possibly even unrecognized.

Subordination is a form of accommodation in which the weaker party accepts the will of the victor. "Unconditional surrender" in warfare, acceptance of slavery, and ending a strike by returning to work with no contract would all be examples. Other examples would include the acceptance of reservation life by the American Indians a century ago, and acceptance of second-class citizenship by American Negroes after the Civil War.

Compromise develops when both parties wish to avoid or end conflict, and neither party is powerful enough to impose subordination upon the other. Each party makes some concessions, and the resulting compromise should reflect the respective power positions of the contestants. If, through clumsy negotiation, one party fails to gain concessions proportionate to its power, or if the power balance changes later, then the compromise will be opened for renegotiation under threat of renewed conflict. For example, black Americans today have greater power to resist subordination than they had a century ago, for a number of reasons—economic, political, and philosophical. Under threat of violence (along with other appeals) they are demanding that the old accommodation be replaced by a new one, granting equal opportunities to black people.

Answer frame 1[6]

1. False. Cooperation is the most pervasive. Even competing and conflicting groups depend on extensive cooperation among their members.
2. True. Cooperation tends to encourage sensitivity to others and nonaggressiveness. Competition encourages ruthlessness, selfishness, and insensitivity to others, creates insecurity and anxiety, and promotes individuality. It develops independence, initiative, self-confidence, and ambition in those who succeed and feelings of inadequacy, frustration, apathy, and withdrawal in those who fail.
3. True. It is a culturally patterned process. In some societies most social behavior is cooperative and in others, like the United States, every institution is characterized by competitiveness.
4. False. Group competition stimulates unity, loyalty, and cooperation within the group, and is often deliberately used by group leaders for this purpose.
5. True. Every competitive situation has its rules, and there is a constant temptation to violate the rules in pursuit of victory.

If you missed any of the above, you should restudy Frame 1[6] before turning to Frame 2[6] on page 32.

Answer frame 2[6]

1. True. Sometimes group conflicts divide old friends or separate families. Those who try to remain neutral are likely to be attacked by both sides.
2. True. Within each group, members reassure one another of the justice and rightness of their cause, and of the venality of the opposing group. The violence and bitterness escalates.
3. True. One function of group conflict is to increase the unity, solidarity, and dedication of groups in conflict, while conflict within a group has the opposite effect of creating disunity and inability to act. Frequently groups reduce internal conflict by increasing conflict with another group or nation.
4. False. This is a rare event in human history. Generally group conflict is replaced by some form of accommodation and perhaps eventually by assimilation.

If you missed any of the above, you should reread Frame 2[6] before turning to Frame 3[6] on page 33.

Frame 3[6] continued

Mediation, conciliation, and *arbitration* are third-party techniques of arranging compromises. The terms *mediation* and *conciliation* are used almost interchangeably to describe third-party efforts to help the contestants arrive at an agreement. In *arbitration,* the arbitrator makes a decision which the contesting parties have agreed in advance to accept.

Toleration is a form of accommodation in which the parties agree to interact peacefully without any settlement of certain differences. It is practical only when the nature of the differences is such that the parties *can* interact peacefully in other areas of interaction without coming to agreement upon their points of difference. Employer and employee can cooperate in production without agreeing on questions of politics or religion; but they *must* reach some agreement on wage rates or there can be no economic cooperation. Catholic and Protestant can interact peacefully as neighbors, or as fellow workers in the factory, without coming to any common agreement about papal infallibility. Of course, they *can* argue endlessly about it, but they need not, for the difference is irrelevant to their amiable interaction as neighbors and workers. A "tolerant" man accurately perceives where agreement is not essential to peaceful interaction in other areas, is critical of unsubstantiated rumors, and respects the right of others to their opinions.

Institutionalized conflict resolution procedures are a part of many cultures. Many primitive societies have institutionalized certain contests, ordeals, or magical tests as means of resolving conflicts. Some of these involve a ritual mock battle in which hostility is released with little or no bloodshed. The judicial system serves this function for civilized societies.

Assimilation

Assimilation is the process of becoming culturally similar, so that the points of conflict are erased. It is unconsciously acting out the old adage, "If you can't lick them, join them!" The immigrant group may, within a very few generations, absorb the culture of the host population (while giving a few traits to the host population) so that the two groups are culturally indistin-

guishable. If there is no racial difference to make them permanently identifiable, the immigrants are likely to be both culturally assimilated and socially accepted. High racial visibility, and sometimes religious differences, may prevent the assimilated minority from becoming socially accepted. Thus the Dutch, Germans, and Scandinavians have become assimilated and accepted in the United States, and have virtually disappeared as indentifiable categories. The Jews have become assimilated but not completely accepted, while the Negroes are assimilated but even less fully accepted.

As the present black-white conflicts in the United States reveal, assimilation does not necessarily remove all sources of group conflict. It only resolves those conflicts which are rooted in cultural dissimilarity. As long as there are identifiable groups, with differing ideas or clashing interests, conflict is never far away.

True or false?

_____ 1. Unlike conflict and competition, accommodation is final and fixed.

_____ 2. Compromise develops when neither conflicting group is powerful enough to impose subordination on the other.

_____ 3. Institutionalized conflict resolution procedures are a part of many cultures.

_____ 4. Racial visibility may prevent an assimilated minority group from becoming thoroughly integrated into a society.

Now turn to Answer frame 3⁶ on page 36 to check your answers.

Answer frame 3[6]

1. False. Accommodation is a temporary and precarious set arrangement among parties who are in present or potential conflict. It is highly unstable.
2. True. Compromise develops when both parties wish to avoid or end conflict. Each party makes some concessions, and the result should reflect the relative power positions of the contestants.
3. True. Among these are contests, ordeals, and magic tests. The judicial system serves this function for civilized societies.
4. True. If there are no visible racial differences to make them permanently identifiable, immigrants are likely to be both culturally assimilated and socially accepted.

If you missed any of the above, you should restudy Frame 3[6] before continuing on to Chapter 7.

chapter 7

CULTURE

Frame 1[7]

Animals live largely by *instincts*—by inborn behavior patterns which unfold reliably and uniformly in all healthy members of a particular species. Isolate some honey bee larvae, and when they mature, they will predictably build honeycombs and establish a bee colony with the same social structure as any other bee colony. Man has no such instincts. Man has a few *reflexes* (knee-jerk, eye-blink, pain-withdrawal), but these are uncomplicated muscular contractions in response to a specific stimulus; they are not complicated behavior patterns comparable to nest or beaver-dam building. Man also has certain inborn needs and appetites which we call *drives*—for food, sleep, sex, and a few others—but these drives are not accompanied by any inborn behavior patterns for satisfying them. Thus man

lives largely by a series of habits we call "culture."

The Definition of Culture

Sir Edward Tylor's early definition (1871) views culture as "that complex whole which includes knowledge, belief, art, morals, law, custom, and any other capabilities and habits acquired by man as a member of society." Thus a culture consists of *all the learned patterns of acting, feeling, and thinking shared by the members of a particular society.* Our culture includes the literature of Shakespeare along with unprintable folk ballads, the "King's English" and the obscenities, the manners of the drawing room and those of the bar room. It includes our beliefs about religion, our praise for hard work and "getting ahead," our fondness for mechanical gadgetry, our desire for speed and punctuality —the list is almost endless. Such responses and feelings become so much a part of us that they seem to be natural—a part of our inborn natures —but this is a mistake. Every one of these characteristics is cultural, that is, each is learned in our society and each varies from society to society. There are many societies in which speed and punctuality are of no concern and new gadgets are scorned. Each society has a culture differing somewhat from that of all other societies. A *society* is therefore defined as *all the people who share a common culture.*

A distinction is sometimes drawn between the *material culture* (man made objects such as clothing, tools, houses), and *nonmaterial culture* (ideas, beliefs, traditions, values, ceremonials, etc.). This is not a very useful distinction, since a physical object is a part of the culture only through the uses and ideas which accompany it. Thus a "chair" may be something to sit on, a rack to dry fish on, or fuel for a fire. But since these concepts occasionally appear in the sociological literature, the student must recognize them. Some sociologists prefer to confine the term "culture" to the nonmaterial characteristics, and use the term "cultural objects" or "cultural equipment" for physical objects.

A *simple, irreducible unit of culture is called a trait.* Some traits in our culture would include shaking hands, applauding a performer, driving on the right, and sitting on chairs. When an activity involves *a cluster of functionally related traits,* this is a *culture complex* (or cultural complex). Football, dating, and Christmas are culture complexes. In each case, there is a cluster of behavior traits, together with a supporting set of ideas, sentiments, values, and ceremonials.

Indicate whether each of the following statements is true or false by writing "T" or "F" in the space provided.

_____ 1. Human beings live in houses because the human species has a house-building instinct.

_____ 2. A human drive stimulates activity to satisfy that drive, but the particular forms and modes of activity followed in a society are determined by habit and custom, not by inborn instinct.

_____ 3. "Culture" and "society" are closely related terms.

_____ 4. A "trait" is a more inclusive term than is a "culture complex."

Now turn to Answer frame 1⁷ on page 38 to check your responses.

Frame 2⁷

Origins of Culture

Is culture an expression of inborn urges, drives, and instincts which unfold as the human being matures? Or is culture simply an accumulation of accidental choices among possible alternatives? Obviously, it is neither. Instinctivist versus environmentalist arguments have raged for ages. For most of the present century, scientific opinion has been discarding instinctivist explanations in favor of environmentalist explanations. Recently, a number of scholars who have come to be known as *ethologists* (not to be confused with ethnologists) have revived the nature-nurture controversy. Coming mainly from the field of zoology, writers such as Robert Ardrey, Robin Fox, Konrad Lorenz, Desmond Morris, Lionel Tiger, and Nikolaas Tinbergen claim that sociologists have misjudged the importance of biological impulses and drives in human behavior. They claim that observations of the higher animals suggest that responses such as aggression and conflict, defense of territory, status seeking, and possibly others are genetically determined as parts of mankind's original nature. They propose that there is an instinctual human urge to claim and defend territory, for males to establish domination over

Answer frame 1⁷

1. False. Human beings have no house-building instinct, and in many parts of the world people do not live in houses.
2. True. For example, man's food drive stimulates him to seek and eat food; but the particular foods chosen, methods of preparation, rituals of eating, etc., vary widely between societies according to each society's customs.
3. True. A *society* is defined as all the people who share a common *culture*. A *culture* is defined as all the learned patterns of acting, feeling, and thinking shared by the members of a particular *society*.
4. False. A culture complex is a *cluster of traits*, together with a supporting set of ideas, sentiments, values, and ceremonials. Christmas activities are an example of a culture complex.

If you missed any of the above, you should restudy Frame 1⁷ before turning to Frame 2⁷ on page 37.

Frame 2⁷ continued

females and other males, and to fight with one another. Their books have had an enormous popularity, bringing such terms as "territoriality" and "dominance structures" into popular vocabulary.

The proposal that violence, domination, and selfishness are genetically determined does provide an attractive excuse for some of our more unpleasant ways of treating one another. But is it true? Critics have pointed out that for each of these "genetically determined" forms of behavior, at least a few human societies can be found in which these behaviors are entirely absent. There are at least a few societies in which there is no physical combat among human beings, and no legends or accounts of fighting, nor even any words in the language to name the activity. There are several societies in which the male urge to defend territory, establish dominance over other males, or to accumulate and monopolize women are entirely absent. If anything is genetically determined, it can be expected to appear reliably in all human groups. Critics also challenge the ethologists' data. They object that

the ethologists' observations of animal behavior have too often been conducted upon animal groups in the artificial living conditions of a "game park" or glorified zoo. Other scholars who have observed, for example, baboon groups in a more natural forest setting have reported findings which conflict with those reported by the ethologists. Furthermore, whether animal behavior can be extrapolated upon human beings can be argued. Consequently, the ethologists have focused great popular interest upon the genetic factor in human behavior, but whether they have made a major scientific contribution or merely created a fashionable parlor diversion is not yet clear.

All that can be said with certainty is that mankind inherits a common set of basic drives and needs whose exact composition is a matter of debate. These can be satisfied through an immense variety of ways. Each drive or organic need thus becomes culturally conditioned, and each culture consists of one of the many possible systems for satisfying them.

Label each of the following statements as true or false.

_____ 1. For most of the 20th century scientific opinion has been favoring environmentalist explanations of culture rather than instinctivist ones.

_____ 2. Ethologists argue that responses such as aggression and conflict, defense of territory, status seeking, and others are determined primarily by environmental factors.

_____ 3. There is little or no evidence to challenge the theories of the ethologists.

_____ 4. There seems to be agreement that man's biological impulses and drives are conditioned by the culture.

Now turn to Answer frame 2⁷ on page 40 to check your answers.

Frame 3⁷

The Structure of Culture

People can live comfortably and efficiently together only if they know pretty well what they can expect from one another. Therefore, every society has developed a set of *norms*, which are *the customary, conventional, expected ways of acting, thinking, and feeling in that society*. Norms thus include those actions, ideas, values, rules, and relationships that most people share in a particular society.

An early sociologist, William Graham Sumner, coined the term *folkways*—literally, *the ways of the folk*—to describe the action norms of a society. American folkways include shaking hands, wearing neckties on certain occasions, eating three times a day, sleeping in beds, and all the other common ways of doing things. Each presumably originated in response to a particular need. Sumner reports that the first clothing consisted of a particular genera of leaves that would repel body flies. Today clothes are not only worn for protection and comfort, but are even worn at times when nudity might be more comfortable. Clothes are also worn for decoration, and because wearing clothes is now one of the folkways. We would feel embarrassed without them. The folkways are "proper," and one either conforms or faces social disapproval. Thus, customs arise to meet a practical need, but may outlive that need and continue simply because they have become customary.

Some of the folkways are believed to be vital to group welfare, and are therefore supported by the *mores*. The mores are the *ideas of right and wrong* which surround certain behavior. To wear a bikini to a wedding would violate the folkways, would be a breach of good manners, in "bad taste"; to go nude to a wedding would violate the mores, and be termed "immoral," for (rightly or wrongly) our society has for generations considered that public nudity would be socially harmful. The mores are, then, a society's ideas of right and wrong which forbid certain acts and require others. Our mores forbid cannibalism, infanticide, incest, and murder, and require that we pay our bills and take care of our children and aged parents.

Like folkways, mores emerge gradually from the social life of a people, representing their conclusions as to what practices are beneficial and harmful to people. Sumner said, ". . . the mores can make anything right and prevent the condemnation of anything," meaning that right and wrong become whatever the members of a society agree is good or bad for people. Having agreed that an act is harmful, these mores forbidding it are passed down from generation to generation until the circumstances of origin are forgotten. By this time, the mores have acquired a sacred character, to be accepted and obeyed without question. Our remote ancestors with a perfectly clear conscience could have as many wives and concubines as they could afford; our mores today condemn polygamy and concubinage. Unchaperoned "dates" are approved by our mores, but condemned by the mores of most Latin Americans. Mores differ dramatically in time and place. During the present decade, our traditional mores approving large families and condemning abortion are rapidly changing. Especially under conditions of rapid social change, the exact moral status of some actions may be in doubt.

In civilized societies, the most important mores may be written into *law*. Violations are then punished with legal penalties in addition to social disapproval. But not all mores are written into the law, while many laws deal with technical matters (building codes, business regulations) which are not covered by the society's mores. Occasionally a law is passed which conflicts with the mores of large groups of people (prohibition, for example); such laws are difficult if not impossible to enforce.

Social institutions are clusters of related norms

Answer frame 2⁷

1. True. The instinctivist versus environmentalist arguments have raged for years, but for most of this century the environmentalist explanations have been favored.
2. False. The ethologists argue just the opposite view—that these responses are caused by biological impulses and drives and therefore are genetically determined.
3. False. Critics point to societies in which each of the "Genetically determined" forms of behavior are absent. They also argue that ethologists' data are based on animal behavior in an artificial living situation. The question also arises as to whether animal behavior can be extrapolated upon human beings.
4. True. Each culture provides a different system for satisfying the basic drives and needs of man.

If you missed any of the above, you should reread Frame 2⁷ before turning to Frame 3⁷ on page 39.

Frame 3⁷ continued

centered upon a major human concern. Major social institutions are family, religion, government, economy, and education. In each case, a vital human concern is met through an appropriate series of norms, together with a set of supporting attitudes, values, beliefs, and sentiments. The clusters of norms surrounding some less vital human interests are also sometimes called institutions, such as baseball or Christmas, and there is no firm boundary dividing institutions from lesser culture complexes.

Behavior is *institutionalized* when it has been formalized and standardized, has been defined as proper and good, and surrounded with supporting safeguards and arrangements to protect people from being hurt. In our society, dating is institutionalized, while premarital intercourse is not.

Subcultures and Countercultures

A subculture is a cluster of somewhat divergent norms shared by a group or category of people within a society. The "youth subculture" in our society today includes a set of values of work, music, dress, and morality, and a special vocabulary which set youth somewhat apart from their elders. Not many youth fully accept the "hippie" subculture, but most of today's youth are in some degree affected by it.

There are countless subcultures in our society. The occupational subcultures of the jazz musician, the Christian missionary, and the college professor differ dramatically. There are numerous racial, religious, social class, regional, and special interest subcultures. The most rapidly growing magazines today are those aimed at a special interest subculture (*Boats and Boating, Guns and Ammo, Popular Photography,* etc.). There are, of course, varying degrees of involvement; not every owner of a surfboard has dipped very deeply into the "surfing" subculture, but one is there for him to share if he wishes. One person may share in a considerable number of subcultures, some highly important to him (sex, race, class) and others more trivial (recreational subcultures).

Most subcultures serve to reinforce the dominant culture by providing opportunity for individual expression of special interests without abandoning the dominant culture. But some subcultures are in opposition to the dominant culture, and some sociologists term these *counter-cultures* (or perhaps contracultures). The counterculture rejects major elements of the established normative structure. Examples would include delinquent gangs, revolutionary movements, and some aspects of the hippie subculture. Those who embrace the counterculture have separated themselves from the dominant culture and operate by their own normative system. They are often feared or disliked by conventional people, usually rejected, and sometimes persecuted.

Is each of the following true or false?

_____ 1.   All "folkways" are "norms," but not all "norms" are "folkways."

_____ 2.   "Mores" are ideas of right and wrong and are constant from society to society.

_____ 3.   One can belong to various subcultures and have differing degrees of involvement in them.

_____ 4.   Subcultures always serve to reinforce the dominant culture.

Now turn to Answer frame 3[7] on page 42 to check your answers.

Frame 4[7]

Real and Ideal Culture

Every society has a system of behavior norms defining the behavior that is proper and moral. This is the *ideal culture—the norms people are supposed to follow.* But in all societies, the actual behavior of people deviates somewhat from this ideal. The *real culture* consists of the *norms most people actually follow,* while possibly paying lip service to the ideal norms. Our ideal culture includes obedience to law, premarital chastity, and marital fidelity; in our real culture, exceeding the speed limit by a few miles an hour is normal, while premarital and extramarital intercourse are fairly common.

To some extent, the discrepancy between real and ideal culture may be a measure of human frailty—few people live up to their standards all of the time. Some may be due to normative confusion; not all persons or groups share the same norms, and some subcultures are in conflict with the norms of the dominant culture. Or it may be due to social change; the norms of the ideal culture are likely to change only after most people have already abandoned them in practice. In such a manner our ideal norms respecting marijuana use, premarital intercourse, and abortion appear to be changing today.

Ethos and Ethnocentrism

The *ethos* of a culture is *the characteristic core of values which is central to a culture.* For example, American culture is noted for its materialism, competitiveness, technological progress, and demand for speed and punctuality; Latin American cultures are more relaxed, more emotionally expressive, less materialistic, and less concerned with change and punctuality. The "joie de vivre" of the French, the taciturn reserve of the English, the methodical diligence of the Germans, and the informality of the Americans are reflections of differing ethos. The term "national character" is a popular term which comes quite close to the concept of ethos.

The term *ethnocentrism* has been coined to describe *the tendency of all known human groups to assume the superiority of their culture* (or subculture, or group) over all others. To an American, our monogamous marriages and free choice of marriage partners is evidence of our cultural superiority over "uncivilized" peoples. With an equal ethnocentrism, these "uncivilized" peoples define their bride purchase prices and parent-arranged matches as evidence of their culture's high respect for womanhood. All societies, and all known human groups within societies, are ethnocentric. (Our fraternity is, somehow, better than all others!) Ethnocentrism is not a rational conclusion, but an automatic, emotional response, a "taking for granted" of something so obvious that it does not need to be demonstrated.

Ethnocentrism is revealed in the unthinking way virtually all people make statements which betray their value judgments and impose them upon others. Such statements as: "There is nothing good on TV tonight," "The new styles are perfectly hideous," "Never trust anyone over 30," or "Nobody would want to buy that stuff," are all ethnocentric. All assume the correctness of the speaker's value judgments. But to say, "There's nothing on TV that interests me," or "I don't like the new styles" is not ethnocentric,

Answer frame 3⁷

1. True. They both refer to the habitual behavior or normal, customary ways of doing things in a particular society, but norms also include mores, laws, values, and relationships.
2. False. While mores are ideas of right and wrong which surround certain behavior (i.e., not going nude to a wedding), they are not constant from society to society or even in the same society over time. Mores of a society at a particular time are whatever the members of a society agree is good or bad for people.
3. True. One person may share in a number of subcultures, some highly important to him (racial, religious) and others more trivial (recreational subcultures).
4. False. Some subcultures are in opposition to the dominant culture in that they reject major elements of the established structure. Examples of such subcultures (or countercultures) are delinquent gangs, revolutionary movements, and so on.

If you missed any of the above, you should review Frame 3⁷ before turning to Frame 4⁷ on page 41.

Frame 4⁷ continued

for one is merely stating a personal preference, not announcing it as a standard which others should follow.

Ethnocentrism promotes group identity and loyalty, unites the group, and makes it more cohesive. Organizations and nations actively promote ethnocentrism for this reason. Schools are expected to distort history to our advantage, and to cultivate a self-righteous condescension to other peoples in the name of "patriotism," while churches cultivate a disdain for other belief systems in the name of "faith." Ethnocentrism discourages the adoption of culture traits from other cultures. Depending upon circumstances, this may protect the culture from damaging influences, or prevent it from making necessary adaptations. For example, the technological and commercial development which many countries desire is retarded by many traditional norms of political and family life which they are reluctant to change. Ethnocentrism, with its bland assumption that any rational people must think as we do, leads nations into many mistakes in their dealings with other nations. A set of highly ethnocentric assumptions about Vietnam, in the opinion of many observers, led the United States into one of the greatest political and military disasters in the nation's history, where a more realistic appraisal of the wishes and needs of the Vietnam people might have spared the nation this blunder. Thus, ethnocentrism may either strengthen or weaken a nation, and sustain or undermine a culture, according to circumstances.

Cultural Relativity

The concept of *cultural relativity* means that *the effects of a culture trait or complex are relative to its cultural setting.* Whether a particular practice is "good" or "bad" depends upon the network of norms and values into which it fits. Early marriages and high birth rates are necessary in a society with high death rates. When death rates fall sharply, high birth rates are a certain road to disaster. In order to understand how a cultural trait or complex operates in its own cultural setting, it is necessary to understand what meanings and functions it carries for the people who practice it. To most Americans, wife purchase seems to be a degrading custom. Our ethnocentrism betrays us into visualizing women being purchased like slaves or cattle and treated as property. But among people who practice wife purchase, it carries no such suggestions. Typically it is a complicated property arrangement between the respective families, showing mutual respect and acceptance, and serving as a pledge for good behavior. Thus a wife who is neglected and mistreated may return home, and the bride-price is forfeit, giving the husband the task of persuading his family to part with another bride-price unless he wishes to remain lonely. But if the wife is at fault, the husband may return her for refund or replacement, and one can imagine the reception she gets from her family under these circumstances. Thus the bride-price helps to arrange "appropriate" matches and to stabilize the marriages. For almost any "quaint," "odd," or "revolting" custom of another people, a more careful examination will generally reveal some useful functions it fulfills. For Americans, wife purchase would fill no useful purposes, and would conflict with many of our traditions and values. The concept of cultural relativity thus reveals how wife purchase works very well and is very "good" for some societies, but would work badly and would be "bad" for our society. Whether a trait is "good" or "bad" cannot be decided without first determining what its consequences are within its own cultural setting.

Cultural Integration

A culture is more than a collection of traits; it is an organized system of traits, norms, values, etc. *Cultural integration* refers to *the degree of harmonious interrelatedness of the various elements of a culture.* Our culture is integrated around its technological-industrial-commercial system, and many of our norms and values are adjusted to complement that system. Eskimo culture was integrated around hunting seal and walrus, the Plains Indians around buffalo hunting, the Southwest Indians around maize growing. When the buffalo was exterminated, the Plains Indians were defeated and demoralized. So much of their culture revolved around the buffalo hunt and the many uses of the buffalo that when the buffalo disappeared, the "bottom dropped out of everything" for them. The different parts of a culture must "fit together" harmoniously if it is to function efficiently. For example, the patri-archal family, ruled by the father, was fully compatible with an agricultural society where the family all worked together under the father's direction, but when wives and children began earning individual paychecks, such authority became difficult to maintain. In many developing nations, the family institutions include obligations which conflict with the rational operation of industrial and commercial enterprises. Many social problems are problems of cultural integration—of incorporating new social changes into the culture without unendurable disharmony.

Cultural integration and cultural relativity are two very closely related concepts which are easy to confuse. They are two different ways of looking at and describing the interrelatedness of the many parts of a culture. Integration describes the degree to which the different parts fit together harmoniously. Relativity describes how the working of one part depends upon the other parts which surround it. When using the concept of cultural integration, we look at the entire culture to see how smoothly it all fits together. In rural agricultural America of a century ago, we would note how the high birth rates, the patriarchal family, and the values of hard work and thrift all fit together. In modern urbanized industrialized America, however, low birth rates, the democratic family, and a value system oriented toward leisure and consumption all fit together. When we use the concept of cultural relativity, we look to see how a particular trait relates to the rest of the culture. Thrift was a useful value a century ago; it fits the needs of a people with a frontier to settle and a shortage of capital. If we all became "thrifty" today, buying only what we absolutely needed, the result would be depression and unemployment, and, if we persisted, the transformation of our culture into a quite different one.

True or false?

_____ 1. There are differences between the *ideal* culture and the *real* culture in all societies.

_____ 2. The ethos of our culture includes materialism, competitiveness, technological progress, demand for speed and punctuality, and informality.

_____ 3. There is a tendency for all human groups to assume the superiority of their own culture, group, or value judgments.

_____ 4. Cultural integration and cultural relativity mean the same thing.

Now turn to Answer frame 4[7] on page 46 to check your answers.

chapter 8

SOCIAL AND CULTURAL CHANGE

Frame 1[8]

All societies and all cultures are constantly changing—some rapidly and some slowly. Even the most static culture is gradually changing. Language slowly changes, as one finds if he compares successive editions of the dictionary. Legends are forgotten or modified in their retelling. But while some cultures have changed so little that one could be "time-machined" back a thousand years and notice little difference, others change so rapidly that people become misfits within a single lifetime.

There is a technical difference between social and cultural change. *Social change is change in social structure and social relationships*—in status systems, sex relations, population distribution, power systems, organizations, etc. *Cultural change is change in the culture of a society*—in its norms, values, technology, art, literature, lan-

guage, etc. This distinction is not very important, and the terms are often used interchangeably; or the term "social change" is simply used to include both.

Processes of Social and Cultural Change

There are three major processes of change—discovery, invention, and diffusion. A *discovery* is *a human perception of a condition or relationship that already exists*. Men discovered that the earth rotates, that germs cause disease, that self-concept affects performance. An *invention* is *a new combination of existing objects or knowledge to make a new product*. A stick, a stone, and a length of animal tendon are simply natural objects; when man ties the stone to the stick with the tendon and makes a club, he makes an invention. The term *innovation* is sometimes used to include both discovery and invention.

Diffusion is the spread of knowledge and culture traits, both among the members of a society, and from one society to another. Diffusion is an acceptance process, and not all discoveries or inventions are accepted. Some are rejected, only to be rediscovered or reinvented and accepted later. Diffusion is selective. When two societies come into contact, each accepts some traits and rejects others. Diffusion between societies is a two-way process, with the more simple societies usually accepting more from the complex societies than they give to the complex societies. Thus the American Indians accepted a great many traits from the American settlers, while contributing a few, such as tobacco, corn, and the canoe.

Diffusion is an adaptive process, for culture traits are generally modified in the diffusion process. Every trait has *form, function, and meaning*, any or all of which may change during diffusion. Tobacco diffused from American Indians to settlers and Europeans, who added to the form (retaining the pipe while adding cigarettes, cigars, snuff, and tobacco chewing), but changed the function (ceremonial) and the meaning (religious) which Indians found in tobacco. Form usually diffuses more easily than function and meaning. The rituals and outward forms of Christianity, democracy, and corporate capitalism have been far more widely copied than their functions and meanings.

A fourth process of change, not always mentioned, is the gradual, unconscious change through imperfect learning and copying. Words die out or change in meaning; legends die out or become modified; some folkways disappear or gradually change. In the most static societies, their very limited change is mostly of this type.

Factors Influencing the Rate of Change

Changes in physical environment are rather rare, but their impact can be very great. They may stimulate mass migrations, or revolutionize the lives of those who remain. Major climatic change in North Africa thousands of years ago transformed a well-watered farmland into a thinly populated desert. Man-made changes in physical environment have been locally important. Irrigation can make the desert bloom; but in time, salinization may return it to desert again, as in the ancient Tigris-Euphrates river valleys. Man-made changes today are potentially catastrophic. Reckless, destructive coal mining practices in Appalachia have produced such deforestation, erosion, and river pollution as to force a heavy migration from the area. Man is even well on his way to changing the physical environment so that it will no longer support human life. To date, however, physical environmental change has been a relatively rare factor in social change, with most changes arising from other factors.

Population size, distribution, and composition are factors in social change. A large population has a large number of innovators, and an innovation need be conceived by only one person to be copied and shared by all. Youthful populations are more receptive to change than aging populations. Rapid change in population size, in either direction, brings inevitable changes.

Contact and isolation affect social change. Isolation discourages diffusion and encourages conservatism. All the most primitive peoples are highly isolated, while the world's crossroads have always been centers of change. Peoples who wish to protect their culture from diffusion from other societies have always sought to prevent contacts with other societies (ancient Hebrews, modern China).

Values and attitudes which prevail within a society may encourage or discourage change. A reverence for the past and for the aged discourages change, while pride in "progress" and the cult of youth encourage change. Values also affect the kinds of change in a society. Ancient Greeks were highly innovative in art, architecture, literature, and philosophy, but relatively static in technology, since gentlemen were unconcerned about lightening the work of slaves.

Social structure affects change. Authoritarian societies promote some changes while forbidding others. Church power, and unity of church and state, tend to discourage change. Democratic organization anywhere—in family, school, church, or state—is more conducive to social change.

Perceived needs of a society encourage and

Answer frame 4[7]

1. True. The ideal culture consists of the norms people are supposed to follow, while the real culture consists of the norms most people actually do follow. There are differences between the two in all societies.
2. True. These are the characteristic values which are central to our culture.
3. True. This phenomenon is referred to as ethnocentrism and is an automatic, emotional response rather than one based on rationality.
4. False. They are closely related but do not mean the same thing. In using cultural integration we look at the *entire culture* (i.e., rural agricultural America) to see how smoothly it all fits together. When using cultural relativity we look to see how *a particular trait* (i.e., low birth rates) relates to the rest of the culture.

If you missed any of the above, you should restudy Frame 4[7] before beginning Chapter 8 on page 44.

Frame 1[8] continued

direct change. But it is important to note that the only "needs" which stimulate change are those which are perceived as needs by a people. Many innovations languished until a need was perceived (usually as a result of other social changes), whereupon they were accepted.

The *cultural base* is perhaps the most important factor in the rate of change. The cultural base is the accumulation of earlier discoveries, inventions, and technical skills which the innovator can use. A basic invention, like the wheel, is used in thousands of later inventions. The principle of the steam engine was known for thousands of years, but a practical steam engine could not be built until metal-working technology had advanced far enough to machine parts to a tolerance of a few thousandths of an inch.

Often an innovation in one field will provide raw material for innovations in unrelated fields. This is called *cross-fertilization*. The vacuum tube, and later the transistor, developed for use in radio communication, made the electronic computer possible. From the nuclear physicist's search for more deadly weapons has come radioactive materials that are used in many kinds of medical research, diagnosis, and treatment. One cannot know in what remote fields his discoveries and inventions may find application.

The *exponential principle* states that, as the cultural base grows, the possibilities for new inventions and discoveries grow in a geometric ratio. As an illustration, everyone who plays Scrabble knows that with six letters one can spell not merely twice as many words as with three, but several times as many. This helps explain the accelerating rate of invention in the modern world. Cave man could invent very little, no matter how innovative he might have been, because he had so little to work with. Modern man has a steadily growing cultural base, providing the raw materials for a flood of innovation which has not, as yet, shown any signs of slowing down.

Indicate whether each of the following statements is true or false by writing "T" or "F" in the space provided.

_____ 1. All societies and all cultures are constantly changing.

_____ 2. The function and meaning of culture traits diffuse more easily than the forms.

_____ 3. Of the various factors that influence the rate of change, changes in physical environment are quite rare.

_____ 4. The social structure is the most important factor in the rate of change.

_____ 5. The *Peter Principle* explains the accelerating rate of invention in the modern world.

Now turn to Answer frame 1[8] on page 48 to check your responses.

Frame 2[8]

Acceptance and Resistance to Change

Attitudes toward change not only affect the rate of innovation, but also affect whether an innovation is diffused throughout the society. Attitudes which value "progress," the awareness of unfulfilled needs, and an absence of reverence for the past all encouraged the acceptance of innovation.

Demonstrability of innovations hastens their acceptance. Innovations which can easily be tested on a small scale, and shown to be workable, will be more readily accepted. Most mechanical inventions can be demonstrated quite easily and cheaply. Most social inventions, such as the alphabet, the decimal system, pacifism, or world government were more difficult to demonstrate.

Compatibility with the existing culture simplifies acceptance. If the innovation does not conflict with any values or practices of the existing culture, so that it can be added without displacing anything (or without any awareness that it will displace anything), its acceptance is encouraged. But an innovation may be incompatible in several ways.

1. The innovation may conflict with established patterns, as, for example, the proposed legalization of marijuana conflicts with a number of traditional attitudes and values. When an innovation conflicts with the existing culture, this conflict may be resolved in three ways: (*a*) the innovation may be rejected (as many people, probably a majority, reject the legalization of marijuana); (*b*) it may be accepted and the conflicting cultural values or practices may be adjusted to remove the conflict (removing marijuana from the list of "narcotic" drugs and defining it as harmless); (*c*) it may be accepted and the conflict evaded by rationalization (claims that marijuana is harmless; that it is less harmful than alcohol or tobacco; that prohibition makes matters worse).

2. The innovation may demand new patterns not present in the culture. When the Plains In-

dians acquired horses from the Spaniards, they had no norms for the ownership and inheritance of private property, and were forced to develop some.

3. Some innovations are substitutive, not additive. An innovation which can simply be added, without displacing any of the existing culture, is accepted more readily. Thus, American baseball and "western" movies have been accepted more widely than American democracy. Innovations which demand immediate discard of a traditional value or practice, like free love or communism in America, or rational business enterprise in the underdeveloped countries, are less readily accepted.

Costs of change discourage acceptance. Nearly all social changes involve some costs to somebody. The "jumbo jets" require costly rebuilding of airport facilities. A metric system of measurement would be far more efficient than our clumsy, archaic system based on the length of a dead English king's arm. But the costs of the changeover would be so great that we keep postponing it.

Often a change would be beneficial to some but costly to others. *Vested interests* are those who profit from things as they are, just as property owners benefit from the private property system, welfare clients have a vested interest in the welfare system, and college students are gaining a vested interest in the cash value of a college degree. Vested interests generally oppose change. Wagon masters opposed the railroads, and the railroads opposed building canals and seaways. But sometimes vested interests support changes which they perceive will benefit them. Most social reforms are finally achieved when powerful vested interests come to redefine their vested interests, that is, they come to believe that the change will benefit them. Thus Medicare was opposed by medical associations, but supported by hospital associations, nursing associations, labor unions, and organizations of the aged.

Answer frame 1⁸

1. True. Even the most static culture is gradually changing. The rate of change varies among societies, but all societies and culture are constantly changing.
2. False. Form usually diffuses more easily than function and meaning. For example, the rituals and outward forms of Christianity have been far more widely copied than their functions and meanings.
3. True. Although they are rare, their impact can be very great.
4. False. Social structure is important, but the *cultural base* is perhaps the most important factor in the rate of change. The cultural base is the accumulation of earlier discoveries, inventions, and technical skills which the innovator can use.
5. False. The *exponential principle* states that, as the cultural base grows, the possibilities for new inventions and discoveries grow in a geometric ratio.

If you missed any of the above, you should restudy Frame 1⁸ before turning to Frame 2⁸ on page 47.

Frame 2⁸ continued

Is each of the following true or false?

_____ 1. Attitudes toward change affect whether an innovation is diffused throughout the society.

_____ 2. Innovations may conflict with existing culture, but this conflict can frequently be resolved.

_____ 3. Substitutive innovations are more readily accepted than are additive inventions.

_____ 4. Vested interests generally oppose change.

Now turn to Answer frame 2⁸ on page 50 to check your answers.

Frame 3⁸

Social Change and Social Disorganization

Social Effects of Discovery and Invention. An innovation always sends shock waves throughout the culture. Ogburn compiled a list of 150 social changes which he attributed to the invention and acceptance of the automobile. Gunpowder ended feudalism, machine guns ended cavalry, and nuclear weapons have made it impossible to "win" a major war. No important invention fails to set in motion an almost unending series of social consequences.

Change and Cultural Lag. Since culture is interrelated and integrated, an innovation that produces changes in some parts of the culture requires adjustments in the related parts of the culture. Jumbo jets require new airport facilities, to a cite a very simple example. But needed adjustments take time, and this time interval is called *cultural lag,* a concept coined by Ogburn. He observed that workmen's compensation laws were not passed for about 50 years after workers started entering large factories where they could not individually protect themselves against accident and injury. We did not establish the Social Security system until long after urbanization and industrialization had destroyed the ability of the worker, or his family, to insure his old age security. For a current example, it is widely recognized today that zero population growth is our only alternative to population disaster, but it will take time to change the idea that each couple has the right to bear as many children as they wish. In a rapidly changing world, cultural lags are numerous and persistent.

Personal and Social Disorganization. All change disrupts established routines and relationships and requires new adjustments. Some changes which look quite innocuous may actually produce major disruptions. The invention of barbed wire produced range wars, ended the open range, and simplified the survival of small ranches. The automobile is given credit for the growth of suburbs, but the electric pump and the septic tank were equally important.

Even "desirable" changes may be painfully disruptive. Our population explosion arises from our success in the humane endeavor of promoting good health. Either societies must "adjust" by voluntarily limiting family size, or Malthusian misery will set the limits for them.

People's capacity to absorb and adjust to change is not unlimited. The changes can be too great, or the nature of the changes may be so disruptive, that people become *disorganized*. This means that they are confused and uncertain. The rules they have learned don't seem to apply, and their behavior becomes uncontrolled and erratic. When large numbers of people have become uncertain what to believe or how to act, the society has become disorganized. *Social disorganization is the disruption of established social arrangements and social controls through social change.* In a disorganized society, the traditional rules have become undermined, while no new rules have yet gained general support or firm binding power. Thus the traditional rules and laws forbidding drug use are being disregarded by many of the young, but no new rules defining "proper" and "improper" drug use have yet emerged. Change undermines established beliefs and values. Thrift and large families have long been highly approved values, but today, overindulgence in either is socially injurious. Thus the change-disorganization-reorganization cycle is continuous in all societies today.

Changes may be so numerous and disruptive that the goals people have been socialized to seek may no longer be attainable or look desirable. When this happens, people become *demoralized*. They lose their morale, and become listless and apathetic. The culture of the Plains Indians was so highly integrated around the buffalo that the intentional extermination of the buffalo by the white man not only ended the Indian wars but left the Indians demoralized. The disappearance of the buffalo left their economy destroyed, their religion a useless shell, and their status system completely unworkable. Their traditional goals which made life worth living were now unattainable, and (aside from the difficult problem of learning another set) they were excluded from any real participation in the white man's culture. In a few instances where Indians had made a successful transition to a peaceful, productive agricultural economy, such as the Cherokee in northern Georgia, this adjustment was soon destroyed by the white man's greed for the Indian's land. There was little left for the Indian but to drink, dream, and die—which he often did. Demoralization is often accompanied by population decline, and a number of human societies have become extinct. American Indian population today is growing rapidly, but problems of disorganization and demoralization remain.

To prevent social and cultural change today would be impossible. The constantly expanding cultural base provides endless materials for innovation, and we have institutionalized the promotion of change in the form of organized research. Whether human beings have the capacity to absorb and integrate such great change remains to be determined.

Label each of the following statements as true or false.

_____ 1. An innovation that produces changes in some parts of a culture will not usually require changes in other parts.

_____ 2. Desirable changes are never painfully disruptive.

_____ 3. The reduction or even the loss of social control is a product of rapid social change.

_____ 4. According to the authors, human beings do not have the capacity to absorb and integrate increasingly rapid and endless change.

Now turn to Answer frame 3[8] on page 50 to check your answers.

Answer frame 2⁸

1.   True. Attitudes which value "progress," the awareness of unfulfilled needs, and an absence of reverence for the past all encourage the acceptance of innovation.
2.   True. Existing values and norms are frequently adjusted to remove the conflict, or the conflict is evaded by some rationalization that makes the innovation easier to accept.
3.   False. An additive innovation, e.g., baseball, is accepted more readily than substitutive innovations, e.g., free love, because it can be added without any obvious costs or sacrifices.
4.   True. Vested interests are those who profit from things as they are, and often a change would be costly to them. Vested interests generally oppose change. For example, the American Medical Association opposed Social Security and Medicare.

If you missed any of the above, you should review Frame 2⁸ before turning to Frame 3⁸ on page 48.

Answer frame 3⁸

1.   False. Since the parts of a culture are interrelated and integrated, an innovation that produces changes in some parts of the culture requires adjustments in the related parts of the culture.
2.   False. All change disrupts established routines and relationships and requires often painful new adjustments. Our population explosion arises from our success in the humane endeavor of promoting good health.
3.   True. If change is too fast or too disruptive, rules that regulated conduct under an earlier set of conditions may not regulate conduct later. Social disorganization is the disruption of social controls through rapid social change.
4.   False. The authors suggest this as a possibility—not a fact. Whether human beings have this capacity is unknown. The promotion of social change is now institutionalized in our society.

If you missed any of the above, you should reread Frame 3⁸ before beginning Chapter 9.

chapter 9

SOCIAL INSTITUTIONS

The word "institution" has so many popular meanings that it is difficult to define concisely. In popular usage, "institutions" may refer to formal organizations such as a church, a state legislature, or a university; to a culture complex such as marriage or baseball; to cultural objects such as the American hot dog or television sets; or to a sentiment-laden social role such as the village blacksmith or the country school teacher. Even within sociological literature the term appears both as an important cluster of norms and values and as large-scale organizations or associations such as the Red Cross or the army. Most sociologists today, however, are defining an *institution as an organized system of social norms and relationships which embody certain common values and procedures which meet basic needs of the society. Associations,* as distinguished from institutions, are *groups of people organized for a particular purpose.*

The institution consists of the norms, values, statuses, roles, and relationships which surround an important activity. The institution of religion includes sets of common values and norms (doctrine, faith, devotion), with sets of common procedures (worship, rituals, ceremonies), with defined roles and statuses (lay member, priest, deacon, convert). The First Methodist Church on Main Street is not an institution; it is an association of people who share a particular faith. The body of beliefs, values, rituals, and relationships comprise the institution; the membership of a congregation or of a denomination from an association. Likewise, the institution of the family is not a single family, but consists of the values, norms, and patterns of family life followed in a society.

Institutions originate in the patterns that emerge as people live together. As people grapple with common problems, standardized modes of behavior gradually emerge and norms and values develop around them. *Institutionalization* is the process whereby standardized patterns are developed and integrated into the normative structure of the society. For example, people in the exchange of goods develop certain patterns and rules for this exchange. Direct barter is one kind of pattern which a number of societies institutionalized with different tribes or groups meeting at specified intervals and conducting exchanges according to well-understood rules and traditions. Money is another institutionalized means of exchange. Appropriate rules are standardized, defining what constitutes a fair exchange, and eventually written into the law. Thus the economic institutions of a society are developed.

Institutionalized Roles

Within each institution there are specific statuses and roles. In the family there are the statuses of parents, children, and various relatives, with appropriate roles for each status. The institutionalized roles provide predictable behavior patterns through which the activities can be carried out, efficiently and without confusion, with strong sanctions for proper role performance. An institutionalized norm originates as a practical way of getting something done; but these conditions of its origin are soon forgotten, and the institutionalized norm acquires an aura of sanctity and timelessness which protects it from criticism or rational appraisal. One does not challenge private property, motherhood, the flag, baseball, or apple pie unless he is willing to be branded as un-American. As Wilson says, institutions provide "frozen answers to fundamental questions."

Manifest and Latent Functions of Institutions

The functions of an institution include both the *manifest functions, those which are intended and recognized,* and the *latent functions, those which are unintended and perhaps unrecognized.* The manifest functions of our military institutions are national defense and implementation of our foreign policy; their latent functions include educating youth, providing jobs and profits, stimulating some kinds of scientific research, spreading venereal disease, and exercising a disputed degree of influence upon foreign policy and domestic politics. Our health institutions have the manifest function of reducing illness and death; their latent function has been to create the population explosion. The latent functions of religious ceremonials sometimes seem to overshadow the manifest functions. The manifest function of the Indian rain dance was to bring rain; the latent functions included opportunities for sociability, display of family wealth, courtship, and others. The manifest function of the corporation was to organize resources efficiently for large-scale business enterprise; the latent functions included promoting the growth of labor unions—a development unintended and certainly not desired by the incorporators.

Interrelationships of Institutions

Institutions do not function independently; they overlap and affect one another. Changing economic institutions have been largely responsible for changes in the family—receiving their own paychecks has increased the independence of wives and children; working hours and daily routines have been rearranged; families move far more often; and a reduced need for child labor has made large families uneconomic. The "welfare state" has arisen mainly because of changes in economic and familial institutions. No institution operates in a vacuum; each is part of a culture that must be somewhat integrated.

Institutional Change

All societies change continuously, some more rapidly than others. The effect of change is to make some of the old institutional norms ineffective and to create new needs for the institution to fulfill. This results in institutional change, a modification of the normative and value structure of the institution. The family today is far less a working team or a producing unit than formerly, and far more a consumption and companionship unit. Educational and political institutions have assumed many tasks that used to be fulfilled by family and church. Churches are attempting to revise their message and program to meet the needs of an urbanized, industrialized society. All institutions must be adapted to social and cultural change, but institutions are the most tradition-encrusted part of a culture, and are highly resistant to change. For example, "property rights" are often perceived, not as a set of practical compromises among people, but as something natural, fixed, and eternal, with which it is wicked to tamper. The social ideal of the large family persisted for a long time after it became clear to demographers that the world was becoming desperately overcrowded. Thus, the institutions of a rapidly changing society are generally somewhat out of date. By the time one set of quaint anachronisms has been updated, others have developed.

Indicate whether each of the following statements is true or false by writing "T" or "F" in the space provided.

_____ 1. The First Methodist Church on Main Street is an *institution.*

_____ 2. *Bureaucratization* is the process whereby standardized patterns are developed and integrated into the normative structure of the society.

_____ 3. Institutionalized norms acquire an aura of sanctity and timelessness which protect them from rational appraisal.

_____ 4. Institutions are functionally autonomous.

_____ 5. Institutions are the most tradition-encrusted part of culture, and are highly resistant to change.

Now turn to Answer frame 1[9] on page 54 to check your responses.

chapter 10

TYPES OF GROUPS

Frame 1[10]

Groups are important. A person has as many selves as he has groups—a somewhat different self for each group. We become socialized through group experience; most of our satisfactions and disappointments come through group relationships.

The various definitions of *group* usually include both a *common identity* or *awareness of membership* and *social interaction between members*. A bus load of passengers is not a group; if the driver stops for a few drinks, they quickly become a group. The term group is often confused with the terms *category* and *aggregation* or *collectivity*. A *category* is composed of *people who share some common characteristic* but have no shared interaction. Males, whites, college graduates, bankers, adolescents, ex-convicts, and persons with type B blood are categories, not groups. A *collectivity* or *aggregation* is a *physical gathering of people* without a shared sense of identity or interaction. The people gathering in a stadium are a collectivity or aggregation; when

the game begins, they become an audience (one kind of group), but this group may dissolve back into a collectivity any number of times when nothing is happening to center their attention.

Some Major Group Classifications

In-Groups and Out-Groups.   *In-groups* are those *for which one has a feeling of membership*, such as one's family, clique, fraternity. *Out-groups* are *all groups toward which one has no feelings of membership or belonging*—other families, other cliques, other clubs and organizations. References to our in-groups are prefaced by "we" or "my," and out-groups by "they" or "them." Obviously, every group is both an in-group and an out-group—an in-group to its members, and an out-group to everyone else. And there can be in-groups within in-groups. For example, Alpha Kappa Delta members are an in-group when interacting with members of Phi

Answer frame 1[9]

1. False. It is an *association* of people who share a particular faith. The *institution* of religion is the organized set of values, norms, practices, roles, and statuses which surround religious activity.
2. False. *Institutionalization* is the process described. *Bureaucratization* is the process whereby voluntary associations are formally structured and activities are rationally coordinated (due to large size).
3. True. One normally does not rationally appraise such institutionalized normative systems as private property, motherhood, democracy, and free enterprise.
4. False. Institutions do not function independently; they overlap and affect one another. Example: a changing economy produces a changing family.
5. True. The institutions of even the most rapidly changing society are generally somewhat out of date.

If you missed any of the above, you should restudy Frame 1[9] before turning to Chapter 10 on page 53.

Frame 1[10] continued

Delta Theta; but when interacting with "barbarians" who belong to no fraternity, all fraternity men join together in an in-group against these outsiders.

The in-group and out-group responses are also extended to categories in which we are included or excluded—my age group, religion, occupation, sex, race, home town, nation—and all others. Let any man drop a thoughtless remark about "crazy women drivers" and watch all the women bristle! In-group and out-group feelings are important because the responses are different. Toward our in-groups (or sometimes categories with which we identify) we tend to be sympathetic, helpful, trusting, and protective. Note how men "stick together" when women criticize them, and how most people react defensively when their occupation, religion, or age category is attacked. Toward out-groups (and categories), the responses may be of many kinds —indifferent, hostile, competitive, suspicious, defensive, exploitative—but never the same as toward the in-group. The two sex categories certainly are not indifferent to each other, and not always hostile; yet men definitely respond to women differently than they respond to other men!

Much behavior can be understood only in terms of in-group and out-group responses. Note the political candidate's efforts to establish an in-group relationship with every group and category among his electorate. Soap operas thrive on stories of the in-group/out-group relationships involved in family and professional problems. In-groups encourage group loyalty and serve as a mechanism of social control, as shown by teen-aged conformity to current youth dress styles and vocabulary. In-groups encourage ethnocentrism and may even violently oppose outgroups. Soldiers are trained in the art of exterminating out-group nationalities. Even when the enemies are racially and culturally similar, the conflict process creates out-group feelings and responses toward them.

The ethnocentrism of in-groups encourages the rejection of out-groups. This feeling of rejection toward out-groups is called *social distance*, a measure of the degree of acceptability or nonacceptability of other groups and categories. For example, a student taking a social distance test might indicate that he would accept English, Hungarian, and Turk as fellow student, English and Hungarian as roommate, but only the Englishman as brother-in-law. War propaganda is an effort to increase social distance from the enemy. War atrocities are understandable as acts against enemies who have practically ceased to be defined as members of the human race. Thus, the civilians who were casually killed in Vietnam were "gooks," not human beings.

Indicate whether each of the following statements is true or false by writing "T" or "F" in the space provided.

_____ 1.   The term "group" means the same thing as the term "collectivity."

_____ 2.   Every group is both an in-group and an out-group.

_____ 3.   In-groups discourage ethnocentrism and encourage cooperation among out-groups.

_____ 4.   *Social distance* is a measure of the degree of acceptability or nonacceptability of other groups.

Now turn to Answer frame 1[10] on page 56 to check your responses.

Frame 2[10]

Primary and Secondary Groups. *Primary groups* are small groups, seldom over a dozen or two, *in which the relationships are informal, intimate, and personal.* Examples include the family, play group, clique, or small circle of close friends, and possibly work crew or neighbors. Primary groups must be small, for it is impossible to know *intimately* all the members of a large group. Large groups often include a number of primary groups, as cliques form within the membership of a fraternity or student body. In *secondary groups, the relationships are formal, impersonal, segmental, and instrumental.* Examples might include formal organizations such as labor unions, chambers of commerce, P.T.A. or church, but also such small, temporary groups as salesperson and customer. Secondary group contacts are *impersonal* (the salesperson is expected to treat all customers with the same courteous consideration, regardless of his personal reaction to them); *segmental* (involving not the total person, but only that segment of the person which is relevant to the task at hand); and *instrumental* (for the purpose of getting some job done). Primary groups are *relationship-oriented*, filling our need for warm, intimate, human relationship; secondary groups are *goal-oriented*, and exist for the purpose of getting some task done. True, the union or the medical society may provide some pleasant relationships, but these are incidental to their main purposes.

Conversation in primary groups is unplanned, relaxed, rambling, and sometimes confidential. Members are interested in each other, and *care* about one another. Conversation in secondary groups is more scheduled, planned, reserved, and

businesslike, with reminders to "get to the point" if one rambles. Secondary groups are evaluated according to their efficiency in getting tasks done. Primary groups are valued for the satisfactions they bring through intimate human interaction. Whenever people are thrown into an impersonal world—at college, in military service, in a large factory—they promptly form primary groups.

Both primary and secondary groups maintain standards, norms, and expectations for behavior. Rejection is the penalty for disregard of group norms. The influence and informal social control of primary groups is much stronger than for secondary groups. One can endure rejection by the P.T.A., but not by parents or close friends. The primary group is the more influential in setting standards for personal behavior. Even the difference between heroism and cowardice may lie in one's group relationships. Stouffer's famous study of *The American Soldier* showed that soldiers do not fight for their country or for democracy, but, rather, their greatest concern in battle is to protect their buddies (primary group members). Excellently trained soldiers are undependable in battle unless they are part of a tightly-knit primary group whose members trust and feel responsible for one another. The military has reorganized training to encourage primary group identification, with the "team approach" making each soldier directly responsible for the rest of the platoon.

Voluntary and Involuntary Groups and Associations.   Most application blanks ask one to list his organizational memberships. These memberships are one way of classifying or "sizing up" people. And organizations are an effective way of

Answer frame 1[10]

1. False. Members of groups have a shared sense of identity and they interact, but members of a collectivity have neither a shared sense of identity nor do they interact.
2. True. A group is an in-group to its members and an out-group to its nonmembers.
3. False. In-groups encourage ethnocentrism and may violently oppose out-groups.
4. True. The feeling of rejection toward out-groups is called *social distance*.

If you missed any of the above, you should restudy Frame 1[10] before turning to Frame 2[10] on page 55.

Frame 2[10] continued

getting certain things done. They are ways of organizing the work of society.

Membership in many groups and organizations is *involuntary*. One has no choice about his family, and the small child has only a very limited choice of play group and no choice of classroom group. Servicemen cannot pick their platoon, and civilians generally cannot pick their neighbors or fellow-workers. One's only alternative generally is to withdraw, with no guarantee of better luck next time. Inability to easily escape involuntary groups gives these groups a measure of control over us. We must conform or suffer.

Many groups and organizations are *voluntary;* one is free to stay out or to join as he wishes, provided he can gain acceptance. Many groups and organizations welcome all comers; others are more exclusive. Those primarily devoted to the direct enjoyment of the members—cliques, recreational organizations, clubs, fraternities, etc.— are likely to be somewhat exclusive. Since enjoyable human relationships are the goal, they act to exclude persons they consider unacceptable. Those which are organized to promote a vested interest—unions, professional societies, trade associations—are generally open to all those who share that vested interest. Those which are organized to promote a cause or to "do good"— pressure groups, taxpayers' associations, churches, welfare organizations, political parties, reform movements—are generally open to all who will join in support of their cause.

Voluntary organizations provide a means for expressing and expanding individual interests and goals. They become a channel for purposive social action and social change. Separate voluntary organizations can sometimes perform certain tasks more efficiently than government can. Voluntary organizations become part of a network of interlocking groups and associations which knit a heterogeneous, diverse society into a more integrated unity.

Formal and Informal Organizations. Formal organizations have a formal structure of official positions, ranks, duties, and goals. Most formal organizations, such as the military or government, have a definite chain of command and responsibility, with proscribed procedures for operation. This *formal structure* can easily be diagrammed on an organizational chart. Formal organizations also have an *informal structure,* a network of influence which depends not upon formal rank or title, but upon prestige and personal relationships. The informal structure of an organization cannot easily be diagrammed, and can be detected only by extended observation of the people involved. One who "knows how to pull strings" is one who is familiar with the informal structure of the organization.

Informal organizations such as cliques, street gangs, most small clubs, and most other primary groups have no formal structure, since by definition informal organizations are those with no formal structure. But they do have an informal structure. As in all groups, there are leadership roles, patterns of influence, petty rivalries and jealousies, and other human relationships which structure the interaction within the group.

Reference Groups. Groups of any kind may serve as reference groups. *Reference groups are groups whose standards we respect and use as models or referents for our own behavior.* We respect the norms and goals of the group and accept them as our own. They become "significant others," and provide models for role taking and role playing. Examples might be our own family, a professional association, the YMCA, Boy Scouts, Methodist Church, Communist Party, a delinquent street gang, the S.D.S., the Black Panthers, the "hippies," or practically any other group or organization whose standards have become our standards. (The term "reference groups" is often applied to organizations or categories which are not actually "groups"; yet while technically incorrect, this is a common usage.) One follows the norms of the reference group when one encounters a situation in which the expectations of the reference group seem applicable. Yet, one does not have to be a member of a group to value its standards; groups to which we would *like* to belong may influence our behavior as greatly as some in which we now claim membership. In fact, the social climber who aspires to membership in the Hillside Tuesday Flower Club may follow its dictates even more slavishly than the current members, who dare risk a little laxity.

Gemeinschaft and Gesellschaft Groups and Communities.   The concepts of *gemeinschaft* and *gesellschaft*, proposed by the German sociologist Tönnies, denote types of group relations or communities somewhat similar to primary and secondary groups. Gemeinschaft relations are personal, informal, traditional, primary, and homogeneous, somewhat similar to those of the small rural town of 1900. Gesellschaft relations or communities are more impersonal, formal, contractual, utilitarian, secondary, and heterogeneous, more like urban communities today.

The primary-group nature of social relations in the gemeinschaft communities leads to more effective social control and greater stability with less deviance. The predominance of primary-group relations makes a person's behavior highly observable and makes him accountable for any violation of norms. Greater variation in behavior is tolerated in gesellschaft communities, as in the large cities today.

These various group classifications—in-groups and out-groups, primary and secondary groups, voluntary and involuntary groups, formal and informal groups—are not mutually exclusive. The city council is a formal, voluntary, secondary, gesellschaft-type group, while the Saturday evening poker group is an informal, primary, voluntary, gemeinschaft-type group. So groups and organizations or associations are found in endless variations, all serving the diverse needs of mankind.

Is each of the following true or false?

_____ 1. Both primary and secondary groups maintain standards, norms, and expectations for behavior.

_____ 2. Involuntary groups exercise more social control than voluntary groups.

_____ 3. Formal organizations have leadership roles, but informal organizations do not.

_____ 4. One has to be a member of a group to value its standards and to follow its norms.

_____ 5. The various group classifications—in-group and out-group, primary and secondary, formal and informal, etc.—are mutually exclusive.

Now turn to Answer frame 2^{10} on page 58 to check your answers.

Answer frame 2¹⁰

1. True. All groups exercise social control over their members. The social control of primary groups is stronger than that for secondary groups.
2. True. Inability to easily escape involuntary groups gives them control over us. We must conform or suffer.
3. False. All groups—formal and informal—have leadership roles, patterns of influence, and structured interaction.
4. False. Groups to which we would like to belong may influence our behavior as greatly as some in which we now claim membership.
5. False. One group (example: city council) may be formal, voluntary, secondary, and gesellschaft.

If you missed any of the above, you should review Frame 2¹⁰ before beginning Chapter 11.

chapter 11

URBAN TRANSITION

Frame 1¹¹

Early man lived in tiny bands of no more than a few families, for only a few people could subsist in any single area in a hunting and food gathering economy. Only after the development of agriculture and the domestication of animals could people collect enough sustenance in a single locale to support a community.

The various definitions of *community* include the ideas that it is a locality whose residents have a fairly complete social life, a feeling of local unity, and an ability to act collectively. Communities are commonly classified as *rural*, being small, relatively simple and homogeneous, and based upon agriculture; *urban*, being large, heterogeneous, and based mainly upon commerce and industry; and *suburban*, variable in size, rel-

atively homogeneous, and based upon urban employment and an attempt to flee the city without sacrificing urban life.

The Rural Community

The first communities were rural communities. Until very recently most of the world's people lived in rural communities. In much of the world, farm families were gathered into hamlets, located a mile or two apart, and tilled the lands within walking distance. In the United States, the farmers lived on their farms instead of in hamlets. Villages were several miles apart and populated mainly by people not engaged in farming. County seat towns served as political and commercial centers for a number of villages.

The anthropologist Robert Redfield developed a folk-urban continuum to characterize the differences between rural and urban communities. The rural community, a folk society based upon gemeinschaft relations, was small, informal, homogeneous, and tradition-bound. Rural people led an isolated life on the scattered farmsteads (in the United States). The urban communities were described as large, impersonal, heterogeneous, gesellschaft or commercial, and more subject to change.

Certain personality differences emerged from the differing conditions of rural and urban social life. To cite one example: In most urban social contacts, one does not know intimately many of the persons he deals with, so must judge them by what he can see—their dress, grooming, manners, title, organizational connections. In the rural community, most people are well known to one another. One's reputation is widely known, and his responsibility, efficiency, and income can easily be judged from the condition of his crops, buildings, and livestock. Putting up a "front" would fool nobody. Hence the emphasis upon outward appearances in urban life, and the lack of affectation in rural life, are natural products of the social life in each type of community.

The Changing Rural Community. American rural life is rapidly changing, and has been changing for decades. Farming as a "way of life" has been replaced by agriculture as a business. Gone is the farmer who is proud of producing on his own farm everything his family eats; today's farmer is a specialized producer of cash crops for the market. Modern transportation and communications have ended rural isolation. Mechanization, together with the agricultural sciences, has multiplied output per farm worker almost beyond belief, multiplied by several times the acreage one farmer can handle, and multiplied the amount of capital investment per farm. In consequence, the average size of farm has grown, the number of farms and farm workers has declined, and farm specialization has been encouraged. The end is not yet in sight. Current development of a variety of picking machines, together with new varieties of produce especially developed for mechanical harvesting, are continuing to feed these trends.

Agriculture today has become professionalized. Today's successful farmer, in contrast to the stereotyped hayseed chewing a timothy stalk, is, at the very least, a careful reader of agricultural magazines and Department of Agriculture bulletins, and a frequent consultant with the county agent. Often he is a college of agriculture graduate, managing a quarter- or half-million dollar enterprise, who consults regularly with his broker on market conditions. This professionalization of agriculture, together with the mounting capital needed to farm on a profitable scale, has made many small farmers "marginal." These are farmers who lack enough land, equipment, capital, and skill to make a decent living. Most of them are middle-aged or older, and are not good candidates for learning a new occupation. They are kept from destitution by the farm price support program, which is of doubtful economic wisdom, but which keeps them on the farm instead of on urban direct relief.

These changes have other consequences. The decline in farm population means the migration of the youth of both the farms and of the rural trading towns. These decaying small towns, offering little future to youth, are so "dead" that young people are anxious to flee them.

The Urbanization of Rural Culture. The rural community is rapidly becoming urbanized as urban patterns spread into rural areas. No longer do mail order houses carry different lines of apparel for the rural and urban customers. The new-found freedom of mobility for rural people, the mass media of communication, and the professionalization of the business of farming have all led to a gradual diffusion of the urban culture to create an amalgam of the old and the new culture in rural areas. Today's true provincials are no longer the rural people. Of all people in America, those who live the most narrowly confined social life may be the urban poor.

The Urban Community

Cities first developed along the ancient river valleys, where annual floods provided the fertility for highly productive agriculture while the river provided the transportation. Later, cities of many types developed—fortress cities, capital cities, temple cities, trading cities, industrial and commercial cities, resort cities. An early sociologist, Charles Horton Cooley, developed the "break in transportation" theory, noting that cities grew wherever there was a transfer from one kind of transport to another—at river mouths (New York, London), at the confluence of rivers (St. Louis, Pittsburgh), at the base of mountain ranges (Denver), or wherever shipments had to be repacked.

In the Western world, urbanization and industrialization have complemented each other. Industrialization requires an abundant supply of labor, plus distribution, transportation, and communication systems. Industries locate in urban areas, thus contributing to further urbanization.

Indicate whether each of the following statements is true or false by writing "T" or "F" in the space provided.

_____ 1. Until very recently most of the world's people lived in rural communities.

_____ 2. Gemeinschaft-gesellschaft typology does not apply to modern communities.

_____ 3. The urban poor may live the most narrowly confined social life of all people in America.

_____ 4. In the Western world, urbanization and industrialization have complemented each other.

Now turn to Answer frame 1¹¹ on page 62 to check your responses.

Frame 2¹¹

Patterns of Urban Growth. Most cities show little evidence of design as one drives through the haphazard assortment of factories and junk yards, interspersed with housing developments and shopping centers. There is, however, a design which several scholars have attempted to describe.

Burgess derived his *concentric zone pattern* from the study of Chicago in the early 1920's. He found a series of concentric zones radiating from the business district core at the center. The second zone is a zone of transition from businesses to slums and lower-class housing, then a circle of middle-income housing, ending with a circle of elite housing and a commuters' zone on the fringe of the city. Burgess' model is an "ideal type," and no city has the clearly defined zones that he defined. Among several other objections, it makes no provision for heavy industry, and takes no account of topography.

Noting that Burgess' zones seldom completely surround the city, Hoyt developed a *sector theory* of city growth. He held that a particular kind of land use in one area of the city tends to

be continued, gradually shifting outward as the city grows. The lower-class residential area is located close to the smoky industrial sector, with elite housing cleanly separated in the more scenic areas.

Another approach, the *multinuclear theory*, is based upon the fact that most large cities have engulfed several smaller towns as they grew. Each of these formerly separated towns now forms one of the multiple nuclei of the city. Thus there are several business districts, many residential areas, etc. The above theories are illustrated in Figure 11–1.

A very simple theory relates topography to land use. Railroads tend to follow river beds through town, and heavy industry locates near both. Lower-class residential areas develop near industry with upper-class residence along the scenic high ridges and wherever the view is nice and the smells are distant.

None of these theories is completely satisfactory in explaining any particular city's development, but most cities (in the United States) show some degree of similarity to all of them. The develop-

FIGURE 11–1

Three Theories of City Structure

The concentric zone pattern takes no account of topography, and makes no provision for several kinds of land use, but is a generalized pattern. The sector and multiple nuclei patterns would vary for each city, with the diagrams below representing two of countless possible variations. (Adapted from C. D. Harris and E. L. Ullman, "The Nature of Cities," *The Annals,* 242: 13, November, 1945).

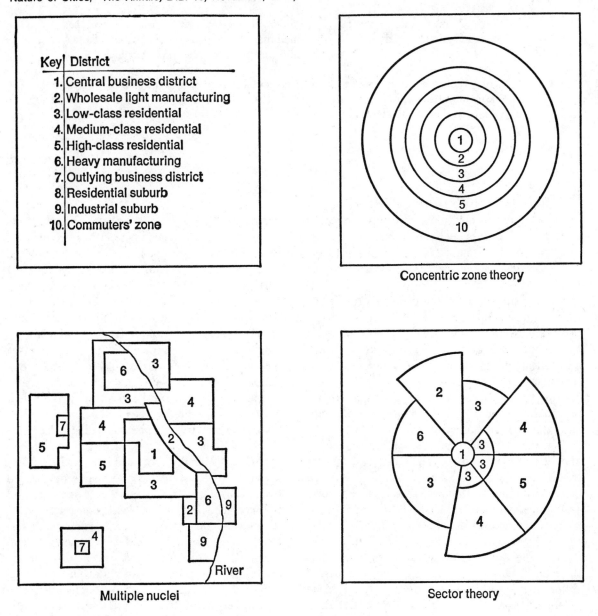

Key	District
1.	Central business district
2.	Wholesale light manufacturing
3.	Low-class residential
4.	Medium-class residential
5.	High-class residential
6.	Heavy manufacturing
7.	Outlying business district
8.	Residential suburb
9.	Industrial suburb
10.	Commuters' zone

Concentric zone theory

Multiple nuclei

Sector theory

ment of suburbs and suburban shopping centers is causing haphazard city reorganization, and contributing to the decline of inner-city regions.

Urban Life and Personality. Urban social life is different from rural social life. Urban life is more time and speed conscious, more crowded, more impersonal, more regimented. In some respects, the urbanite has less freedom to act with-

Answer frame 1[11]

1. True. Until recently most of the world's population has lived in small, relatively simple and homogeneous communities based on agriculture. The period during which man has lived in urban societies has been very brief.

2. False. Robert Redfield's "folk-urban" continuum—used to characterize differences between rural and urban communities—includes within it the gemeinschaft-gesellschaft topology.

3. True. Today's true provincials are no longer rural people. Urban culture has spread to rural areas through the combined means of mass media of communication, new-found freedom of mobility of rural people, and the professionalization of farming.

4. True. Industries create urban communities out of small towns. Industries tend to locate in urban areas, thus contributing to further urbanization.

If you missed any of the above, you should restudy Frame 1[11] before turning to Frame 2[11] on page 60.

Frame 2[11] continued

out concern for his neighbors (the noise he makes and what he does with his garbage affects others), yet the urbanite is less sensitive to his neighbors' evaluations of him. In rural social life most of one's associations are primary group associations, subject to all the primary group controls. In urban life, primary groups are equally necessary to the individual, but most of one's associations are secondary group associations, and reflect the impersonal, segmented nature of secondary groups. To substitute folk language for this sociological discourse, country folks are informal, friendly, and hospitable, while city folks are more cold and distant!

The urban population is more heterogeneous and behavior is more varied. Nearly all the extremes of personality and behavior are more common in the city. Nonconformists of most sorts —sex deviants, drug addicts, political extremists, hippies, and misfits of all sorts drift to the city, in most cases to the slum, where they have greater freedom to do as they wish with others of their kind. Different sections of the city attract different types of people and styles of life. The cheap hotel and bar section attracts the rambling rejects of society, those who are unable to hold a steady job because of alcoholism, emotional instability, or physical disability, and who seem barely to live from day to day. Other sections are variously known as the financial district, the entertainment section, and the "tenderloin,"

where prostitution and other unapproved attractions are available. Racial and ethnic groups tend to accumulate and establish (or have imposed upon them) a set of shifting boundaries for their part of town. The German and Irish districts, products of an earlier immigration, have disappeared as these groups became assimilated and accepted. Little Italy and Little Poland are almost gone, but Chinatown remains and the black belt steadily grows larger. There is some evidence that personality maladjustment is greater in the city than in rural areas, but it is unclear whether urban life produces personality maladjustment, or merely attracts the maladjusted.

The *anti-urban bias* is an evaluation of city life which is deeply rooted in our rural past. For ages, rural critics and prophets have denounced the sins, vices, extravagances, and decadence of the city. The anti-urban bias is one reason why, for decades until recently, city voters were discriminated against in legislative apportionment.

"Goodness of life" is not easy to measure in any objective manner. The widely held conviction that rural life and rural people are somehow better, more sturdy, honorable, and basically decent than urban life and urban people is a value judgment, not a fact. Most of the qualities of life that can be measured statistically—mortality and morbidity, education, income, books and magazines purchased, etc.—come out to the city's advantage. But not everything important is statistically measurable. So the question remains a fruitless debate and the anti-urban bias a widely shared value judgment.

The Suburb. Only in the twentieth century have any significant fraction of the world's people failed to live within walking distance of their work. The suburb is a product of modern transportation. It is by far the most rapidly growing part of our country; suburbs are exploding while most central cities and most rural areas are losing population. While there are working-class suburbs and shanty-town suburbs, most suburbanites are from the upper and middle classes, or from the top layers of the working class. The typical suburb is quite homogeneous in race and class, and carefully insulated from less "desirable" people. Zoning regulations and building codes are deliberately designed to prevent any poor people from slipping in. This is done by setting minimum lot sizes and apartment sizes which make housing too expensive for the poor. Since the majority of black people are poor, this effectively screens out most of them, while a variety of subtle and not-so-subtle pressures keep out most of the rest of the nonwhites, so that most suburbs are lily white. The suburb drains the central city of much of its talent and income, leaving the central city overloaded with the poor, the nonwhite, and the dependent.

Not only people, but also industry and trade are migrating from the central city to suburban industrial sites and shopping centers. This means that jobs are migrating to the suburbs, where the middle-class whites can follow, but where the poor and the blacks are not permitted to live. In these and still other ways, the suburbs are parasitic upon the central cities, whose financial burdens are soaring while their local revenues are sinking. These are among the reasons why every major city in the country is in the grip of a crisis which it is unable to solve. It is significant that big-city mayors are no longer moving up to governorships, senatorships, and the presidency; the unsolvable problems of the big city —unsolvable within the present institutional context—make the big-city mayoralty the graveyard rather than the springboard for political aspirations.

Future Prospects for the City. A semi-popular literature has arisen, questioning whether the city is doomed. This is like asking whether the right side of one's body is doomed. Cities will survive because they are inevitable and indispensable parts of a modern society. The urban crisis is genuine and severe—of that there is no question. Sweeping and costly changes in urban life and organization will be necessary. But the problems of the city cannot be solved by changes in the city alone; changes in the structure and functioning of the entire society will be involved. After all, we have been living for less than a single lifetime in the first urban civilization the world has ever seen. Most of our traditional institutions are geared to a rural society. Many institutional changes need to be made if urban civilization is to remain civilized.

The direction of some of the necessary changes is no secret from city planners and social scientists. The city cannot continue to be the dumping ground for a growing proportion of the nation's poor, and pay the cost itself. Either the drift of the poor and the dependent to the cities must be arrested, or cities must share more greatly in state and federal revenues. We have been subsidizing the destruction of intracity public transportation by subsidizing automobile transportation while public transportation deteriorated. Our property tax, by taxing vacant land lightly and property improvements heavily, encourages property deterioration. These are but a few of the many institutional arrangements which will need to be changed if cities are to be places where very many will live by choice.

True or false?

_____ 1. There is no design or pattern to cities.

_____ 2. In urban communities most of one's associations are secondary rather than primary.

_____ 3. The urban population is more heterogeneous, and behavior is more varied.

_____ 4. Rural life and rural people are better, more honorable, and basically more decent than urban life and urban people.

_____ 5. The suburb is a product of modern transportation.

Now turn to Answer frame 2[11] on page 66 to check your answers.

chapter 12

SOCIAL STRATIFICATION

Frame 1[12]

The simplest societies, where all persons of the same age and sex have much the same duties and privileges, we call relatively *unstratified* societies. There would be individual differences in status, resting upon personal prestige, ability, and personality; but where such status differences are individual, nonhereditary, and not associated with any particular division of labor or function, they are not part of any stratification system. By *social stratification* we mean *a ranking of people in status levels according to some criteria of superiority or inferiority*. The criteria for ranking may be race, religion, family lineage, kind and amount of property or income, occupation, or some other characteristic. A few sociologists draw a distinction between social stratification and social class, including age and sex status

differences in stratification, but this is not the customary usage. Most sociologists use the term "stratification" as the process of developing status levels or social classes.

Ascribed and Achieved Role and Status

Roles and statuses are of two kinds—*ascribed* and *achieved*. *Ascribed* statuses and roles are *those which are assigned and according to birth or other factors unalterable by the person.* Age, sex, and race are common bases of ascription. *Achieved* statuses and roles are *those that one attains through his own choice or actions.* Examples in our society include occupational and marital status. One is normally ascribed the social class status of his parents, but in our society it is possible to achieve a different class status through one's own actions.

Social Class

The Origin of Social Classes. Most primitive societies had no class system. Most persons of the same age and sex did the same kind of work and had about the same possessions. There might be great differences in individual prestige, based upon personal qualities, but such personal prestige was not usually inheritable, nor was the society organized into prestige levels.

A few societies had status levels based upon property ownership. For example, in some African societies, all families kept cattle, with the size of the herd determining the social status of the family. In most societies, however, the development of a class system arose from specialization or the division of labor. Wherever there is a division of labor, some kinds of work come to carry greater prestige than others, and the persons doing such work hold a higher status and are generally rewarded with higher income or other special privileges. Scholars have sought, unsuccessfully, to find a logical, rational basis for the prestige ranking of occupations. But, no matter what "principle" is used—social importance of the work, difficulty or hazards of the work, intelligence and abilities required, length of training needed—enough exceptions can be found to question any "rational" basis for the prestige ranking of occupations. We can only say that, for whatever reasons, certain occupations have come to carry higher prestige than others, and this varies greatly in time and space. In classical China, the warriors had the power and the loot, but the scholars had the highest prestige. In medieval Europe, land ownership was the basis of upper-class membership, while those "in trade" (businessmen, merchants, manufacturers) could hope for no more than middle-class status; today, this is changed.

Early in the twentieth century, the American economist Veblen in his *Theory of the Leisure Class,* observed that when people's income exceeds their subsistence needs, they use this excess income in forms of conspicuous display which advertise their superiority over other people. He called this "conspicuous consumption" and offered it as an explanation for the high price of mink and diamonds.

Karl Marx found the origin of social classes in the historic clash of interest between the workers, or the "proletariat," and the "bourgeoisie," or the owners of productive wealth (land, factories, machines). Within each class, according to Marx, a feeling of class unity emerges from the common experiences and common interests of its members. Workers share a common poverty and insecurity and suffer a common exploitation, while the bourgeoisie share a common affluence and a common interest in preserving the system of values which protects their privileges. Marx predicted that the middle class would gradually be eliminated by monopolistic big business, and would be "proletarianized"—turned into salaried workers who would discover that their interests were the same as those of the workers. The increasingly miserable workers, joined by this "proletarianized" middle class, would eventually overthrow the bourgeoisie in a violent revolution, seize the "instruments of production," and operate them for the benefit of all.

Contrary to Marx, however, workers in the industrialized nations have grown more affluent, not more miserable; the middle class has expanded enormously, and has not identified itself with interests of workers. Even the workers, instead of uniting against the owners and managers, have often formed alliances with managers in defense of their joint interests, against those of other alliances of workers and managers. In other words, political alignments often transcend class lines and are based upon special interests rather than class interests; for example, American textile workers' unions and textile manufacturers are presently united in support of higher textile tariffs. While Marx's predictions did not come true, his conceptualizations of class interest and class conflict remain important in the analysis of stratification.

Nature of Social Classes. Just what is a social class? While definitions vary somewhat, a *social class* is usually defined as *a stratum of people who hold a similar social status.* There are no distinct boundaries between classes comparable to the ranks of the army; instead, each class is a section of a status continuum, just as

Answer frame 2¹¹

1. False. There is a design which several scholars have attempted to describe. Examples are concentric zone, sector, and multinuclear patterns.
2. True. In urban life, primary groups are necessary to the individual—as in rural life —but most of one's associations are secondary group associations, and reflect the impersonal, segmented nature of secondary groups.
3. True. Nearly all the extremes of personality and behavior are more common in the city. Nonconformists of most sorts drift to the city where they have greater freedom to do as they wish with others of their kind.
4. False. This is a value judgment, not a fact. It reflects an anti-urban bias. "Goodness of life" is not easy to measure in any objective manner.
5. True. Only in the twentieth century have a significant fraction of the world's people failed to live within walking distance of their work. Suburbs are by far the most rapidly growing part of our country.

If you missed any of the above, you should restudy Frame 2¹¹ before beginning Chapter 12 on page 64.

Frame 1¹² continued

"young," "middle-aged," and "old" are sections of an age continuum, with no clearly defined boundaries.

People of similar class status will show considerable similarity in income, education, prestige level of their occupation, values, interests, and life style. All these factors are in a circular cause-and-effect relationship with social class. One's social class background influences his income, choice of occupation, life style, etc., while these characteristics serve to determine in which class he belongs.

How many classes are there? Each class is composed of all those people who recognize one another as approximate status equals, and with recognizable status distinctions separating them from other classes. A simple rural village might have only two or three such status levels, while a large city has a greater number. Warner's six-level class system has been widely used in studies of class, with upper-upper, lower-upper, upper-middle, lower-middle, upper-lower and lower-lower classes. The two upper classes in the United States are composed of wealthy land-owners, owners of inherited wealth, professional people, and gentleman farmers, whose families have for several generations been wealthy enough to carry on an upper-class pattern of gracious living (a little longer for the upper-upper class). The upper-middle class is drawn from the same occupations, and its members are sometimes nearly as prosperous but are newcomers to affluence. The lower-middle class is composed of white-collar workers, clerks and secretaries, semi-professionals and technicians, and possibly the top levels of skilled workers, foremen, supervisors, etc. The upper-lower class is composed of regularly employed workers. The lower-lower class includes the irregularly employed and casual workers, migrant farm workers, welfare families, and others at the bottom of the heap. While this outline of Warner's is probably roughly accurate, it is applicable only to urban and suburban America, and has some imperfections. Whether, for example, skilled workers are upper-lower or lower-middle class can be argued. But this description is widely used by social scientists.

Indicate whether each of the following statements is true or false by writing "T" or "F" in the space provided.

_____ 1. The development of a class system normally arises from the division of labor.

_____ 2. According to Veblen, the high price of mink and diamonds is due to "conspicuous consumption."

_____ 3. In American society there are clear and distinct boundaries between social classes.

_____ 4. Sociologists agree that in all communities there are four social classes.

Now turn to Answer frame 1¹² on page 68 to check your responses.

Frame 2¹²

Determinants of Social Class. One's class position is revealed by noting who gets invited to whose dinner party. This is not mere "snobbishness." Persons of similar class generally share similar interests, values, and viewpoints, follow similar manners, and are comfortable and relaxed with one another. Social contacts across class lines are likely to be strained and uncomfortable unless they are rigidly structured and utilitarian, such as master-servant, customer-salesperson, etc. The prosperous home owner (lower-upper class) may chat comfortably with his gardener (upper-lower class) in the flower garden, but both might be ill at ease having a drink together at the tavern or country club. For relaxed companionship and satisfying primary group relationships, we prefer our own social class.

Total way of life thus determines class membership (just as, in turn, it is largely shaped by class background). In most research studies of social class, three measures of class status are used—wealth or income, occupation, and education. These criteria are easily available (at least for census districts), can be quantified, and are fairly accurate when applied to substantial numbers of people, even though inaccurate in individual cases. For example, income does not always indicate social class of an individual, for there are exceptions. Airline pilots earn more than university professors, and construction workers earn more than many ministers. The "old rich" have higher class status than the "new rich," and money from a salary is better than money from wages, while money from investments is best of all. "Family background" is highly associated with class status, but it is not easy to measure or quantify. Although total way of life really determines class status, "way of life" cannot easily be objectified or quantified. So the three criteria of occupation, education, and income are used in most research on social class,

and are fairly satisfactory indexes when applied to enough people so that individual exceptions will cancel out.

Significance of Social Class. A significant function of social class lies in _determining life opportunities_. The class status one inherits will influence the schools he attends, the ambitions he forms, the language he speaks, the books he reads, and the people with whom he comes into contact. The patterns of irregular employment and haphazard work habits of the lower-lower class present a barrier to achievement which the middle-class youth need not surmount.

Perhaps the most significant function of social class lies in _socializing children to their class subculture_. The social class subcultures vary in almost every respect. Virtually every aspect of thought and behavior, even including techniques of making love (according to Kinsey) differ among the social classes. The middle and upper classes generally set the standards of conventional morality, from which lower-class behavior frequently deviates. Some forms of "crime" are nothing more than normal lower-class behavior which deviates from the middle-class norms which are written into law.

Lower-class family life is less stable, with more ill health, frequent unemployment, more parental desertion, economic deprivation, larger family size and greater crowding, and more verbal and physical violence. Middle-class family life is more stable, economically more comfortable, with smaller families and more individual attention, less verbal and physical violence, and greater achievement orientation. One striking characteristic of the middle class, largely absent from the lower class, is the _deferred gratification pattern_, or the habit of postponing immediate satisfactions in order to achieve a long-term goal. Middle-class values encourage the postponement of marriage, prolonged education, and studious

Answer frame 1¹²

1. True. The simplest societies generally have no class system. Wherever there is a division of labor, some kinds of work acquire greater prestige than others, and the persons doing such work hold a higher status and are generally rewarded with special privileges.
2. True. Veblen asserted that excess income was used to purchase extravagant symbols of one's membership in the leisure class. He called this "conspicuous consumption" and offered it as an explanation for the high price of mink and diamonds.
3. False. Each class is a relatively arbitrary section of a status continuum. The definition of the number of classes and their dividing points is usually determined by the sociologist.
4. False. A simple rural village may have only two or three classes, while a city may have a large number. Warner's six-level class system is applicable only to urban and suburban communities; it is not applicable to the national society.

If you missed any of the above, you should restudy Frame 1¹² before turning to Frame 2¹² on page 67.

Frame 2¹² continued

application in hopes of eventual occupational success and status advancement. Present sacrifice for long-term goals is less common in the lower classes, where people typically have little confidence in their ability to do anything which will affect their fate, but tend to take each day as it comes. Middle-class families prepare their children for upward mobility, while lower-class families prepare their children for survival.

A third function of the class system is to *allocate duties and privileges*. This is done in many subtle ways, too many to enumerate. To mention a few, school prods middle-class children for academic achievement and counsels them into the professions; from lower-class children, the school often demands no more than obedience, and counsels them into menial occupations. The "dirty work" is done by the lower classes; the police treat them less respectfully and the courts treat them more severely, while the law is written mainly to protect middle- and upper-class interests. Community power is virtually a middle- and upper-class monopoly, while the lower classes are quite conscious of their lack of power and influence. Thus, they become an alienated segment of the population with considerable active hostility against the middle-class establishment of police, courts, judges, teachers, preachers, and social workers who seem to be everlastingly pushing them around.

Social Mobility

Caste and Class. Social mobility refers to *changes in class status in either direction.* One occasionally finds the concept defined to include both "vertical mobility" (changes upward or downward in class status), and "horizontal mobility" (changes from one position to another at the same status, such as change of job or residence). The more common usage among sociologists, however, is to apply the term social mobility to changes in class status, and to describe "horizontal" changes as "occupational mobility," "residential mobility," etc.

Class systems vary in the degree to which changes of class status are possible. In an "open-class system" of the ideal type, all levels of class status would be equally open to achievement by everyone. In practice, no society has ever had a perfectly open class system. In all societies, families at each class level socialize children to continue life at that class level, and thus discourage upward or downward mobility. Furthermore, families at the higher class levels contrive to assist their children in retaining their present class status, or in advancing it, by providing educational advantages, and by encouraging the ambitions and attitudes which promote upward mobility. Thus, an "open-class" society does not really provide equal access to the higher class ranks; it is one with no rigid barriers to mobility, and which provides the ambitious with some facilities for upward mobility. At the opposite pole is the *closed-class system,* in which class status is strictly ascribed at birth with no means for achieving a different status. In its ideal type, it is called a *caste,* wherein one's status is ascribed at birth, intermarriage and all equality-type contacts between members of different castes are forbidden, and there is no way to change caste status. The caste system in India and the black-white castes in America are often cited as examples. In both countries, caste distinctions are legally prohibited today, yet many discriminations remain.

Caste and class may both exist in the same society. Our black-white caste system strongly discourages intermarriage, and in some respects assigns to blacks a status inferior to all whites; meanwhile a class system classifies both whites and blacks into several class levels according to much the same criteria.

True or false?

_____ 1. Social interactions across class lines are likely to be strained and uncomfortable unless they are rigidly structured and utilitarian.

_____ 2. Income or wealth is the only reliable measure of social class status.

_____ 3. The most significant function of social class lies in socializing children to their class subculture.

_____ 4. Types of class system vary in the frequency of social mobility.

_____ 5. Caste and class may both exist in the same society.

Now turn to Answer frame 2^{12} on page 70 to check your answers.

Frame 3^{12}

The Process of Social Mobility. The techniques of achieving upward (or downward) mobility vary in different societies. In America today, upward mobility for a boy normally involves his gaining an education, occupation, and income appropriate to the next higher class level, and also developing the appropriate attitudes, values, and viewpoints, and then copying the life style of that class until he can "smoothly" act as expected, and until others have forgotten his humble origin. For a girl, the usual technique is to latch onto a mobile boy or a higher status man, meanwhile cultivating the appropriate attitudes, life style, etc. Unless the disparity is great, wives are usually accorded the class status of their husbands.

Upward mobility rarely exceeds one class level per generation (on the Warner six-class scale), for few people, even if they can get the necessary money, can handle the enormously intricate unlearning and relearning of the requisite values, habits, language, diction, interests, and life style needed to jump two or more levels.

Downward mobility, though less advertised, also takes place. Loss of money does not entail immediate loss of class status, for one retains his class subculture; as long as he can retain some semblance of the old life style, he retains his class status. A number of upper-class Americans can keep the roof on the crumbling mansion only by opening it to gaping tourists part of the year. When one abandons the life style of his class, or drops to a lower status occupation (not temporarily, as students do while "working their way" through college, but permanently), a loss of class status follows. Women who marry "beneath their station" usually drop to the class level of their husbands. Most of the "skid-row bums," and some of the permanent "welfare class" are products of downward mobility.

Channels of Social Mobility. The amount of upward mobility depends upon the number of openings in the higher class levels. In a relatively static society, the upper-class openings are generally filled by persons born into that class, so there is little opportunity for others to climb. In revolutionary periods, the existing upper and middle classes may be exterminated

Answer frame 2¹²

1. True. Persons of different classes do *not* share identical interests, values, viewpoints, and attitudes. For relaxed companionship and satisfying primary relationships we prefer our own social class.
2. False. In most research studies of social class, three measures of class status are used—income, occupational prestige, and education. Income does not always indicate social class of an individual.
3. True. The social class subcultures vary in almost every respect. The family is the primary agent of socialization for each social class.
4. True. In an open class system such as in the United States, social mobility is far more frequent than in a caste system, as in India or South Africa.
5. True. Our black-white caste system strongly discourages intermarriage, and assigns to blacks a status inferior to all whites; meanwhile, a class system exists within each caste.

If you missed any of the above, you should restudy Frame 2¹² before turning to Frame 3¹² on page 69.

Frame 3¹² continued

or exiled, making room for a wholesale replacement from below. Rapidly changing societies are likely to have more openings, as some persons in the middle and upper classes may fail to make the adaptations necessary to retain their class rank in a changing society. Social change may also alter the proportion of class openings at the different levels. In our society, technological change has greatly increased the openings in the middle-class occupations (professional, semiprofessional, technical, managerial, clerical), and decreased the proportion of people employed in lower-class occupations (unskilled and semi-skilled labor, domestic service, farm labor). This has meant a rapid expansion of the American middle classes. It has also created the possibility of a substantial number of permanently unemployed, who lack the training for the jobs available, living on odd jobs and "welfare."

Whether it is becoming easier or more difficult to achieve upward mobility is a common debate. Recent studies show that the rate of upward mobility in the United States has not greatly changed within recent decades, and that mobility rates appear to be about the same throughout the industrialized world. In communist states, the destruction of the old class system has been followed, not by Marx's "classless society," but by a new class system in which the upper classes are composed of the top party and government officials, generals, and managers, plus the distinguished professors, scientists, artists, and writers. In the Soviet Union, where free university educations are supposedly open to all on a competitive merit basis, studies over a period of years have shown a growing proportion of students coming from middle- and upper-class backgrounds, with a declining proportion of students coming from the families of peasants and workers. As mentioned before, successful parents in all societies will find ways to get special advantages for their children.

Upward mobility is not equally open to all categories of people in any society, for in every society there is discrimination against some. Immigrants have typically entered the American class system at the bottom, but those who were racially, culturally, and religiously similar to our WASP (white, Anglo-Saxon, Protestant) majority found the greatest social acceptance and the most rapid mobility. Even today, the greater the deviation from WASP physical and cultural characteristics, the greater the barriers to upward mobility.

Individual Consequences of Social Mobility. Upward mobility brings certain rewards—prestige, power, and usually affluence, plus perhaps a feeling of personal accomplishment that may be most gratifying. Many men are addicted to fond and tiresome accounts of their struggles, sacrifices, and victories. But, even beyond this struggle for success, upward mobility often exacts a price from the individual.

Status anxiety arises from the stress of competition for status. A closed-class society seeks to provide everyone with a role and status commensurate with his birth. Children can be trained from birth to find fulfillment and contentment in their ascribed roles, free from the prod of ambition or the fear of failure. An open-class system encourages all to aspire to a higher status, thereby dooming most people to failure. Even those who succeed are only provisionally successful, for there are others who climbed still higher. Meanwhile, any of a variety of misfortunes may snatch away the fruits of success, for whatever is won in competition may be lost tomorrow. The anxiety produced by the "rat race" is managed by many people, but some develop physical or emotional illnesses, while some others simply "drop out" of the competitive struggle.

Role strain arises from the need to adapt to new roles. Upward mobility means new responsibilities, including new patterns of behavior and life style. Occasionally a promotion is rejected because one shrinks from the strain of the new responsibility.

Disruption of primary group relations is a price of upward mobility. Mobile children become alienated from parents and other relatives, with whom they come to have less and less in common. Husband and wife often are unequally ambitious for mobility, or unequally skillful in adopting new class-type behavior. The wife of a highly mobile man, who may in fact have struggled to help him get his start, is often ruthlessly discarded for a new wife who is more "suitable" in his new class status. Possibly for all these reasons, studies of successful men have found that those who climbed to their present status are suffering more psychosomatic illnesses than those who were born into that status.

Frustration of downward mobility is one of the costs of an open-class system. Those who lose class status also face the strain of new role adjustments and the disruption of primary group relations, plus the humiliation of failure. While some of those who "lose out" or voluntarily "drop out" may claim to have found happiness and contentment, the evidence suggests that most of these are rationalizing their failure.

Social Consequences of Social Mobility. It can be argued that the best of all societies is one with a high proportion of ascribed statuses, including a relatively closed-class system, wherein each can receive an appropriate role training and can find contentment within his ascribed role and status. If one assumes some justice in the distribution of rewards, such a society may very well minimize frustration and maximize contentment. But such a society will remain relatively static, and it is debatable whether a static society can be contented for very long in today's world. Those countries with the most rigid stratification today also appear to be those most likely to suffer violent social upheaval in the not distant future.

A society with a high rate of mobility may increase certain kinds of anxiety and frustration while reducing others. The open-class society avoids the frustration of the talented person who is trapped in an ascribed role which offers little opportunity to express his talents. It is often claimed that a closed-class system turns talented people into revolutionists (as they attack the system which blocks them), while an open-class system co-opts potential revolutionists by turning them into social climbers. Yet the noisy revolutionists in the Western world today come from the more privileged classes in relatively open-class societies. Whether an open-class system creates more frustration and social discontent than it allays is not entirely clear.

A closed-class system is highly wasteful of talent, while an open-class system allows a talented, ambitious person to rise to greater responsibilities. A static society has only a limited need for talent, for most ascribed roles can be filled successfully by mediocre people, given appropriate training. But a highly dynamic, changing, industrialized society cannot waste talent so casually. An open-class system better fits the needs of the modern world, whatever its costs. This may be why, as traditional societies become modernized, there is a tendency for the class system to open, and for mobility to increase.

Label each of the following statements as true or false.

_____ 1. Wives generally are accorded the class status of their husbands.

_____ 2. The amount of upward mobility is highly affected by the rate of social change in a society.

_____ 3. In the United States it is clear that it is becoming easier to achieve upward mobility.

_____ 4. The consequences of upward mobility are all rewarding.

_____ 5. In all societies open-class systems are unquestionably superior to closed-class systems.

Now turn to Answer frame 3[12] on page 74 to check your answers.

chapter 13

BASIC ECONOMIC FOCUSES AND ELEMENTS

Frame 1[13]

Economics in Cultural Perspective

Economics, as applied to societal functions and systems, manifests itself as a fundamental and universal cultural institution. In this context, economics' main concern centers on the multiplicity of actions and interactions that evolve when man and society undertake various roles and activities that, together, provide the means of making a living. In short, and as described by the eminent economist Alfred Marshall, economics is "a study of mankind in the ordinary business of life." (Alfred Marshall, *Principles of Economics*, 8th ed., New York: Macmillan, 1948, p. 1.)

Within the family of social sciences, economics may be viewed and studied as a singular discipline. However, as one of several cultural institutions, it borders on and is closely oriented to the principles and doctrines set forth in the disciplines of sociology, political science, psychology, and anthropology. It can also be said that economics draws heavily on the study of history; for example, the historical roots and sequence of events constituting the Industrial Revolution remain fundamental concerns of the economist as well as social scientists in other domains. Thus it becomes evident that doctrines, concepts, structures, functions, and techniques that, together, comprise economic institutions and related systems are basically products of combined cultural forces that influence and, in turn, are influenced by the material and service components which are involved in the development and application of economic theory and principles.

The foregoing is cited as a basis for the approach to the study of economics that follows. In essence, the information provided is not specifically attuned to the economists' preoccupations with the theory, principles, and abstractions involved in the internal functioning of an economy but rather to emphasize the broad fundamental concepts and concerns that serve to shape economic institutions and to gauge their influence and impact on patterns of behavior that bear on the total cultural milieu of society.

As is the case of all disciplines dealing with the social institutions of man and society, economics and economic systems influence and are influenced by the established ideology, tradition, value, and belief patterns existent within a given society. As will be seen, the power effect of economic factors in this cultural linkage is often direct and positive. Some societal scientists feel the influence of economics over other cultural forces shaping the social order is overwhelming. However, few would go so far as to accept the Marxian thesis that economics alone is the controlling institution within any society. After all, man is a complex social creature whose life-styles and satisfactions impose demands that clearly negate the concept that man can live by bread alone.

Indicate whether each of the following statements is true or false by writing "T" or "F" in the space provided.

_____ 1. Economics is a discipline that is distinct and separate from other disciplines within the social sciences.

_____ 2. The author is going to focus his attention on the theory, principles, and abstractions involved in the internal functioning of an economy.

_____ 3. The influence between economics and the established ideology, tradition, value, and belief patterns within a given society is a two-way relationship.

_____ 4. Economists agree that economics alone is the controlling institution within any society.

Now turn to Answer frame 1[13] on page 74 to check your responses.

Frame 2[13]

In her book, *Patterns of Culture*, Ruth Benedict makes the point that various cultures reflect commonality to some degree with respect to norms and behavioral patterns but never to the point of totality. (Ruth Benedict, *Patterns of Culture*, Boston: Houghton Mifflin Company, 1959, pp. 45–49.) This is the essence of the problems facing those concerned with the culture concept and its relationship with human behavior. Specifically, the major task is that of ascertaining the shared as well as variable patterns among cultures and to isolate the causative factors.

In this initial stage of our overview of economics, data presented will be focused primarily on those forces and factors that, in general, have

led to the development and institutionalization of economic systems within all societies. As you will note, biological, environmental, and technological factors are the key elements of what evolves as a common process. In later chapters we will inject into our analysis varying ideological, philosophical, and political concepts that have served as the prime catalysts in creating elements of diversity among various economic systems.

Basic Forces

Economic institutions and systems are universally powered by the material needs and wants of individuals and groups constituting a

Answer frame 3^{12}

1. True. This is usually the case, and a technique of upward mobility for girls is to marry boys of higher status.
2. True. In a relatively static society there is little upward mobility. Rapidly changing societies are likely to have more openings, or some persons in the middle and upper classes may fail to make the adaptations necessary to retain their class rank. Social change may also alter the proportion of class openings at the different levels.
3. False. Whether it is becoming easier or more difficult to achieve upward mobility is debatable. In the United States the evidence suggests that the rate of mobility has not changed in recent decades and mobility rates appear to be about the same throughout the industrialized world.
4. False. Upward mobility often produces negative consequences for the individual. Examples: status anxiety, role strain, mental illness, and the disruption of primary group relationships.
5. False. Open-class systems better fit modern societies but not traditional societies.

If you missed any of the above, you should reread Frame 3^{12} before turning to Chapter 13 on page 72.

Answer frame 1^{13}

1. False. Economics is closely related to other social science disciplines such as sociology, political science, psychology, anthropology, and history.
2. False. He is going to emphasize the broad fundamental concepts and concerns that shape economic institutions and also measure the impact of these institutions on society.
3. True. Economics influences and is influenced by these patterns within a given society.
4. False. Karl Marx held this view but few other economists would go this far.

If you missed any of the above, you should restudy Frame 1^{13} before turning to Frame 2^{13} on page 73.

Frame 2^{13} continued

society. The human-needs factor is viewed as an imperative in as much as man's biological nature imposes an uncompromising demand for the provision of food, drink, and, in almost every environment, shelter and clothing. Within the limitations imposed by the physical aspects of the environment, cultural forces integrate with biologically imposed needs in determining the material and social functions and norms applicable to a society concerned with servicing its members' basic physiological demands. Involved are the economic responsibilities of providing materials necessary to satisfy need demands as well as imposed social norms with respect to kinds, types, styles, mannerisms, taboos, and so on, related to the usage of the various material components.

Concurrently, economic and cultural progression sets into motion man's desire for material items that are not absolutely essential to the maintenance of life but, nevertheless, serve to expand and enhance human capabilities and patterns of existence. In contrast to human needs, we will call these demands human wants. Man's creativity and desire for personal fulfillment and satisfaction move him beyond simple needs satisfaction into the realms of the arts, literature, recreation, comfort items, technical-mechanical devices, and the like. Once exposed to the availability of such products, human demand tends to become insatiable. This is evident in our society and every other society that has progressed beyond the subsistence stage of economic development.

It would be well to pause here in order to discuss materialism as a characteristic of society. For example, our society has been characterized by a wide spectrum of indigenous and foreign social scientists as being unduly concerned with material possessions and gain. No doubt there is some validity to their position. However, often overlooked by those of this disposition is the cultural truism that material satisfaction has remained a central force in all social orders subject only to the inhibitions imposed by the availability and attainability of material products within any given society. Of course, wantless societies still exist but only in small areas far remote from the mainstream of economic and cultural progression. It is interesting that most of the underdeveloped nations of the world have centered their ideologies on material imperatives of economic development primarily to meet the growing challenge of both needs and wants satisfaction among their populations.

Can material wants items that are marginal to human existence at any one time be transformed into the needs category within a society? An affirmative response can be easily supported within our own society. Thus automobiles that not too long ago were classified as luxuries have now become absolutely necessary in providing physical mobility. The mechanical refrigerator, once a device nice to own is recognized today as essential to the general health, welfare, and convenience of members of our society.

Indicate whether each of the following statements is true or false by writing "T" or "F" in the space provided.

_____ 1. Only in certain societies are economic institutions and systems related to the needs and wants of the individuals and groups in the society.

_____ 2. Human demand is a fixed quantity that is capable of being completely satisfied.

_____ 3. Many social scientists feel that the U.S. society is overly concerned with material possessions and gains.

_____ 4. Within a given society, items that at one time are marginal to human existence may later become essential needs.

Now turn to Answer frame 2^{13} on page 76 to check your responses.

Frame 3^{13}

Genesis of Economic Activity

We must now investigate how various economic functions and activities are organized and integrated into systems designed to service the needs/wants demands of a society. Some initial insight into the nature and scope of the elements involved is set forth rather precisely in the following functional definition cited by Paul A. Samuelson in his text, *Economics:* "Economics is the study of how men and society end up choosing . . . to employ scarce productive resources which could have alternative uses, to produce various commodities and distribute them for consumption, now or in the future, among various people and groups within society." (Paul A. Samuelson, *Economics,* 8th ed., New York: McGraw-Hill Book Co., 1970, p. 4.)

Reducing the foregoing to essentials, we see that economics imposes the concept of scarcity, involves society in the economic decision process, and incorporates the functions of production, distribution, and consumption.

Law of Scarcity. Economics as a discipline and as an institution of society would not exist except for the fact that the means for satisfying human needs and wants, even among the most affluent societies, are scarce. Thus if all goods and services could be produced in unlimited amounts with all needs and wants satisfied

Answer frame 2¹³

1. False. In all societies economic systems and institutions are related to the wants and needs of the various components that make up the society.
2. False. Once the human is exposed to the arts, literature, recreation, and so on, his demand tends to become insatiable.
3. True. Many American and foreign social scientists feel that our society is very materialistic.
4. True. An excellent example in the American society is the automobile.

If you missed any of the above, you should restudy Frame 2¹³ before turning to Frame 3¹³ on page 75.

Frame 3¹³ continued

fully, there would be no need for economics or economizing. Like the air we breathe, all goods and services would be free, thus negating the need for societal decisions on such key economic concerns as what to produce, how to produce it, and for whom.

In comparison with their historical economic capabilities, or relative to the current status of the underdeveloped nations of the world, today's modern industrial societies produce an enormous amount of goods and wealth in servicing human demand. Yet higher production and technological advancement tends to generate ever-growing consumption standards within a culture. In economics, things are scarce only in relation to man's desire for them. However, since this desire tends to be limitless, society through its economic institutions must always contend with scarcity as a fundamental and continuing problem of universal proportions within the social order. Thus no society can escape the fact of scarcity nor the attendant responsibility of providing decisions which are essential to the establishment of viable economic and social systems.

The Economic Cycle. Every economic system is structured around the processes of production, distribution, and consumption. This economic triad constitutes a cycle of interdependent, self-perpetuating functions organized and directed in accordance with society's traditions, values, and beliefs coupled with existent economic capabilities factors with respect to technological development, availability of material resources, and the qualitative-quantitative abilities of the populace.

Elaborating further, decisions relative to which of alternative goods and services and the volume—how much will be produced—for the most part, fall under the purview of a society's goals, values, and beliefs as modified by existent economic capabilities factors. Thus a democracy attuned to the fulfillment of consumer demand responds to such decisions in one way; a military-oriented authoritarian government, in quite another. Except under a command-type economy, cultural forces within a society exercise a high degree of direction and consistency with respect to the nature and intent of economic decisions. Nevertheless, pressures may arise causing major alterations. For example, during World War II, the United States shifted from a consumer-oriented democracy to a military-production economy functioning under what was virtually authoritarian direction.

Another decision evolves from the question of how the various resources of a society will be combined in the process of producing goods and services. Economists agree the essential elements involved integrate under the heading "factors of production" that include land, labor, capital, and management.

Is each of the following true or false?

_____ 1. If all goods and services could be produced in unlimited amounts, there would be no need for economics.

_____ 2. Industrial societies, because of their vast wealth, rarely have to contend with the problems of scarcity.

_____ 3. All economics systems are structured around three interdependent functions—production, distribution, and control.

_____ 4. The production process involves three elements titled "factors of production"—land, labor, and capital.

Now turn to Answer frame 3[13] on page 78 to check your answers.

Frame 4[13]

Land, both a natural and original resource, incorporates the soil itself as well as mineral deposits, waters, forests, harbors, rainfall, and climate. Labor, also considered an original economic resource, involves all forms of human effort expended in the production-distribution processes and is measurable in terms of time and energy outputs plus abilities requirements. The labor equation of production is directly influenced by such factors as the composition of the populations with respect to age levels, size, education, and technological capabilities. Also of major import is the cultural disposition toward material progress to include attitudes and motivations toward work.

Capital as the third factor is a product of land and labor. In economic terms, capital is not money but rather the physical necessities for further production including tools, machinery, buildings, transport equipment, tractors, and the like. Within all productive systems, capital infers investment and investment demands deferred consumption or savings. To produce the capital necessary for production, man and society must sacrifice to the extent of curbing outlays of money for consumer items in favor of investment via savings accounts, tax revenue payments, or corporate stocks and bonds. Money saved but not invested may give personal satisfaction but, in economic terms, this is hoarded wealth that is useless and, as a practice, harmful to the growth and expansion of productive enterprises.

Two further considerations regarding capital —first, it is interesting to note that every economic system must employ both savings and profits concepts in order to provide initial or expanded levels of productive equipment. Thus capital is not singular to a capitalist society. Sec-

ond, of the myriad of problems facing the economic planners within the underdeveloped world, none has the dimensions of the capital formation concept. With poverty dominant, how can savings or the incentive to save exist or be created? Also, with per capita income generally at or below subsistence level, the possible revenue gains from government-imposed tax programs can only become marginal, at best. Internal sacrifice coupled with aid and assistance from abroad afford the only possible solutions to the dilemma.

Management, as the fourth factor, is essentially a specialized owner-administrator kind of labor. Here we are concerned with the internal decision makers of the production-distribution processes and the availability of personnel skilled in these areas is absolutely essential to the economic well-being and progress of a society. Management includes the entrepreneur who, as a risk taker and innovator, initiates economic enterprises, combines and coordinates the other factors of production, and may direct and manage operations. Management also includes those concerned solely with administrative functions at each of the various levels within organizations and enterprises.

In the decision-making process, management is concerned not only with productive factors but also with societal influences such as those related to the ecology, work conditions, government and consumer priorities, monetary and fiscal policy, pricing and profit margins, labor relations, unemployment, employee welfare, taxation, and tariffs policies. Management, therefore, provides the proximate link between economic processes and related cultural norms manifested by society with respect to the functioning of its economy.

Answer frame 3¹³

1. True. Everything would be free, thus eliminating the need to determine what to produce, how to produce it, and for whom.
2. False. All societies must contend with scarcity as a fundamental and continuing problem.
3. True. This structure is present in every economic system.
4. False. There are four—land, labor, capital, and management.

If you missed any of the above, you should review Frame 3¹³ before turning to Frame 4¹³ on page 77.

Frame 4¹³ continued

True or false?

_____ 1. Capital is money raised to aid in the production of goods.

_____ 2. Management includes both the entrepreneur and the individual performing administrative functions.

_____ 3. Today management is concerned not only with producing goods, but also with social questions such as working conditions, unemployment, employee welfare, and so on.

_____ 4. Capital exists only in capitalistic societies.

Now turn to Answer frame 4¹³ on page 80 to check your answers.

Frame 5¹³

The next logical step following the production element of the economic cycle is the determination of who gets what and how much of the goods and services are made available to a society or, in short, the distribution-consumption process. Of all decisions confronting society, those in this realm are the most difficult mainly because of the sociological, political, and even psychological determinants and variables that bear on this facet of the economic process.

Historically, most philosophers concerned with the economic well-being of man and society have confronted the problem by proposing idealistic, egalitarian concepts that reflect equality for all in sharing the products and wealth of a society. This has been particularly true of those espousing the philosophic aims of utopianism, socialism, communism, and various forms of humanism.

Yet, except perhaps for a few traditionally directed, communally organized societies existing at subsistence levels, all social orders evidence the existence of continuing overt inequality in the distribution of goods and services among populaces. Thus, despite idealistic protestations and variable levels of affluence, the society of man has yet to create a social order wherein the economic system and goals totally eliminate the existence of the haves and the have-nots.

Each economic system imposes criteria for the distribution of wealth and products among its public. A feudal system is organized around ascribed social statuses with distribution priorities set by fixed levels of rank within each estate organization. In some social orders, work output serves as the singular guide concerning levels of participation in the distribution process as evidenced by the San Blas Cuna Indians. Under an authoritarian, planned economy, such as the USSR, the leadership decides not only what will be produced, but also distribution criteria and priorities involving state, group, and individual requirements.

Among other societies, such as our own, the distribution factor functions under the less precise and impersonal forces created primarily by economic specialization, competitive markets, and the division of labor. In substance, the free play of these forces intensifies the levels of economic interdependence, thereby creating demand for a wide range of products and services. Differentials in demand priorities, productive skill requirements and availabilities, plus socially accorded power and prestige are the essential determinants of reward levels. As a result, rewards or incomes vary; some people are highly rewarded while others receive minimal or less than minimal returns. Since income levels reflect purchasing power, quite obviously varying income results in unequal sharing in the products and services of society. In short, distribution is directly oriented to wage differentials.

Overviewing distribution vis-à-vis consumer demand within the broader dimensions of the total world order, one can only conclude that inequality predominates on an extreme scale. Over two thirds of the world is classified as economically underdeveloped, thereby being incapable of providing much more than a subsistence standard of living to a majority of the world population existing within its confines. The remaining one third comprising the economically advanced nations enjoys vastly superior standards of living made possible by modern technology, massive industrialization, and huge expenditures of human skills and material resources in support of consumer-related productive enterprises. Unfortunately, the economic gap between the have and have-not nations of the world continues to widen despite the latter's priority efforts toward industrialization, including large measures of aid and assistance support which has been provided by advanced industrial societies.

Indicate whether each of the following statements is true or false by writing "T" or "F" in the space provided.

_____ 1. In very few modern societies does equality exist in the distribution of goods and services among the population.

_____ 2. Market forces determine the distribution of wealth and products in all economic systems.

_____ 3. Generally, the one third of the world population that resides in industrial nations has a much higher standard of living than the remainder of the world.

_____ 4. In the USSR decisions on production and distribution are made by the leaders of that nation.

Now turn to Answer frame 5[13] on page 80 to check your responses.

Frame 6[13]

Internal Institutions. All economic orders, whether simple or complex, are functionally dependent upon a variety of social norms and understandings that together facilitate, stabilize, and afford predictability to systems operations. Because of their import on the social, political, and economic framework of society, such norms are formalized under the institutional headings of property, contract, and economic role or occupation. Within a simple economy, such institutions exist, if only implicitly, within the total fabric of society. However, among the more complex industrial societies, institutions become singular elaborations of shared rules, laws, and procedures concerning the conduct of economic affairs.

The institution of property sets forth societal rights, privileges, and obligations regarding economic items intrinsically valuable and transferable among persons. Property items may be classified as tangible or intangible with respect to susbstance; private or public, regarding ownership.

Recognized societal rights and privileges regarding property generally relate to the factors of use, control, transfer, and disposal. Related

Answer frame 4¹³

1. False. Capital is not money, but rather the physical necessities for further production.
2. True. Management encompasses both the risk taker and administrators.
3. True. Management is concerned with many societal influences including pricing, consumer priorities, taxation, and tariffs.
4. False. Capital is not unique to capitalistic societies.

If you missed any of the above, you should restudy Frame 4¹³ before turning to Frame 5¹³ on page 78.

Answer frame 5¹³

1. True. In most societies there exists inequality in the distribution of goods and services.
2. False. Each economic system has its own criteria for the distribution of wealth and products to its public.
3. True. Over two thirds of the world in underdeveloped nations are struggling to give their people a subsistence standard of living; in contrast, the advanced nations enjoy high standards of living.
4. True. In an authoritarian planned economy, such as the USSR, the leadership makes production and distribution decisions.

If you missed any of the above, you should restudy Frame 5¹³ before turning to Frame 6¹³ on page 79.

Frame 6¹³ continued

laws and regulations vary among societies. Some reflect large measures of flexibility in application with the result that most members of society can enter into personal property and service arrangements either as owners, users, sellers, or in combination. In broad application, flexibility in property rights and privileges has enhanced personal satisfactions and stimulated economic motivations especially in the areas of entrepreneurship and investment. Among societies that have achieved economic takeoff, the concept has been a major force in facilitating the development and expansion of highly productive enterprises capable of servicing a wide variety of demands within all sectors of society.

Conversely, within societies organized under authoritarian rule, property, with attendant rights, rules, and regulations, is closely regulated and controlled by a central authority. Normally, decisions and actions affecting property as well as related economic processes reflect a delimitation of the private in favor of the public domain concept with the state functioning as the supreme authority. Property functions are thus fused into an inflexible arrangement that tends to negate the incentives, motivations, and efficiencies that accrue under the privately oriented, flexible concept of property. In this regard, there is adequate evidence to indicate that command-type societies have been relatively unsuccessful in recreating these attributes by instituting planned substitute measures in the form of production quotas, incentive awards, or punishments.

Contract is the institution that guides and facilitates exchanges involving property and/or services. As such, it encompasses the shared values and norms that govern and legitimatize those elements of economic activity concerned with bargaining and transfer operations.

Contract is a fundamental and commonplace feature of our daily lives. In almost every action of an economic nature, there exist promises among the parties concerned with respect to labor in return for wages, food in exchange for money, education in exchange for fees, an automobile for a promissory note, stock certificate for a given cash collateral outlay, and so on.

To be effective, contract as a principle and in specific application, must be enforced by society through established laws, rules, and regulations. If such were not the case, either economic life would come to a standstill or it would become a matter of the survival of the fittest. Thus by guaranteeing the fulfillment of terms of exchange (with or without the use of sanctions) the institution of contract provides necessary credibility, predictability, and functional direction to economic systems, thereby contributing immeasurably to the maintenance of stability within social order.

The operation of an economic system, whether simple or complex, incorporates the accomplishment of various activities and functions considered necessary for the continuity and material well-being of a society. Such activities and functions are the delineators of economic roles in terms of specific occupations that, in total, reflect the work demands and objectives of society.

All societies have found it expedient to institutionalize occupational roles by surrounding them with clusters of norms. Because of high levels of economic interdependence among peoples of advanced industrial societies, related roles and functions must be delineated precisely. For example, there must be an understanding of the functional orientation and contributions of a given occupation as well as obligations of those who perform the economic role with respect to knowledge, skill, and responsibility. Further, there are culturally defined role delineations with respect to sex, age, division of labor priorities, and occupational qualifications. In every society marked by a high degree of specialization and division of labor, economic roles of major magnitude and complexity must be coordinated. They must be meshed into an effectively integrated process; otherwise, chaos, inefficiency, and limited productivity will plague the system.

Is each of the following true or false?

_____ 1. Flexibility of property rights and privileges has been a major force in facilitating the development of highly productive enterprises in economically developed societies.

_____ 2. Property may be classified as private or public with respect to substance.

_____ 3. Enforceable contracts contribute to the orderly conduct of an economic system.

_____ 4. In advanced industrial societies occupational roles are not carefully defined.

Now turn to Answer frame 6¹³ on page 82 to check your answers.

Frame 7¹³

Exchange

The rationale for economic systems, including supporting institutions achieves fruition on implementation of exchange processes. Conceived and structured on the basis of shared expectations and understandings, exchange incorporates the totality of interactions that take place when goods and services are marketed for transfer and acquisition with both the seller and buyer expecting to benefit.

Exchange involves the entire spectrum of marketable items within a society. In addition to commodity items, the process incorporates labor, money, services, and related human resource factors that compose demand forces within a society.

Exchange may take place either indirectly or directly. The former is best exemplified by those transactions wherein goods and services are provided recipients, usually by a third party, without direct regard to the ratio of individual or group payment for value received. A case in point is taxation wherein governments widely

Answer frame 6¹³

1. True. Flexibility in property rights and privileges has helped in the development of highly productive enterprises in societies that have achieved economic takeoff.
2. False. Property may be classified as tangible or intangible with respect to substance; private or public regarding ownership.
3. True. Contracts provide credibility, predictability, and functional direction to economic systems.
4. False. In advanced industrial societies occupational roles and functions must be delineated precisely.

If you missed any of the above, you should review Frame 6¹³ before turning to Frame 7¹³ on page 81.

Frame 7¹³ continued

redistribute wealth drawn from their taxable members without regard to the magnitude of individual or group contributions. Direct exchange, either through barter or money purchase, normally involves bargaining and haggling between the seller and buyer on a head-to-head basis in a marketplace with each seeking to benefit under compromise arrangements. In complex economies, the exchange function normally involves a number of agencies including the producer, wholesaler, retailer, and consumer. Because of the time factor as related to the huge volume of business, haggling has become impractical except in areas where there is considerable price fluctuation or values are not generally standardized, for example, works of art, used cars, real estate, including land and property speculations.

Money. Except among a few tradition-oriented societies, money has almost totally superseded barter procedures in the exchange process. As the medium of exchange in commodity and service transactions, money best meets the essential requirements for portability and facility of usage in value computations (standard of value). Also, serving as the store of value, money affords both predictability and continuity to economic functions extended over time.

Money has often been described as the life blood of an economic system with a smooth, uninterrupted flow through all functional elements being essential to continued progress and prosperity. Such concerns as inflation, deflation, tight or loose credit, concentration, and decentralization of monetary wealth are reflective of the impact of the money equation on the total operations of societal systems.

The real value of money in the exchange process and general economic functions is geared to its universal acceptance. Money, of itself, normally has little or no intrinsic value with the result that money is what society thinks it is based on the psychological factors of faith and trust. True, such objective factors as reserve backing, state of the economy, political stability, and government policy formations influence the status of monetary values but, in the main, it is the public regard toward this instrument that mark its value.

So far we have been concerned with the basic decisions, functions, and forces that influence economic concepts, institutions, and systems within the social order. The question of how various societies have shaped and patterned these factors within the framework of their cultures now becomes significant and will be elaborated on in the following chapter.

True or false?

_____ 1. In an exchange, both the buyer and seller expect to benefit.

_____ 2. The redistribution of wealth by a government by use of taxation is an example of direct exchange.

_____3. In the main, the value of money in an economy is a function of public regard toward it (money).

_____4. Money has completely replaced barter in all societies.

Now turn to Answer frame 7[13] on page 84 to check your answers.

chapter 14

EVOLUTION OF ECONOMICS

Frame 1[14]

General

From the very beginning, humanity has had to cope with the task of survival. In contrast with the multitude of forces within the environment that endanger human existence, man as an individual represents a relatively weak counterforce, both physiologically and psychologically. Thus in the continuing battle for self-preservation, man has found it necessary to organize his defenses around the cooperative power base afforded by the social group and its supporting institutional structure. The resultant elaborate mechanism constitutes the culture base required for the development and survival of a society.

That society has been able to overcome environmental challenges to its survival over the centuries is reflective of man's superior innovative and creative powers. Included is the ability to employ science and technology in problem resolution arising from social demands and issues that bear on the development and perpetuation of cultural systems. It is interesting to note that while engaged in overcoming dangers imposed by the natural environment, society succeeded in creating advanced cultures encompassing a complexity of functions, tasks, and organizations so meshed and interdependent that should some fail of mission accomplishment, all or a major part of the social order could suffer serious disruption or possibly chaos. In short, human frailties have tended to supersede environmental factors as the prime threat to the well-being and survival of culturally advanced societies.

Basic Economic Systems

The continuity and viability of a society is directly related to the adequacy and effectiveness of its economic system in providing materials and services in support of social demand. Throughout the long sweep of history, there have evolved within various social cultures that embody and govern discernible economic processes three types of system which, separately or in combination, have made it possible for humanity to counter successfully the economic

Answer frame 7¹³

1. True. In an exchange goods and services are marketed for transfer and acquisition with both the seller and buyer expecting to benefit.
2. False. Such redistribution is an example of indirect exchange.
3. True. Public regard is a crucial factor influencing the value of money.
4. False. Barter still exists in a few tradition-oriented societies.

If you missed any of the above, you should restudy Frame 7¹³ before beginning Chapter 14 on page 83.

Frame 1¹⁴ continued

challenge. Specifically referred to here are the socioeconomic system designs governed by tradition, command, and the market.

Tradition.   The oldest and most simplistic mode employed by society in shaping and guiding its economic organization and functions is that of tradition. It affords a static design for the total organization of society, including the economy, since it is based on policies and procedures drawn from the past and applied to the present under accepted social restraints of custom, law, and belief.

Among societies based on tradition, the economic function becomes tightly interwoven into the total fabric of human activity, thereby becoming a simplified pattern of behavior with few characteristics of a singular social institution. Based on ascribed statuses and the hereditary linkage of personnel to specific skills, functions, and tasks, tradition employs the concept of an unchanging, repetitive cycle of activity and custom in providing for the material needs and wants of society, including regulation of their distribution.

A tradition-directed economy engenders a high degree of orderliness, stability, and continuity. Further, being devoid of the vast technical and organizational trappings associated with modern industrial society, its constituents quickly become oriented to the workings of the entire system without the added help and direction of learned social philosophers, including economists.

The forces of tradition have lost ground in the economic world under the pressures of science, technology, and industrialization. Thus today, only among the primitive agrarian or nonindustrial societies can one find tradition as the mainstay of economic and social organization and activity.

Still, vestiges remain even among the most advanced societies. Within our own economic system, one can still discern such traditional practices as pay differentials between male and female for identical work, tips for service personnel, bonuses based on length of service, sons succeeding fathers in occupational roles, and the selection or nonselection of an employment based on social status factors.

Custom-bound, repetitious, and routine, tradition-directed economies seldom institute change or suffer change as a result of internal forces. On the other hand, the external pressures of technology, cultural diffusion, war, acts of nature, and political incursions have effectively undermined the power and capabilities of tradition as the locus of economic and social activity, especially during this and the preceding century.

Thus, within an ever-changing world, tradition still provides answers to economic problems to some societies but always at the cost of economic progress with resultant stagnation.

Indicate whether each of the following statements is true or false by writing "T" or "F" in the space provided.

_____ 1. A socioeconomic system based on tradition relies on what has occurred in the past.

_____ 2. In the modern world, tradition-directed economies are found in moderate-sized industrial economies.

_____ 3. Sex discrimination in employment is an example of a traditional practice in the American economic system.

_____ 4. Internal pressure is usually the impetus for change in a tradition-directed economy.

Now turn to Answer frame 1^{14} on page 86 to check your responses.

Frame 2^{14}

Command. As a second economics mechanism, the reign of command approximates that of tradition in guiding and directing societies in efforts to secure their economic well-being. Based on the concept of imposed direction by a central authority, command involves the organization of a viable system responsive directly to the dictates of political rulers. Normally, wherever the command method is accepted practice, it usually has been superimposed on a traditional social base with the result that part of the economic effort reflects the endless customs of the past and the remainder, the desires, directives, or even whims of the central authority.

Command affords the most direct, and in relation to time, the most efficient method for directing human efforts toward the resolution of economic problems. In crisis situations, it may be the only way society can get the economic job done and still survive. Thus, as indicated earlier, the economic system of the United States during World War II was reconstituted under a central authority in order to facilitate actions in response to the emergency situation.

In addition to its usefulness in emergency situations, command has the additional attribute of facilitating and even forcing economic change. In effect, it provides the means for keeping up with the times with respect to technological and social developments and provides a spur to progress.

With respect to the past, command in its most dominant form guided the economic destinies of ancient Egypt, medieval China, and the societies of England and Europe during the time of feudalism. Currently, we can see its application very precisely within authoritarian communist societies such as the USSR, Mainland China, Cuba, and the like. While no modern society is without some elements of command, the matter of its employment is one of degree and permanency within a social order. Command as employed within a democratic society becomes a tactical device; within an authoritarian society it is the fundamental feature of the ruler's strategy.

The Market. The third economic system applied by society to the problem of survival is known by the rather abstract title as the market or marketplace. In comparison with tradition and command, the market is functionally far more complex, its energizing mechanisms less precise, its rationale less evident, and its overall cultural impact far more involved and extensive in application.

A product of events leading to the Industrial Revolution and the revolution itself, the market encompassed a new concept that removed economics from the constraints of tradition and command and replaced them with a system oriented to individual self-interest directed toward the attainment of profit and rewards provided to those motivated toward accomplishing the labor and tasks necessary to the establishment and maintenance of a viable economy.

Self-interest and the lure of personal gain provide the impulse for production and distribution but, unless inhibited, it is unlikely that society could endure. Accordingly, the system incorporates the regulatory mechanism of competition to curb man's selfishness while servicing the material demand of society as a whole. The essence of competition within the market is to pit seller against buyer, labor against wages, seller against seller, price against service, quality versus quantity, and the like. With all things being equal, the competitive battle would result in the proper allocation of labor, just rewards, efficiency of operations, stimulation of self-interest, and accomplishment of necessary

Answer frame 1¹⁴

1. True. A traditional system is based on the past; it relies on the concept of an un-changing, repetitive cycle of activity and custom.
2. False. Today, only among the primitive agrarian or nonindustrial societies can one find tradition as the mainstay of economic and social organization and activity.
3. True. Pay differentials between male and female for identical work is an example of traditional practices.
4. False. External factors such as war or acts of nature are usually the impetus for change in a tradition-directed economy.

If you missed any of the above, you should restudy Frame 1¹⁴ before turning to Frame 2¹⁴ on page 85.

Frame 2¹⁴ continued

economic tasks in a manner advantageous to the total social order.

One can view the market both as a warehouse of the end items of production and as an institution which coordinates occupation, property, and contract; facilitates the exchange and distribution processes; brings together the buyer and seller; and serves as the focal point of competition executed under terms of the law of supply and demand. On the other hand, a market may be visualized in the concrete terms of a grocery or clothing store as well as in an abstract or diffuse sense such as labor, investment, capital, and professional services, to cite a few.

Finally, it must be made evident that the mar-

ket system has never functioned in a pure state wherein competition under the law of supply and demand has been afforded total free play. Command in the form of government regulation has injected itself into the market in growing increments as the economic base of society progressively expands. In this regard, some economists feel political interference has served to degrade the efficiency and effectiveness of market operations; others are of the opinion that the motivational and regulatory elements incorporated within the system are inadequate and must be buttressed by government legislation or regulation to achieve proper effectiveness and balance.

Is each of the following true or false?

_____ 1. A command-directed economy is based on imposed direction by a central authority.

_____ 2. A command-directed economy does not facilitate economic change.

_____ 3. In a market-directed economy, profit and rewards are provided to those performing the labor and tasks necessary to the smooth functioning of the economy.

_____ 4. In advanced industrial nations the market system functions in a pure state wherein competition under the law of supply and demand is afforded free play.

Now turn to Answer frame 2¹⁴ on page 88 to check your answers.

Frame 3¹⁴

Economic Systems in Transition

General. The injection of the market concept into the economic picture had far-reaching effects on the human cultural patterns that evolved over the centuries. From the changeless, easily comprehensible and rather secure life-styles and arrangements that obtained under the forces of tradition and command, society had now to contend with a system demanding of change, dubious with respect to its security aspects and, above all, totally perplexing in doctrine, organization, and functions except to a few newly arrived intellectuals with the title of economists.

The inevitable transition of society from the dictates of tradition and command to the forces of the market system was primarily an evolutionary process, but the resultant impact on the social order achieved the magnitude of full-scale cultural upheaval of worldwide proportions known as the Industrial Revolution. With its roots extending deep into events of history, the Industrial Revolution became the catalyst for cultural change that resulted in revamping society into its modern social and organizational structure.

The information that follows portrays, in polarized contrast form, the essential variables between the communal-traditional society and modern industrial society. Promoted by the Industrial Revolution, these variables are particularly revealing, not only with respect to the magnitude of the transition but also the sometimes forgotten cultural roots of the social order we know today.

In elaborating on the diverse cultural elements, cognizance was taken of the fact that their total applicability to societies in the several stages of development may be questionable. However, as generalizations, they make quite evident the dimensions of culture existent at both ends of the economic spectrum as well as the nature of the social upheaval involved in the transition. Our first look will be toward the traditional society and its basic characteristics with emphasis on economic factors.

Traditional and Industrial Society Variables.
As indicated earlier, traditional society is unchanging and custom-bound with beliefs, roles, statuses, and patterns of behavior affixed to the past. Life, living, and cultural forces are totally integrated, with the economy and its related activities remaining embedded within all other institutions that shape the way of life.

Organized on a small scale in tribal or village formations with the extended family the locus of economic and social activity, a tradi-

tional society remains oriented to the primary economic functions of agriculture, hunting, fishing, and forestry. Production generally remains at a subsistence level with little or no surplus available for market exchange or to enhance living standards. The low level of technology imposes heavy demands on human and animal energy in the accomplishment of production and service tasks. Except perhaps in the case of cottage industries, specialization and the division of labor do not exist.

There is little, if any, distinction of economic roles and statuses with the individual being both the producer-distributor and consumer of commodities that service his needs and wants. Social mobility through personal achievement, skills, and ambitions is negated by the twin forces of ascription and the sacred dogma that man's position and duties on earth are preordained with the good life to come in the hereafter.

Profit, savings, and investment as part of the economic way of life are considered unnecessary and amoral. After all, the custom-directed production and distribution methods adequately correlate personal living standards with prescribed roles and statuses; to seek change or to gain profit at another's expense are considered marked deviations from accepted norms.

In sharp contrast, an industrial society evolves what is essentially a new way of life. The environment is viewed as a challenge, a phenomenon to be conquered and recast to the service of humanity. Consequently, under the aegis of science, technology, pragmatism, and efficiency, the static concept of custom and tradition fall victim to the forces of progressive change.

Organized in mass, large-scale, and urbanized settings as demanded by the processes of industrialization, the social order assumes a structure and organization reflective of highly differentiated roles, functions, and statuses coupled with increased levels of interdependence among all elements of society. Within the economy, specialization and the division of labor prevail along with a recognized distinction between the roles of producer, distributor, and consumer.

The family no longer constitutes a basic economic entity, thus eliminating the extended family concept with replacement by a nuclear organization. Social statuses and mobility are ori-

Answer frame 2¹⁴

1. True. A command-directed economy involves the organization of a viable system responsive directly to the dictates of political rulers.
2. False. A command-directed economy facilitates and even forces economic change.
3. True. A market system provides reward to those who perform the labor and tasks necessary to the establishment and maintenance of a viable economy.
4. False. The market system has never functioned in a pure state.

If you missed any of the above, you should review Frame 2¹⁴ before turning to Frame 3¹⁴ on page 86.

Frame 3¹⁴ continued

ented toward achievement rather than ascribed qualities, thereby assuming a very open and flexible pattern. Concurrently, the sacred concept of a preordained life role for the individual or group is superseded by the here and now ethic of work, ambition, and achievement as accepted means of attaining the good life as well as one's spiritual goals bearing on the hereafter.

The basic industries are encompassed within the whole pattern of industrialization with productive capacity far exceeding subsistence levels, making possible advanced standards of living, surplus items for exchange, and profits for savings and investment. Human and animal labor and energy are replaced by mechanical processes that facilitate productivity, limit human drudgery, and facilitate man's escape from the traditional constricts of his economic role.

True or false?

_____ 1. In a traditional society, production generally remains at a subsistence level.

_____ 2. In a traditional society there are sharp distinctions between the roles of producer, distributor, and consumer.

_____ 3. In an industrial society the family is a basic economic unit.

_____ 4. In an industrial society human and animal labor and energy tend to be replaced by mechanical processes.

Now turn to Answer frame 3¹⁴ on page 90 to check your answers.

Frame 4¹⁴

The Industrial Revolution

General. The Industrial Revolution that gave rise to the social upheaval marking the transition from traditionalism to industrialism was long getting under way among societies first to feel its influences. However, once momentum was achieved, it moved inexorably forward along pathways that cut through the very fabric of society.

In describing the economic forces that burst asunder the changeless order of tradition-di-

rected societies of the past, one must first take into account a progression of events that set the stage for the coming of industrialization and the market system. With respect to historic time, the processes involved spanned the era extending from the 10th through the 19th centuries. In the discussions that follow, we will take the liberty of generalizing their application. However, it must be borne in mind that few of the many events manifested themselves in any two societies in precisely the same manner during this cited time frame.

Agencies and Forces of Change

The Merchant. Perhaps the first element to come to the fore in creating inroads into the economic stagnation of medieval Europe was the so-called itinerant merchant. Consigned to the very lowest rank of society, these marketeers moved from manor to manor and town to town throughout Europe and England purveying material items produced in one locale but normally unattainable in others through established channels of commerce. Traveling with their wares, they constituted a crude, but nevertheless active marketplace, involving trade, price and profit calculations, simplistic bookkeeping, and basic money transactions. Beginning even before the 10th century and extending through the 15th, such tradesmen gave life and continuity to commercial intercourse throughout England and Europe. In so doing they set the stage for the coming of organized commercial systems extending throughout and beyond the Western world.

Urbanization. Closely related to the activities of the traveling merchant was the slow but steady growth of cities and towns. Inhibited by the constricts of the feudalistic manoral system and a paucity of communications means, especially roads, urbanization of any consequence was delayed until about the 10th century. Thereafter, progress was limited but discernible as evidenced in Europe where, in the next six centuries, some 1,000 new towns came into being. The spontaneous growth of urban life in the interstices of feudal society gave impetus for the development of a new outlook on the future of the social and economic order of society. Eventually, each town encompassed such economic entities as inns, granaries, shops, and toll roads, with the result that market operations and commercial transactions became the new and accepted cultural patterns within a growing social order.

Crusades. The Crusades launched by European forces of Christianity against the "heathen" forces in the Middle East failed to achieve their religious goals, but the resultant economic fallout was quite extensive. Two different worlds were brought together. The Crusaders from out of the economically regressive atmosphere of feudalistic Europe expected to be matched against untutored barbarians of the Eastern realms with cultural patterns of the lowest order. What they found, assimilated, and related on their return was quite to the contrary! Surprisingly, they discovered a civilization far more advanced than their own, luxury beyond comprehension, viable and progressive commercial systems, the application of the profit motive in business transactions, and wealth based on money accumulation rather than on landholdings acquired through ascription. The eventual transmission and internalization of these patterns and concepts among European cultures served to inhibit the forces of feudalism and expand the forces seeking social and economic change.

Nationalism. Another factor with an absolute bearing on the economic transformation of society was the growth of nationalism. Until the beginning of the Middle Ages, both Europe and England represented a conglomeration of fragmented and compartmented political, social, and economic entities living in a state of mutual isolation, fear, and distrust. Any degree of national power and sovereignty was a mere reflection of the will and whims of the numerous independent feudal lords who, from time to time, confederated under central direction to overcome problems and threats of mutual concern.

Under such a system, economic functions remained in a state of chaos. Each small political entity portrayed its sovereignty by imposing its own laws, rules, regulations, weights, measures, monetary systems, tariffs, and tolls. The established propensity toward isolationism negated most early attempts aimed toward political and economic coordination or consolidation.

The movement toward achieving a national spirit and allegiance fostered by a central authority was speeded by the increasing growth and spread of towns and cities, expanded commerce, extended communication means, and the need for the consolidation of power under a central authority to counter growing political, economic, and military capabilities and threats of neighboring powers.

The movement toward nationalism and the nation-state system was a laborious process. Political leaders in towns and cities and the agents of commerce saw the opportunity to disassociate themselves from the autocratic power

Answer frame 3¹⁴

1. True. In a traditional society production is usually at a subsistence level with very little surplus available for market exchange or to enhance living standards.
2. False. There is little distinction in economic roles; the individual is usually the producer, distributor, and consumer of the commodities that satisfy his needs and wants.
3. False. In an industrial society, the family does not constitute a basic economic entity.
4. True. An industrial society uses mechanical processes that facilitate productivity, limit human drudgery, and facilitate man's escape from the traditional constricts of his economic role.

If you missed any of the above, you should restudy Frame 3¹⁴ before turning to Frame 4¹⁴ on page 88.

Frame 4¹⁴ continued

of the feudal lord by joining forces with the central government and supplying it with necessary economic and political support. In turn, the central authority began the imposition of its power on the feudal structure through the implementation of unified codes of law, money, tariffs, plus standardized weights and measures. The national power base was extended and expanded further by provision of subsidy support to private commercial and industrial operations and the creation of national military forces to protect its sovereign status and the populace as a whole. England was the first to break the bonds of feudalism and achieve a unified political, economic, and social system. In logical progression, England was also first to undergo the full process of economic transformation including the Industrial Revolution.

Indicate whether each of the following statements is true or false by writing "T" or "F" in the space provided.

_____ 1. The first force to create changes in the economic tradition of medieval Europe was the itinerant merchant.

_____ 2. Urbanization helped to introduce market operations and commercial transactions into the economic life of Europe.

_____ 3. The Crusades exposed Europeans to a different commercial system and consequently helped to bring about economic change in Europe.

_____ 4. Nationalism was not an important factor in the historical development of current economic systems.

Now turn to Answer frame 4¹⁴ on page 92 to check your responses.

Frame 5¹⁴

Exploration. Closely associated with the growth of nationalism and the unification of societies under central authority was the encouragement given to exploration. Certainly some singular explorations into unknown geographical sectors of the world had been undertaken by adventuresome wealthseekers during the heyday of feudalism. However, the implementation of systematic and broad-scale explorations of the world had to await the coming of national leaders whose power and influence made it possible to buy and equip the fleets and forces necessary for such operations.

The economic results of the many explorations were beyond calculation. First, they created a massive inflow of precious metals into Europe and England, eventually leading to further investment in commerce, industrialization, and business speculation. Second, they uncovered vast new areas rich in material resources and constituting new markets for trade and commerce. Third, they created the economic base leading to the creation of maritime-related commerce and industry throughout the world.

Religious Reform. Concurrent with the substantive and visible evolutionary processes summarized so far, there evolved changes in the theological and philosophical concepts that undergirded the traditional structure of feudalism. One of particular impact to the changing economic scene stemmed from the spiritual thrust of religious reform evidenced during the 16th century.

As indicated earlier, the era of feudalism was marked by the powerful religious dogma of Catholicism proclaiming an aversion to profit and gain; the transient and static nature of life on earth as related to the eternal hereafter, and the related validity of spiritual preordination of all earthly activity undertaken by man.

Unless changed, there can be little doubt that such spiritual constricts on human behavior would severely, if not totally, inhibit progress toward commercialization and industrialization. But change did come in the wake of the so-called Protestant Ethic drawn from the teachings of Protestant reformer John Calvin.

As postulated by German philosopher and sociologist Max Weber, Calvinism placed a premium on man's ability to maximize his inherent capabilities while on earth. To gain spiritual indulgence and favor, one should engage in worldly activity with total dedication, diligence, and energy. Work was the essence of life and the mark of man's worth in the eyes of God; the more successful one became, the more worthy was his spiritual claim.

Thrift, accumulation, investment, profits, and wealth were accepted facets of Calvinism. At the same time, there was no approval of self-indulgence or wealth for wealth's sake. Gain-centered Calvinism gave rise to a new concept of economic life. Powered by work and thrift, it gave new and accepted spiritual meaning to the so-

cioeconomic factors of personal improvement, material gain, and industrial growth and progress.

Enclosures. Another process that undermined the grip of feudalism and pushed society toward an industrialized market economy was the so-called enclosure system. Initiated in England around the 13th century, the process eventually spread to Europe and came to full fruition during the 18th and 19th centuries.

In short, the process was an outgrowth of the changing philosophy of feudal aristocracy with respect to land usage within their estates. With money slowly replacing barter and payment-in-kind arrangements, the lords of the manors began to reevaluate their holdings in terms of cash revenues vis-à-vis economically stagnant fiefdoms. There followed a trend toward expanding land usage for raising larger cash crops and for sheep raising which had become highly profitable on the basis of constantly growing demand for woolen cloth.

In order to meet the increased demands on land usage imposed by commercial farming and sheep grazing, the estate hierarchy undertook to enclose and convert all such holdings, including common land formerly open to all elements of society.

The impact of the enclosure process was far-reaching both positively and negatively. Regarding the former, it brought forth the added efficiency and higher productivity associated with large-scale enterprise, helped dissolve the ties of feudalism, and promoted the development of a market-oriented society.

On the negative side, the results were stark. The process ruthlessly dispossessed the peasant from the land—the traditional source of his livelihood—and forced him into the role of a wandering laborer seeking work for wages in towns and cities. Coupled with the decline of agricultural pursuits was the increasing population that began to crowd the labor market. Together with the unemployed peasants they created what was to become a large urban labor force whose economic salvation rested entirely on the growth of industrialization and the factory system.

In summary, one can say the unplanned but critically important outcome of the enclosure process was that of realigning labor requirements

Answer frame 4¹⁴

1. True. These merchants provided a marketplace involving such things as trade, price and profit calculations, simple bookkeeping, and basic money transactions.
2. True. The development of inns, granaries, and shops in towns resulted in new patterns of market operations and commercial transactions.
3. True. The transmission and internalization of Eastern patterns and concepts among European cultures helped to bring economic change to Europe.
4. False. Nationalism affected the development of economic systems; the development of central authority brought with it unified codes of law, money, tariffs, and standardized weights and measures.

If you missed any of the above, you should restudy Frame 4¹⁴ before turning to Frame 5¹⁴ on page 90.

Frame 5¹⁴ continued

with respect to the argicultural and industrial segments of an expanding economy. It is interesting to note that what was accomplished by enclosure in England had to be implemented by the use of force in the USSR and most all other societies disposed toward totalitarian rule.

Is each of the following true or false?

_____ 1. Nationalism helped promote exploration, which in turn influenced economic patterns in Europe.
_____ 2. The Protestant Reformation had little influence on the economic patterns of Europe.
_____ 3. The "enclosure system" was the custom followed in Europe of enclosing towns behind high walls.
_____ 4. The "enclosure system" helped promote efficiency and productivity.

Now turn to Answer frame 5¹⁴ on page 94 to check your answers.

Frame 6¹⁴

Implementation of the Industrial Revolution

General. The economic pressures and forces surveyed so far in this chapter converged on England during the 18th and 19th centuries setting into motion the first Industrial Revolution.

The specific economic outfalls generated over the centuries previous to the revolution had now become quite discernible and implicit in their effects. Included were the expansion of commerce and trade; establishment of a monetized, market economy based on personal gain and profit; shift of emphasis to production and distribution functions; provision of an industrial work force capable of producing and consuming above subsistence level; advancement of technological processes; creation of a societal propensity to work, save, invest, and achieve material wealth, and finally, to recast economics from its diffuse, traditional application into a differentiated and singular institutional structure of society. With these factors in mind, let us now consider the nature and implications of the industrial upheaval within its original setting.

Britain of the 18th Century. England was first in a long succession of countries to undergo the revolutionary processes of industrialization. The logical question that follows is—why England? The answer involves a multiplicity of influencing factors and considerations, the most important of which would appear to be as follows.

First, by the mid-1700s England had managed to become the richest nation in the world through war, vast explorations, and extensive trade and commerce. Of particular economic import, her riches extended not just to the nobility; rather, they incorporated a large and growing middle-class social stratum involved in numerous business and commercial enterprises. This income spread intensified the forces of demand which eventually activated a large-scale indigenous consumption capability. As a result, there evolved an extensive and viable consumer market—a fundamental and basic requisite to a society undergoing economic development.

Second, England possessed in large measure the natural resources necessary to industrialization especially with respect to coal, iron ore, and water facilities including extensive port and harbor facilities. Her human resources were also a positive factor. Despite the strains impressed on the culture by industrialization processes, the populace exhibited considerable fortitude, skill, and flexibility in adapting to the vast changes imposed on its way of life. In this context, the economic concepts stemming from the "Protestant Ethic" found broad acceptance and, in consequence, had an immense influence on the attitudes, work habits, and economic goals of the English people.

Third, the process of enclosures was a most significant force in setting the stage for industrialization. The resultant commercialization of property held by the landed gentry and subsequent massive movement of uprooted peasants to factory employment were decisive elements in the shift toward an industrialized, market economy.

Fourth, under the aegis of a flexible, stable, and pragmatic political leadership, the ideology of nationalism and the concept of national power became the prevailing and guiding precepts in England's internal and external economic and political policy formulations. By the late 1790s, Britain had become the focal point of international trade and commerce. Subscribing to the concept that national power, security, and prestige were functionally dependent upon economic capabilities, the central authorities shaped the national interest and supporting policy formulations toward the creation of an industrial base designed to transform raw material imports into finished products for export or to meet internal consumption requirements. Concurrently, commercial carrier means and facilities were expanded along with protective sea and land military capabilities. Essentially, it was the economic factor that led to Britain's aspirations to "rule the waves" for the next several centuries.

Fifth, from the period of the Renaissance onward, there evolved in England a popular and enthusiastic interest in scientific research, creative engineering, and technology. By the 18th century, Britain had become the locus of scientific investigations and technical applications in Europe and the world. Of particular import to the industrialization process was the creative genius displayed by such men as John Wilkenson, the father of a dozen or more inventions, including a rolling mill, steam lathe, iron pipes, and iron-plated ships; James Watt who perfected and built the first practical steam-powered engine and Arkwright, inventor of the water frame spinning jenny and chief promoter of England's vast textile industry. While not alone as inventors and innovators on the British scene, these men must be regarded as contributing mainstay elements in providing the technological base for industrialization. In short, they set the stage for the coming of the machine age and the factory system.

Results of Industrialization. Earlier in this chapter we saw the general economic outfalls bearing on England and setting the stage for the oncoming Industrial Revolution. We should not couple these factors with those resulting from the implementation of industrialization.

First and foremost was the sharp increase in both the pace and output of production facilities. Second, the factory and industrial manufacturing processes superseded commerce and agriculture enterprises as the focal points of both social and economic life. Third, with the vast growth of factory clusters, the environmental orientation of the country shifted from the traditional pastoral scene to an urbanized setting reflective of a modern industrialized city.

The impact of industrialization on the social habitat and life patterns was, for the most part, stark and grim. The pace of man's labor was now set by the machine; the freedom of life on the land gave way to the constricted and sterile

Answer frame 5¹⁴

1. True. Nationalism made possible national leaders whose power and influence made exploration possible. Exploration greatly affected the economic patterns of life in Europe.
2. False. The Protestant movement changed the static dogma of the past, for example. Calvinism placed a premium on man's ability to maximize his capabilities while on earth.
3. False. The "enclosure system" involved enclosing large European land estates for the exclusive use of the estate hierarchy.
4. True. Since the estates were large, they had the benefits associated with large-scale enterprise efficiency and high productivity.

If you missed any of the above, you should review Frame 5¹⁴ before turning to Frame 6¹⁴ on page 92.

Frame 6¹⁴ continued

environment of city and the factory; child labor under distasteful and dangerous conditions was commonplace; slum living, long hours of labor with poor pay, lack of safety precautions, and general filthy and unsanitary conditions together complete the picture of conditions that prevailed in the newly created industrial society. Some of these conditions persisted well into the 19th century and gave rise to Marx's and Engels' tirades against industrial capitalism. However, in a more objective vein, it must be remembered that England had to suffer the pain as well as the joys stemming from the Industrial Revolution without benefit of experience or previous knowledge regarding its nature, scope, impact, and consequences.

True or false?

_____ 1. England could have avoided many of the problems she underwent during the Industrial Revolution had her leaders studied the experiences of the other nations that had been experiencing the Industrial Revolution for some time.

_____ 2. The rise of a "middle class" helped promote economic development in England.

_____ 3. Possession of natural resources, interest in scientific research, and the development of naval power all helped promote industrialization in England.

_____ 4. Industrialization brought with it vast social changes.

Now turn to Answer frame 6¹⁴ on page 96 to check your answers.

chapter 15

RISE OF CONTEMPORARY ECONOMIC PHILOSOPHIES

Frame 1[15]

General

It is significant that events of great historical moment have usually escaped recognition as such by those living at the time. Accordingly, participants in the composite of events and actions that configured the Industrial Revolution unknowingly played crucial roles in what eventually became known as one of the greatest liberating forces in human affairs. Certainly it was a painful social experience to those involved; however, in the long view of history, the accompanying wholesale individual misery and social disorientation provide objective insight with respect to the revolution's immense power and profound influence in reshaping the social order.

Since mankind did not understand the full implications of the revolution while it was happening, quite logically neither could it control the application of its power and capabilities in a manner that would efficiently and effectively service expanding economic, political, and social demands. In short, the Industrial Revolution provided the first clear and precise evidence of society's common, yet regrettable, tendency to suffer the consequences arising when social and cultural elements are permitted to lag in the wake of an advancing technological base.

Under the direct pressures of technological applications, nationalistic fervor, and the innovative energies of a burgeoning group of entrepreneurs and merchants, the Industrial Revolution moved inexorably forward along an uncharted path. From the base of Britain, it expanded into the continent of Europe and thence across the Atlantic to America. In each case disruption of the old order was constant, but at the same time the stage was being set for the new industrial era featuring such cultural manifestations as enhanced social mobility, increased wealth and affluency, expanded prosperity, massive productivity, and, of the utmost importance, institutionalized economic systems attuned to the shifting political and social forces and pressures within affected societies.

We shall now investigate the essential elements of the basic economic systems that have evolved consequent to the Industrial Revolution; specifically, mercantilism, capitalism, and socialism. Before undertaking an overview of the model features of each system, cognizance should be taken of the following considerations. First, political rather than economic factors often are the source of variables that exist within like systems as well as among the differing systems. Second, the several systems do not constitute mutually exclusive economic entities in toto; that is, similarities often appear with respect to such concerns as philosophic guidelines, structural designs, basic goals, objectives, and operational procedures. Further, all share to some degree the age-old culture influences of tradition, command, and the market. Third, it is recognized that systems other than those mentioned have evolved at least in name among industrialized nations, for example, syndicalism in Italy

Answer frame 6¹⁴

1. False. England was the first nation to undergo industrialization.
2. True. From the middle class there evolved an extensive consumer market—an important requisite to a society undergoing economic development.
3. True. All of these factors helped promote industrialization.
4. True. Industrialization had a strong impact on social patterns.

If you missed any of the above, you should restudy Frame 6¹⁴ before turning to Chapter 15 on page 95.

Frame 1¹⁵ continued

under Mussolini or the corporate state economy during Hitler's Third Reich. However, it seems quite evident that the root elements of all systems that have developed within industrialized societies of the world—at least up to the present—are encompassed within the framework of mercantilism, capitalism, and socialism, either singularly or in various combinations.

Mercantilism

The period of history wherein mercantilism dominated the economic scene extended from the early 1600s until the late 1700s. National rulers within England and the major European nations caught in the thrust of industrialization were dedicated to the goal of maximizing national power by cornering economic wealth, primarily in the form of precious metals. In essence, mercantilism represented a collectivity of economic principles and practices oriented to the attainment of national power and prestige through wealth accumulation.

Conceived out of the processes that gave rise to the Industrial Revolution, mercantilism became the first comprehensive system for controlling and administering an economy. In addition, the formulators of mercantilist policy viewed the economy as a singular force in support of national political and social aims. Taken together, mercantilism provided the rationale and direction that led to the institutionalization of economics within the total cultural scheme of society.

The fundamental precepts of mercantilism reflect the combination of economic policies with political aspirations thereby giving birth to a concept and philosophy that became known as

"political economy." Incongruous as some of the precepts and policies may seem today, we should not forget their conceptual environment nor the state of the economic processes and political designs existent at the time. Also, one must consider that a number of the mercantilist theories and practices have, in one form or another, remained in effect up to the present day.

What were the fundamental tenets of mercantilism? As mentioned earlier, first and primary was the direct interrelationship of national power to wealth accumulation in the form of money (precious metals) as opposed to material goods. To induce the monetary inflow and retention necessary for wealth accumulation, the central authorities imposed a number of supporting policies and procedures which can be summarized as follows:

1. Maintenance of a favorable balance of trade; that is, the value of a country's exports exceed the value of imports. This was accomplished primarily by the imposition of protective tariffs; curtailment of internal consumption of foreign goods; importing cheap raw materials for processing and exporting as higher priced finished products.

2. Promotion of colonization and imperialism. The aim here was twofold. First, to seize and maintain control of extraterritorial raw material sources. Second, to convert such colonial holdings into profitable export markets for goods processed within the home country.

3. Expansion of military power. Essential to the entire concept of mercantilism was the development of a military capability to protect the national base of power, lend support to colonization ventures, protect trade lanes of communication, and conduct forays against economic

spheres of influences of competitor nations. Not excluded from consideration was piracy and economic plunder.

4. Government subsidy payments. Consigned mostly to the private business interests of the new merchant class, subsidy outlays drawn on the national treasury were used lavishly in support of industrial expansion, merchant shipbuilding, construction and extension of communication means including road nets, ports, and harbors, and military construction projects undertaken by the private sector of the economy.

Internally, the policy of the central authorities was to extend priority to the interests of the entrepreneurs, with the consumer segment of society consigned to a secondary role. While free trade without local restriction was ostensibly the guideline for indigenous commercial and market operations, techniques were applied by authorities that severely restricted the distribution and consumption of goods within the home-land populace. Thus merchants were encouraged to restrict the amount of commodities available for local purchase in order to maintain adequate stocks for export. Also, less expensive and better quality items in short supply at home, but readily available in foreign markets, were either deleted from import lists or restricted by the imposition of high tariff rates.

Mercantilist entrepreneurs working in close harmony with central authorities sought to maintain a strong competitive position in the world market even at the expense of human dignity. Harsh rules and regulations supported by national law prescribed minimal pay to workers for long hours of toil, authorized impressment of personnel into the labor force, permitted child labor, promoted monopoly practices, condemned nonworkers to slavery, condoned inequitable taxation of the populace, and prohibited the exportation of all natural resources except through government channels.

Indicate whether each of the following statements is true or false by writing "T" or "F" in the space provided.

_____ 1. During the Industrial Revolution social reform kept pace with technological change.

_____ 2. The basic economic systems that have evolved consequent to the Industrial Revolution are totally mutually exclusive economic entities.

_____ 3. Mercantilism represented a collectivity of economic principles and practices oriented to the attainment of national power and prestige through wealth accumulation.

_____ 4. All of the following represent policies and/or procedures used by central authorities when mercantilism dominated the economic scene: (*a*) maintenance of a favorable balance of trade; (*b*) promotion of colonization and imperialism; (*c*) expansion of military power; (*d*) government subsidy payments; and (*e*) extension of priority to the interests of the consumer segment of society with the interests of the entrepreneurs consigned to a secondary role.

Now turn to Answer frame 1[15] on page 98 to check your responses.

Frame 2[15]

Decline of Mercantilism. It has been said that industrialism grew out of mercantilism but, in time, served to destroy it. By the latter part of the 18th and early part of the 19th century, the industrialists had succeeded the merchants as the center of power in the industrialized portion of the economic world. With them came a new rationale that, in many respects, undermined the foundation of mercantilism. In the first place, the government imposed restrictions on produc-

Answer frame 1¹⁵

1. False. During the Industrial Revolution social change lagged behind technological change.
2. False. The various systems may be similar with respect to philosophic guidelines, structural designs, basic goals, objectives, and operational procedures.
3. True. Mercantilism was concerned with the attainment of national power through wealth accumulation.
4. False. Policies and procedures (*a*) through (*d*) were true; however, since the central authority gave priority to entrepreneurs over consumers, the statement taken as a whole is false.

If you missed any of the above, you should restudy Frame 1¹⁵ before turning to Frame 2¹⁵ on page 97.

Frame 2¹⁵ continued

tion, and distribution processes came to be regarded as hindrances to the expansion of the economy and barriers to the application of technological innovations within the system. Further, opposition grew with respect to policies inhibiting free international trade while expanding military capabilities and colonial spheres of influence. Pressures were also applied against direct government intervention and control of industry and the marketplace. In addition, and of utmost importance, it became progressively apparent to business interests, industrialists, and even some earlier proponents of mercantilist policies that the wealth and power of a nation were not exponents of the levels of precious metal holdings; rather, the true indices were reflective of production capabilities and related capital assets in the form of factories, machinery, transport facilities, and the like.

In the final analysis, it was from the foregoing critique of mercantilism that new concepts emerged regarding economic systems orientation and design. Included were the ideas of international free trade geared to propositions of economic advantage, open and unregulated markets, mass production of goods in support of consumer demand, and alignment of domestic policies affecting the social order with economic procedures and goals. The key proponent of these concepts was Adam Smith; his economic model was called capitalism.

Capitalism

General. Economic theories and practices may be supplanted in time by new system de-

signs but seldom, if ever, is their demise complete. Thus the fallacies and inequities of mercantilism cited above eventually constituted the basis for its decline as an accepted political philosophy and supporting economic system and set the stage for the application of new system designs based on the tenets of capitalism and socialism. Nevertheless, a number of the practices of the mercantilists have remained in effect in these and all other economic systems that have evolved up to the present day. Included are such applications as protective tariffs, government subsidy payments to both public and private sectors of the economy, adherence to the favorable balance of trade concept, close integration of economic military power, and economic imperialism in various forms. Under the guise of nationalism and the supporting policy of guarding the national self-interest, each modern industrialized nation has seen fit to absorb and retain most of these basic facets of mercantilism within its economic and political system regardless of all other descriptive philosophic features that may be applicable.

Conceived within the political, economic, and social environment that obtained during the early stages of the Industrial Revolution, the philosophy of capitalism began to take root in the economic world, ostensibly as a disclaimer against the concepts of mercantilism coupled with the promises of vast economic expansion attainable under the free market forces of a laissez-faire economy.

The architect and chief proponent of the philosophy, theoretical design, and principles undergirding the capitalistic system was Adam

Smith. A native of Scotland, his early attainments reflected a notable expertise in his chosen field of moral philosophy. Yet, strangely enough, his masterwork was in the realm of economics. Thus in 1776 he brought to fruition 25 years of study, observation, and inspired theorizing in a monumental work entitled *An Inquiry into the Nature and Causes of the Wealth of Nations.* Its scope and content encompassed massive investigations into the fields of psychology and sociology as well as economics and, for the first time, man was afforded precise information and data concerning the theoretical and integrated functional workings of economic systems. By espousing economic factors in concert with the total social functions and institutions of society, Smith's work provided the major leaders and philosophers of the world a basic and understandable picture of human behavior patterns as well as a central prescription for economic and social progress.

By the mid-1700s, economics and related systems and institutions had progressed far beyond the rather simplistic functional arrangements that prevailed within traditional and command-oriented social structures. The abstractions and complexities that marked the economies of industrial societies during this era generated the requirement for a new breed of philosophers attuned specifically to the institution of economics including its functions, principles, and interweaving within the total fabric of society. Adam Smith thus became the world's first recognized economist, even considering the fact that as the pioneering genius of the field he drew heavily on the economic prescriptions of such noted philosophers as Hume, Locke, Turgot, Quesnay, and Dudley North. Smith did not invent economics, but he became economics' first and greatest philosopher and commanding theoretician and the greats that followed him—Ricardo, Mill, Marx, Marshall, and Keynes—were all to stand on his shoulders.

Smith's Classical Capitalism.   The essence of Smith's views and concepts set forth in the *Wealth of Nations* is as follows: First, he vigorously attacked the mercantilist theories that called for government monopoly practices and intervention into the workings of the economy through subsidy payments to merchants and manufacturers; establishment of protective tariffs that inhibited the free flow of commodities; and economic imperialism that in Smith's view eventually constituted a liability rather than an economic asset. Additionally, he destroyed the very foundation of mercantilism by declaring that a society's wealth cannot be measured by its store of precious metals or money but rather by its total production capability. Second, and probably his crowning construction, Smith outlined his concept of the workings of the capitalist system. He argued that, if men functioning within a private enterprise arrangement are given maximum freedom to satisfy their self-interests and satisfactions, the result will not be economic anarchy, but rather an economic equilibrium controlled and governed by immutable laws of economics.

More specifically, to achieve the rewards of wages and profits, self-seeking man retains a propensity to exchange his time, labor, skills, and wealth in making and providing those commodities most needed and wanted by society at large. Within the market, the law of supply and demand works automatically with the exchange process setting prices, profits, wages, quality, and quantity. The finite regulator of the free market process, according to Smith, is competition which propels the entrepreneurs, managers, and workers toward the goal of economic advantage by making things better, swifter, and at a lower price in order to gain the economic vote of the sovereign consumer. Smith visualized that all of the intricacies of his system would mesh efficiently and effectively as if guided by an "invisible hand" provided total freedom of action prevailed. In this regard, government should abandon its economic prerogatives and keep hands off the economy; otherwise its bureaucratic inefficiencies and monopolistic practices would negate the motivational impulses, competitive spirit, and productive power inherent within a privately organized and directed free market system.

Is each of the following true or false?

_____ 1. All of the following contributed to the decline of mercantilism: (*a*) government restrictions on production and distribution began to be viewed as detrimental to economic expansion and technological innovation; (*b*) men came to view the wealth and power of a nation in terms of capital assets instead of precious metal holdings; and (*c*) opposition to restrictions on free international trade.

_____ 2. With the publication of his *An Inquiry into the Nature and Causes of the Wealth of Nations*, Adam Smith was to become the world's first recognized economist.

_____ 3. Smith contended that giving men the maximum freedom to satisfy their self-interests and satisfactions will result in economic disaster.

_____ 4. Smith felt that the government should have a strong hand in runing an economy.

Now turn to Answer frame 2[15] on page 102 to check your answers.

Frame 3[15]

Smith also espoused a positive and strong argument in favor of specialization and the division of labor as a means of enhancing the productive capabilities of the total economy and making possible the achievement of what he termed "universal opulence." As the initial philosopher proponent of modern assembly-line mass production procedures, Smith felt that only the rich could enjoy the limited output of the skilled craftsmen, whereas the division of labor, which emphasized the learning of simple procedures in lieu of complex skills, opened the economic mainstream to all elements of the social order both as producers and consumers.

As the father of a capitalism founded on the precepts of private property, individual initiative, capital accumulation, and the free enterprise system, one might ascribe to Smith the demeanor of a person devoid of liberalistic tendencies. Yet the opposite is true. As already mentioned, his economic goal was to create universal opulence and to make the consumer king. Further, he deplored all evidence of poverty, protested against the achievement of economic affluency by those who did not produce for the common good, and decried collusion in the fixing of prices and establishment of monopolies. A realist, he visualized that uncontrolled mass production methods could create havoc among workers unless closely controlled and regulated

and that businessmen and merchants must be prevented from undertakings that reflect a conspiracy against the public good. He was well aware of the hardships imposed by the Industrial Revolution and openly criticized the use of child labor, long hours with low wages, the dangers of factory machinery, and the squalor existent in the industrialized cities.

For over a century after Adam Smith's era, capitalism served as the locus of economic systems development and activity and, as such, it proved to be the most viable of those so far conceived by man. It demolished almost in toto the long dominant influences of traditionalism and command in shaping economic roles and functions within society. Yet capitalism in the classic sense described by Smith never really existed except in model form, for governments have always injected their powers in economic matters through laws, rules, and regulations as well as in the format of tariffs, excise taxes, fiscal and monetary controls, subsidies, and even public ownership of economic facilities—at least to some degree. By and large, governments have, without exception, gone far beyond Smith's doctrine that their role should be confined to public education, national defense, and public works normally not in the domain of the private sector of the economy, for example, public highways.

Smith relied on the ultimate immense productivity and wealth generation capabilities of his system to provide the means for overcoming the inequities and hardships initially discernible in his highly competitive economic scheme of action. Yet, for all his economic acumen, he was not able to visualize the ultimate force and influence of the Industrial Revolution, including the growth of the massive corporations, rise of the labor unions, the coming of recessions, depressions and unemployment, impact of inflation, deflation and the business cycle, and the infusion of social concerns into the economic process. Today, only the United States among the great industrial powers retains the economic designation as a capitalist nation. But even here the system in effect—managed capitalism—is a far cry from the laissez-faire tenets of Adam Smith's capitalism. Nevertheless, most of the great economic powers of the world employed the essential elements of capitalism in achieving their economic status and even today retain

substantive elements within their so-called "mixed" or socialist-oriented economic systems.

Within this century, the economic situations within most advanced industrial societies has changed to a point in which the populace has become more interested in full employment at high wages than in productive growth, in security instead of economic risk, in inflation rather than depression, in massive government spending in support of public services, in insurance and protection against the harsh demands of competition, and in substitution of public ownership for private ownership in production and service industries affecting the common good. In short, the basic production, distribution, and consumption elements of economic institutions have become geared to the so-called humanistic aspirations of society as reflected in the theories of socialism vis-à-vis capitalism. This area becomes our next concern.

True or false?

_____ 1. Adam Smith questioned the usefulness of specialization and the division of labor.

_____ 2. Smith's ideas were not consumer-oriented.

_____ 3. Capitalism as described by Adam Smith has never existed.

_____ 4. Today the United States is the only great industrial power that retains its designation as a capitalist nation.

Now turn to Answer frame 3[15] on page 102 to check your answers.

Frame 4[15]

Socialism

General. The historical evolution of socialist philosophy has been the most extensive as well as the most imprecise of the several major "isms" discussed in this chapter. From evidence available, it would seem the root elements of theory formulations dealing with socialism extend as far back as Plato's *Republic*, circa 428–348 B.C. Interestingly enough, however, it wasn't until the late 18th and early 19th centuries that the doctrines of socialism began to exercise a discernible influence on the internal economic, political, and social behavior patterns of major societies. Prior to this era, socialism achieved little general ac-

claim or acceptance as a viable force and system design adaptable to society and its functions. Rather, it was viewed by other than its few proponents in terms of an unrealistic social panacea based on the self-serving pronouncements of utopian reformers seeking escape from prevailing cultural forces and institutions. Thus, in a broad sense, the ideas of the early disciples of socialism were destined to remain in obscure disarray until advancing technology and industrialization brought forth social conditions and problems that eventually generated a synthesis of socialist precepts adaptable to their resolution.

In this context, we have seen how the Industrial Revolution effected a massive expansion

Answer frame 2¹⁵ ———————————————————————————

1. True. All contributed to the decline of mercantilism.
2. True. Smith became economics' first and one of its greatest philosophers.
3. False. Smith argued that giving individuals the maximum freedom to satisfy self-interests would produce an economic equilibrium controlled and governed by immutable laws of economics.
4. False. Smith felt that the intricacies of his system would work if government would keep its hands off the economy.

If you missed any of the above, you should review Frame 2¹⁵ before turning to Frame 3¹⁵ on page 100.

Answer frame 3¹⁵ ———————————————————————————

1. False. Smith felt that specialization and the division of labor were useful in opening the economic mainstream to all parts of a society.
2. False. Smith advocated universal opulence; to him the consumer was king. He opposed child labor, price fixing, and monopolies.
3. True. Capitalism as described by Smith has never existed; this is due in part to government actions and policies.
4. True. The United States is considered a capitalistic nation; but our economic system is not like the laissez-faire capitalism pictured by Smith.

If you missed any of the above, you should restudy Frame 3¹⁵ before turning to Frame 4¹⁵ on page 101.

Frame 4¹⁵ continued

of capitalistic productivity marked by the socialization of work; that is, organizing workers en masse in a factory situation under central direction. Among the more positive results achieved were huge commodity output, raised standards of living, division of labor, facilitation of wealth and property accumulation by individuals and groups, substitution of individual motivational impulses in lieu of ascribed social rank as the basis for exploiting opportunities providing social and economic success and status. On the other hand, the system tended to separate the worker from his tools and the farmer from his land, making both subservient to the employer in maintaining a livelihood. It also generated periodic unemployment, led to urbanization with slum growth, and created wide disparities in wealth and income with the rich getting richer and the poor getting poorer. It was from these latter considerations that socialism's early theorists drew strength in developing patterns of reform that became the basis for their several contemporary system designs.

The Essential Elements.   Unlike the rather precise doctrines and concepts that undergird the philosophies and system designs of mercantilism and capitalism, those of socialism tend toward generalities and situational variables that defy implicit definition. In searching for the common denominators of socialist theory, it would appear the social prescriptions incorporated in the philosophies of the so-called humanists and populists are the most pervasive. In this regard, the most common derivatives of socialist dogma include: (1) application of de facto equality throughout the social, economic, and political systems of society, (2) orientation of societal functions and organization in accord with the beneficent forces of natural law including the positive effects of the environment on man's status, rationality, and outlook on life, (3) government direction and regulation of the economy, (4) limitations on the accumulation of wealth and private property, (5) extension of the public domain into the ownership and control of property including the means of production, with government acting as the agent of the people, (6) emphasis on the promotion of social capital vis-à-vis production capital, and (7) provision of an extensive welfare system to service the health, education, and economic well-being of society.

As mentioned earlier, there is no singular design that encompasses the variables of socialist thought; accordingly, the validity of the elements cited above may be argued by the proponents of socialism, but in the main, their rejoiners normally hinge on matters of degree, method, or intent of application rather than scope or control.

So far we have dealt with what can best be described as democratic socialism; that is, where the statuses, actions, and responses of the government and its agencies are subject to the power and control of the people. Socialism shaped to such an ideological base and system design should not be confused with the announced socialist precepts and practices of totalitarian communist states. Using the USSR as a prime example, socialism from the time of Marx was viewed as the final historical step en route to achieving the idealistic goal of pure communism. The goal now appears more elusive and remote than ever before, but in the meantime the self-perpetuating Communist party and dictatorial leadership promote a socialist system that can be characterized by the following principles: (1) maintenance of a command economy, (2) total economic control via state direction and management, (3) elimination of all private ownership of property, industry, and business, (4) elimination of all social classes, (5) distribution of income, services, and goods based on labor performance coupled with need, (6) equality of economic status within the masses, (7) increasing productivity to meet the social demands of the people, and (8) the state and the economy controlled by the proletariat (temporarily under the dictatorship of the proletariat).

In theory and practice, especially the latter, there exists a vast cleavage between democratic and communist socialism. True, both implicitly integrate the institutions of government and the economy in their system designs, but the overall intent is quite different; under democracy, the aim is to manage and direct only those elements of the economy that are essential to maintaining the well-being of society as a whole; under communism, total control by political leaders becomes the prerequisite feature of a command economy servicing the political aspirations of the state. In effect, socialist reformers of democratic persuasion proposed various institutional and social changes of an evolutionary nature designed to cure specific ills stemming from industrial capitalism. The goal was to enhance rather than negate the power and status of the people. Conversely, the communist leadership created socialism from revolutionary principles and actions that promoted the disintegration of the power of the masses, created a dictatorship "over" rather than "of" the proletariat, substituted democratic centralism for democratic socialism, and instituted a command economy oriented to the priority aspirations of nationalism rather than fulfilling long-term demands for social, economic, and political reforms attuned to the best interests of society and its cultural institutions.

Indicate whether each of the following statements is true or false by writing "T" or "F" in the space provided.

_____ 1. The ideas and concepts of socialism extend back only to the 18th and early 19th centuries.

_____ 2. Socialism advocates government regulation of the economy, limitations on the accumulation of private property, and public ownership and control of property.

_____ 3. Elements of socialist doctrine can exist in the economies of both democratic and totalitarian states.

_____ 4. The USSR has a command economy that is oriented to its nationalist ambitions.

Now turn to Answer frame 4[15] on page 104 to check your responses.

Answer frame 4¹⁵

1. False. The root elements of theory extend back to 428–348 B.C. The social conditions and problems of the Industrial Revolution generated socialist precepts adaptable to their resolution.
2. True. Socialist doctrine advocates all of these ideas.
3. True. Elements of socialistic doctrine can be seen in Western democratic nations as well as in the USSR.
4. True. Their economy is oriented to nationalistic ambition rather than the long-term demands for social, economic, and political reforms.

If you missed any of the above, you should restudy Frame 4¹⁵ before beginning Frame 5¹⁵.

Frame 5¹⁵

The Role of Planning. As noted earlier, both mercantilism and capitalism employed the market as the focal point of all economic activity. We are reminded that this extremely sensitive economic and social instrument works almost automatically in bringing together the producer and consumer; integrates the forces of supply and demand; flashes signals of profitability that lure both enterpreneurs and workers into economic action; sets prices, wages, profits, and quantity factors; serves as a mechanism for the allocation of resources and is the spur to capital investment and economic expansion.

But under socialism wherein the government exercises partial or total control over the basic elements of the economic system, the forces of the market are either seriously limited or eliminated altogether. Since such forces constitute economic imperatives, their absence demands the implementation of alternative measures. Under socialism the substitute market mechanism is supplied by the direct orders of a central controlling and planning agency. In effect, the agency assumes the roles and functions of entrepreneurs, producers, and consumers and, as such, determines the goals and objectives of the economic system, sets demand and supply schedules, allocates human and natural resources, establishes production levels, and fixes wage and profit rates. All of the foregoing are encompassed in a master economic plan based on the judgments and desires of the political and economic leadership, possibly in concert with past performance indices and trends.

It should be stated that only a totalitarian economy develops and shapes its plans in a manner that provides absolute control over all segments of economic activity. Where democratic socialism prevails, normally only the most basic elements of the economy fall under the auspices of government control and planning. The remainder remain consigned to the private sector and function under market conditions. In any case, it seems quite clear that, under the system of socialism, the nature of the economy, its goals and objectives, and its functional arrangements are, in part or in total, subject to the control and direction of the political leadership. In contrast, one should recall here the admonition of the classical capitalist Adam Smith for monopolistic and bureaucratic government to stay out of the economy.

Systems Convergence. Evidence clearly indicates the composite forces of economic progress and efficiency, social change, and political expediency have imposed pressures on systems variables. In a number of instances, these pressures have forced a convergence in system designs and orientations. We have already noted how some of the most important elements of mercantilism have become fixtures within all types of economic systems and that industrial capitalism has evolved into managed capitalism with government, economic, and social pressure groups exercising both direct and indirect control over a large segment of the system. It should be added that even totalitarian socialism has undertaken modifications of its system that involve the integration of capitalist designs. For example, some production facilities have already shifted from the established quota system to the cost-profit scheme of capitalist industry. In all societies, economics no less than politics tends to reflect the possible and the attainable with respect to systems and goal orientations. Hence, the variables occasioned by diverse ideological pronouncements eventually become diffused under the pressures of economic reality. Over the long term, systems convergence could well become a norm with the end result reflecting a general alignment of systems in the form of mixed economies.

Is each of the following true or false?

_____ 1. Under socialism the forces of the market are not severely limited.

_____ 2. Under democratic socialism there is limited government control over the economy, while in a totalitarian society the government attempts to control all segments of economic activity.

_____ 3. Today, societies under totalitarian socialism have integrated various elements of capitalism into their economies.

_____ 4. In the long run, economic systems may be a mixture of the various economic systems.

Now turn to Answer frame 5[15] on page 106 to check your answers.

chapter 16

GOVERNMENT AND THE STATE

Frame 1[16]

As we have seen in previous chapters, all societies have a variety of social control mechanisms contained within their cultural packages. No society can long endure that permits unbounded freedom to its members. Within every society, there are activities that are deemed detrimental to the welfare of the group, and the social group has devised sanctions to insure at least minimum conformity.

In preliterate societies, the preeminence of primary relationships throughout the social order is generally sufficient to meet this end. In more sophisticated societies, with their fragmented loyalties brought about by multiple subcultures, minute economic specialization, the rapidity of change, the decline of the extended family unit, and high physical mobility, more direct and obvious means of achieving social compliance are demanded. In such societies, this function is performed by the state and its administrative apparatus, the various levels of government.

Answer frame 5¹⁵

1. False. Under socialism, government control limits or eliminates the forces of the market.
2. True. Under democratic socialism there is limited government control, while in a totalitarian society government control is extensive.
3. True. In some totalitarian societies production facilities have shifted from the quota system to a cost-profit idea.
4. True. In the long run, systems convergence may well become the normal pattern for economic systems.

If you missed any of the above, you should review Frame 5¹⁵ before turning to Chapter 16 on page 105.

Frame 1¹⁶ continued

Nature of the State

The "state" as a concept—at least in political theory—is not the same thing as a nation or a society. A society is the free association of people in families or cultural groups; a nation is a unit of society with common traditions and cultures. The term *state*, that is, the organized political entity which we recognize today as a state, was first introduced by Machiavelli in the 16th century. When Plato and Aristotle discussed political units, they were referring to the *polis* or city-state; the Romans extended their focus to a larger political unit, the *res publica*. But from Machiavelli on, the idea of "nation-states" spread, to be further developed by the Frenchman Jean Bodin (1530–96), who first identified and stressed the importance of the central problem of the state—which is, as we shall see, that of reconciling individual liberties with the power of the state.

The "state" is the most inclusive of man's institutions. It possesses a monopoly of legitimate power within a specified geographic region. In modern industrial societies, the state pervades all other social institutions. The state greatly influences the economic system; it determines the laws relating to marriage and the family; it decides who shall be educated and for how long; it may prescribe what religious practices shall be permitted; and it even determines, to some extent, what recreational activities shall be allowed. The influence of the state touches every member of the modern industrial order.

As an institution, the state possesses the following essentials:

1. Population. Modern nation-states have populations ranging from a few thousand to more than 750 million.
2. Territory. This may range from postage stamp states such as Vatican City to the Union of Soviet Socialist Republics with an area of more than 8 million square miles.
3. Sovereignty. Sovereignty means that a state has authority over and can act directly upon all who live within its borders. Many authorities hold that sovereignty is indivisible, and therefore the state may not share its authority with any external power.
4. Government. Government is that agency of the state through which sovereignty is exercised. It is the administrative instrument of the state.

Through the institution of government men can resolve disputes and reconcile their differences over a broader range of conflict than could the smaller groups—family, kinship group, or clan. The beginnings of government are lost in antiquity. It may be reasonably assumed, however, to have come into existence as man struggled to liberate himself from the bondage imposed by nature. To escape from the necessity of daily forages for food, man harnessed animal power and fashioned tools to break the ground and plant crops. Eventually groups of men banded together to develop irrigation systems for their agricultural needs. As agricultural technology improved, men were released from farming to engage in other pursuits. Some became priests, others toolmakers, and still others merchants. Some, no doubt, decided that through cunning and guile or through brute force they could have the material blessings of life through minimum efforts. Government came into being, in part, to coordinate the activities of the various socially beneficent specialties and to protect their interest from the avarice of the less socially inclined. Further, as specialization emerged and goods and services were exchanged, a monetary system was, quite obviously, demanded. The problem of developing and maintaining the arteries of commerce and of manning an expanding irrigation system—all of those activities beyond the scope of single individuals—called for the creation of a system of law and government. Such a system would be charged with the responsibility of adjudicating disputes within the society and protecting its members from both internal and external threats.

As mentioned, because of its basic purpose, the maintenance of order, and because of its pervasiveness, the modern state, more than any other social institution, must decide the fundamental social question of how much freedom and how much control the social order will permit. If freedom is absolutized, society is deprived of order. Until and unless men become absolutely virtuous, absolute freedom is impossible, for absolute freedom puts the weak at the mercy of the strong.

Societal order requires certain curtailments on freedom of the individual—certain limits must be imposed on one's freedom of action. Thus the state must come to terms with this issue. How it does so largely determines the kind of governmental structure that emerges.

The *form* of government in any state offers only a vague suggestion as to how this question is dealt with. A state may be a monarchy—as are the United Kingdom and the Scandinavian states —and still permit abundant freedom to its subjects. It may have a republican form of government, as do most communist states, and at the same time operate on highly authoritarian or even totalitarian principles. States may possess written constitutions guaranteeing their citizens the widest range of freedoms while on an opera-

tional basis governments in those same states exercise almost unlimited control over the behavior of their populations.

Since the *form* of government offers little help in approaching the question of freedom and control, we shall direct our attention elsewhere. We shall discuss political systems in terms of three major categories: authoritarian, totalitarian, and democratic.

Authoritarian Political Systems

Throughout history most states have been governed under some sort of authoritarian rule —that is, rule imposed from above on the majority of citizens without their consent. The rulers—whether called king, emperor, or czar— based their right to power on inheritance, tradition, or Divine right. They did not recognize any right of the people ruled to question their authority.

The first modern nation-states were made possible by the centralizing of authority in the hands of territorial princes rather than having it diffused among the various local authorities who claimed it earlier. Monarchy, defined at first as the undivided sovereignty of a single individual, goes back to the Greeks and the Macedonians. But the monarchical state rose in the Middle Ages as the power of the Church and the independent nobility gave way to the rule of kings. Absolute monarchy prevailed throughout the 16th and 17th centuries, reaching its culmination when Louis XIV declared, *L'état c'est moi*, "I am the state."

Although it survived in most of continental Europe well into the 19th century, and in Russia until the Revolution of 1917, absolute monarchy came to an end in England in 1689, when the Magna Carta or Bill of Rights established that the king did not rule by Divine right but through the consent of Parliament. Thus began constitutional monarchy, which prevails today wherever monarchy survives at all.

If authoritarian government is thought of as the rule of the many by the few (actually, Aristotle labeled this as *aristocracy* or *oligarchy*), even the United States has been under the sway of a relatively mild authoritarianism for most of its history. When the American Constitution was adopted in 1788, only one white adult male out of six was permitted to vote on ratification. In spite of the 15th Amendment (black suffrage), added in 1868, blacks have voted in significant numbers only in the last three decades. Women, of course, were not enfranchised until 1920. Democracy, as a goal, has moved quite rapidly in the United States, especially during the last two generations.

Indicate whether each of the following statements is true or false by writing "T" or "F" in the space provided.

_____ 1. In modern societies primary relationships are the major mechanism of social control.

_____ 2. Government did not come into existence until man had partially liberated himself from the bondage by nature.

_____ 3. The balance between freedom and control in any society is determined by the *form* of government.

_____ 4. Authoritarian political systems are of recent origin.

Now turn to Answer frame 1[16] on page 110 to check your responses.

Frame 2[16]

Totalitarian Political Systems

All totalitarian doctrines, whether left (communist) or right (fascist) have one thing in common: a basic distrust of the individual. In all totalitarian societies, the individual is compelled to subordinate his interests to those of the state, and the interests of the state are always defined by single individuals or small ruling cliques. The communist ideology, certainly the most prevalent of the world's totalitarian doctrines, masquerades as democratic. It purports to serve the interest of the people. Generally, communist states are even referred to as "People's Democracies." The sham of such designations is revealed by the most cursory examination of the governmental structure, which is proclaimed as a "dictatorship of the proletariat." The Nazis, less adept at semantic games, openly expressed their contempt for the democratic ideal.

States under totalitarian control have tentacles that extend from the political to every aspect of the subjects' lives. The total institutional structure is directed toward the maintenance and enhancement of the totalitarian doctrine. The schools, mass media, and even the church (where it is permitted) become servants of the state. Ideologies that do not harmonize with official state doctrine are ruthlessly suppressed. Where the electoral process is maintained, all candidates are "selected" by the power clique, and the electorate merely ratifies those selections. Through this device the aura of legitimacy is provided to the government.

Until the 20th century, totalitarianism was only a dream of revolutionaries and theorists. Neither the administrative and bureaucratic machinery nor the technological sophistication existed that could have made totalitarian control possible. Even today, those states that we describe as totalitarian are in reality extreme authoritarian. One of the striking facts to emerge from Albert Speer's *Inside the Third Reich* was its revelation of the limitations imposed on Hitler's absolutism. Nazi field commanders frequently operated on the basis of local autonomy; high officials were retained in power long after their effectiveness to the regime had passed in order to appease public opinion; measures that would have enhanced Germany's war-making potential were not undertaken because of the fear of popular reaction.

In the last quarter of the 20th century, for the first time in human experience, total control of the individual has become a frighteningly real possibility. Through the use of the computer, administrative servants of a totalitarian regime can retrieve data (perhaps acquired through electronic eavesdropping and surveillance) on any person in the country. Candidates for service to the regime can be selected—teachers, public service personnel, police—through this means. Enemies of the state can be eliminated through the same technology. Transfers of technical skills from one locale to another can be vastly facilitated through the use of the computer, and efficiency of service to the regime can be more readily and accurately ascertained.

The revolution in the biological sciences suggests the possibility of manipulating the genetic code to determine precisely the potential of future servants of the state. Clonning, the exact replication of any living individual from its cells, has already been accomplished with lower forms of animal life in laboratory experiments. The extension of clonning to human beings could enable a totalitarian regime to create the types of individuals suited to its goals and needs. To biological management, add the specter of psychological control through chemical means and/or a more sophisticated behavioral technology and one can get a glimpse of the enormous potential for absolute control that totalitarianism possesses.

Democracy

Of the three constructs under consideration, democracy, while possibly the least efficient, places the highest premium on the worthiness of the individual. Under both authoritarian and totalitarian models, the individual is subordinate to a greater or lesser degree to a state machinery over which he exercises little or no control. In a democratic society, though the individual definitely has obligations to the state, he controls the machinery through which the will of the state is exercised. The term *democracy* itself means that the people rule. Its origin is Greek, and it literally means the *rule of the many*. In modern usage, however, democracy means rule by the majority, with due consideration for the rights and privileges of minorities.

In order for the democratic model to exist, two minimum requirements must be met. These requirements are (1) popular sovereignty and (2) limited government.

Popular sovereignty means simply that the citizens are the political decision makers in the state. There are two ways through which popular sovereignty can be exercised: (1) direct democracy and (2) representative democracy. Under direct democracy, each citizen can personally influence political decisions, as in the town meetings of earlier days; that is, political power is exercised directly by the whole body of citizens acting under majority rule. Direct democracy can work only when a small population lives compactly in a small geographic region. Direct democracy therefore has limited application in the modern urban industrial state. In such states, democracy is expressed through *representative* government.

Not all representative governments are democratic, however. For popular sovereignty to exist there must be (1) a wide electoral base, (2) frequent and periodic elections, and (3) elections that are free and open. Simply having elections will not suffice. In some authoritarian/totalitarian states, there are frequent elections, and there are large voter turnouts. The elections, however, do not deal with fundamental social questions nor are they free. Candidates are handpicked by the party elite, and opposition (never on fundamental issues) is seldom tolerated.

The second requisite for a democratic state is limited government. Limited government simply means that there are certain areas of the citizen's life to which government is denied entry; there are certain rights, privileges, and prerogatives possessed by the citizen that may not be abridged or denied by government. A synonym for limited government is constitutional government.

Not all states having constitutions are constitutional states. The specific Soviet constitutional guarantees in the very liberal 1945 Constitution did nothing to protect them from the outrages perpetrated by the Soviet secret police.

Nor do all constitutional states have governments that are erected on the basis of single written documents such as we have. Limitations on the powers of government may be the result of a strong democratic tradition within the society and of the existence of contending power blocs of which none is able to gain a monopoly of power.

Chapter 17 will examine the American constitutional system.

Answer frame 1¹⁶

1. False. In modern societies, this function is performed by the state and its administrative apparatus, government.
2. True. As long as man lived on the subsistence level there was no need for the services performed by government.
3. False. The form of government in any state offers only a vague suggestion as to how this question is dealt with.
4. False. Throughout history, most states have tended toward authoritarianism. Even the United States has been under the sway of a relatively mild authoritarianism for most of its history.

If you missed any of the above, you should restudy Frame 1¹⁶ before turning to Frame 2¹⁶ on page 108.

Frame 2¹⁶ continued

Label each of the following statements as true or false.

_____ 1. All totalitarian doctrines increase the freedom of individuals.

_____ 2. Until the 1800s, the reality of totalitarianism was only a dream of revolutionaries and political theorists.

_____ 3. Democracy is the most efficient form of government.

_____ 4. The United States is an example of direct democracy.

Now turn to Answer frame 2¹⁶ on page 112 to check your answers.

chapter 17

THE AMERICAN CONSTITUTIONAL SYSTEM

Frame 1[17]

Among the nation-states of the world, the United States is relatively new; yet it holds the distinction of being the *oldest* state with a written constitution. The longevity of the American Constitution is, in part, the result of the political astuteness of the Founding Fathers and of the beautifully imprecise terminology they chose to employ. This remarkable document has survived two world wars, a four-year civil war, and a depression that endured for more than a decade. By contrast, the French, who established the First Republic in September 1792 (the American Constitution was ratified in 1788), have exhausted four republics, are now working on their fifth and in the same period have had two emperors and one return of the monarchy.

Our Constitution, like that of all democracies, provides for popular sovereignty and limited government. It has features that are shared by some other democracies, and other features that represent uniquely American contributions to the art of government. Our survey of the American constitutional system will explore its seven basic undergirding principles: (1) popular sovereignty, (2) limited government, (3) federalism, (4) national supremacy, (5) judicial review, (6) separation of powers, and (7) checks and balances. After we examine each of these principles, we will discuss our Constitution as a living entity. (See pp. 161–180 for the complete text of the Constitution and its amendments.)

Popular Sovereignty

This was defined in the previous chapter. Acknowledgment of the source of power is recognized in the preamble to the Constitution, in the words, "We the People of the United States . . ." In spite of these opening words, however, the document was ratified by state governments that were committed to elitist rule. With the passage of time, however, the ideal of popular sovereignty has moved far closer to reality. Space limitations do not permit citing all the means through which this transition has occurred, and thus we will confine our listings to (1) the Amendments to our Constitution, (2) congressional enactment, and (3) Supreme Court decisions.

Constitutional Amendments. The 14th Amendment provides us with the only constitutional definition of citizenship and promises that no state shall ". . . deny to any person within its jurisdiction the equal protection of the law." The Supreme Court has used these words (as we shall see later) to strike down state practices that acted as barriers to the political equality of all citizens. This amendment was ratified in 1868.

The 15th Amendment, Black Suffrage, was ratified in 1869 but rendered meaningless by state subterfuge. Through congressional action and Supreme Court decisions, however, its full intent has now moved closer to reality.

Answer frame 2¹⁶

1. False. All totalitarian doctrines—whether communist or fascist—hold a basic distrust of the individual.
2. False. Totalitarianism was not possible until the 20th century. It was not until then that a level of administrative and technological skills existed to make it possible.
3. False. Democracy may be a less efficient form of government, but it places the highest premium on the worthiness of the individual.
4. False. Under direct democracy the citizens express themselves directly on all political issues. It can work only when a small population lives compactly in a small geographic region.

If you missed any of the above, you should reread Frame 2¹⁶ before turning to Chapter 17 on page 111.

Frame 1¹⁷ continued

The 19th Amendment, Women's Suffrage, followed the leadership of a number of western states, some of which actually entered the Union with state constitutions guaranteeing women the right of franchise. This amendment was ratified in 1920.

The 23rd Amendment (1961) permits residents of the District of Columbia to vote in Presidential elections.

The 24th Amendment (1964) denies the states the right to impose a poll tax as a prerequisite to voting in federal elections. Since the states discovered that they would have to maintain two separate voter registration books (one for state elections, one for federal) if they were to retain the poll tax, all found it more expedient to completely eliminate the poll tax.

The 26th Amendment, lowering the voting age to 18, was ratified in June 1971.

The 27th Amendment, granting women equal rights under the law was passed by Congress in March 1972; at the time of this writing, ratification by the states is still pending.

Congressional Enactment. Of particular note in this connection are the Civil Rights Acts of 1964 and 1965. The 1964 act makes it a federal offense for anyone to interfere with the exercise of another's civil rights. This includes one's exercise of the franchise. The Civil Rights Act of 1965 is sometimes referred to as the voting rights act. This act empowered the federal government to send registrars into any state, or part thereof, in which less than 50 percent of those qualified by age to vote were actually registered to vote. The impact of this law was to severely weaken the use of literacy tests as a device to deny citizens the right to vote. Even before the 26th Amendment was drafted, the Congress of the United States had passed, and President Nixon had signed into law, a bill that bestowed the franchise on 18-year-olds in federal elections. The 26th Amendment was drafted because many felt that Congress had gone beyond the grant of power extended to it by the Constitution. It is perhaps worthy of note that all of the previously cited constitutional amendments had their origin in the halls of Congress.

Supreme Court Decisions. No segment of government has been more diligent in its pursuit of the ideal of popular sovereignty than the federal judiciary. The Supreme Court is, of course, the highest court in the judiciary. Even before the passage of the 24th and 26th Amendments, the Court had ruled that the poll tax was null and void in federal elections; it conferred the highest legitimacy to the congressional act lowering the voting age to 18 in federal elections. Beginning at the turn of the century, many southern states had taken the position that political parties were "private clubs," and as such were afforded the privilege of determining qualifications for membership. Since the only viable political party in the South following reconstruction was the Democratic party, it was frequently determined that membership was open only to whites. Blacks were therefore denied participation in the Democratic primaries, through which candidates for public office were selected. In the general election that would follow, the victors in the Democratic primary would run unopposed, and blacks could then vote to ratify the choices that whites had previously made. In 1944, the Court ruled in *Smith* v. *Alwright* that when primaries were tantamount to election, membership in political parties violated the 15th Amendment.

While Article IV of the Constitution guarantees to all states a "Republican Form of Government," the Supreme Court consistently refused to determine just how equitable such representative government had to be. In spite of our rapid urban growth, many state legislatures refused to reapportion to account for shifts in population. The result was, in many instances, that rural voices dominated the proceedings in our state legislatures. In the state of Florida, for example, 17 percent of the population elected 50 percent of the legislature. Urbanites in America were almost as victimized by taxation without representation as were their colonial forebears. In 1962,

the Supreme Court rendered a decision that offered redress to the grievances of the urbanite. In a Tennessee case, *Baker* v. *Carr,* the court ordered that the legislature of that state be reapportioned to reflect the present population distribution. The doctrine established by the *Baker* v. *Carr* decision was "one man, one vote." Subsequent decisions of the Supreme Court made this doctrine applicable to other states and to congressional districts. These decisions were based on the Court's interpretation of the "equal protection of the law" clause of the 14th Amendment.

In our discussion of popular sovereignty, space has not permitted an elaboration of the roles played by public and private education, political parties (with recently more democratized procedures for delegate and candidate selection), pressure groups (particularly civil rights groups), and the mass media. We should note, however, that much of the progress made through the formal machinery of government is attributable to the efforts of these groups in society.

Indicate whether each of the following statements is true or false by writing "T" or "F" in the space provided.

_____ 1. The United States is one of the youngest nation-states with a written constitution.

_____ 2. Although implicit in the Constitution, popular sovereignty has only recently come close to being a reality.

_____ 3. The amendment that lowered the voting age to 18 was a law before it became part of the Constitution.

_____ 4. Until the *Baker* v. *Carr* decision (1962) urban Americans were victimized by taxation without representation.

Now turn to Answer frame 1[17] on page 114 to check your responses.

Frame 2[17]

Limited Government

As earlier stated, the terms *limited* and *constitutional* government are synonymous. Limited government is government based on the rule of law rather than arbitrary rule by a man or men. In constitutional societies, the rulers and the ruled are both subject to the restraints imposed by law. When the powers of government are

limited, there are areas of the citizen's life to which government is denied entry.

Probably the best example of limited government from the perspective of the U.S. Constitution is our Bill of Rights, the first 10 amendments. In reality, the rights bestowed by the first 10 amendments are protections accorded the citizen against the excesses of governments. In 1787, when our national Constitution was writ-

Answer frame 1[17]

1. False. Although the United States is relatively new, it is the oldest state with a written constitution.
2. True. Among the means through which popular sovereignty has been approximated are constitutional amendments and Supreme Court decisions.
3. True. Even before the 26th Amendment was drafted the Congress of the United States had passed, and President Nixon had signed into law, a bill that bestowed the franchise on 18-year-olds in federal elections.
4. True. In this case, the Supreme Court ordered that the legislature of Tennessee be reapportioned to reflect the present population distribution.

If you missed any of the above, you should restudy Frame 1[17] before turning to Frame 2[17] on page 113.

Frame 2[17] continued

ten, most state constitutions already possessed bills of rights. The document that emerged from the Philadelphia Constitutional Convention did not. To allay the fears that the new government might not safeguard human rights, the First Congress, meeting for the first time in New York City in 1789, submitted to the states the 10 amendments known as the Bill of Rights. Without this assurance, it is extremely doubtful that our Constitution would have been ratified.

The Bill of Rights, ratified in 1791, clearly imposed restrictions on the national government. It is significant in this regard to note that the first words of the first amendment (and therefore of the Bill of Rights) are: "Congress shall make no law . . .," and Congress is, of course, the legislative body of the national government. Our Bill of Rights was not considered restrictive on the states, a position affirmed by the Supreme Court in *Barron* v. *Baltimore* (1833).

In 1868, following the American Civil War, the 14th Amendment was added to the Constitution. Through judicial interpretation of this amendment, most of "the rights, privileges, and prerogatives" listed in the first 10 amendments have been made binding on the states as well.

Federalism

Federalism represents one of the finest American contributions to the art of government. Through a federal system, a nation is better assured the twin blessings of unity and diversity. Federalism, broadly defined, is a division of power between a central authority and constitu-

ent parts. Under the American federal system, the division is between the national government and the various state governments. Further, the division of power cannot be changed without the concurrence of both levels of government (see the fifth article of the Constitution).

Under our federal system, certain powers are delegated to the national government (most of which are listed in Article I, section 8). Some of the powers of the national government are exclusive. Exclusive powers include the right to make treaties and declare war, to regulate foreign and interstate commerce, and to coin money. Some powers are shared with state governments. These shared powers are generally referred to as concurrent powers, and include the power to levy and collect taxes, to try and punish criminals, to borrow money, and to maintain internal order.

The powers belonging to the states are not as specifically listed; these powers are often referred to as *residual* or reserved powers. According to the 10th Amendment: "The powers not delegated to the United States by the Constitution, nor prohibited by it to the States, are reserved to the States respectively or to the people." The residual powers of the state certainly include establishing educational policy, enacting all laws relating to marriage and the family, and defining most crimes against the individual and his property. Under our federal system, local governments exist at the pleasure of the states and exercise only those powers granted to them by state governments.

The dividing line between the powers of the

states and those of the national government are not always clearly discernible in our Constitution; even the most casual student of United States history is aware that one of the continuing problems in American government has focused on the dividing line between state and national authority. This ambiguity was at the basis of the nullification controversy of 1832, in which South Carolina contended that the federal government exceeded its constitutional limits when Congress enacted the Tariff Act of 1828. This controversy nearly erupted into armed conflict between South Carolina and the federal authority. In 1860–61, 11 southern states seceded from the Union and justified their position because of what they interpreted as gross usurpations of states' rights by the power of the national government. As late as the 1960s, we had governors standing in schoolhouse doors claiming to do so in defense of their understanding of American federalism.

Federalism is not an essential element of all democracies—many in fact are unitary states. A unitary system is one in which all powers are vested in a central government. Examples of unitary democracies are the United Kingdom, France, and Japan. Federalism, while it may re-

tard the development of authoritarianism or totalitarianism, is no positive check against the growth of such systems. One has but to recall that the Weimar Republic, which immediately preceded Hitler's dictatorship, was a federal republic. Nevertheless, in a system such as ours where political power is dispersed between the central authority and the 50 states, each anxious to preserve its own autonomy, the specter of totalitarianism appears to be less real here than in national states where all political power is centralized.

The authors are aware of the charge that the powers of the states have been diminished to enhance the authority of the power-mad centralists in Washington. Such charges, however, are gross exaggerations. Most instances of federal intervention have been for the purpose of guaranteeing all citizens the equal protection of the law promised by the 14th Amendment. If the cost of government is considered a yardstick by which power can be measured, it is rather interesting to note that the cost of state and local governments has been increasing at a higher rate than has the cost of national government.

Label each of the following statements as true or false.

_____ 1. The Bill of Rights aided in creating limited government in the United States.

_____ 2. Federalism, broadly defined, is when the power of the federal government is increasing.

_____ 3. The powers belonging to the states are specifically listed.

_____ 4. Most instances of federal intervention have been for the purpose of guaranteeing all citizens the equal protection of the law promised by the 14th Amendment.

Now turn to Answer frame 2^{17} on page 116 to check your answers.

Frame 3^{17}

National Supremacy

The doctrine of national supremacy holds that while the authority of the national government is limited, it does possess absolute supremacy in those areas in which power has been

granted to it by the Constitution. The basis for the doctrine of national supremacy is found in Article VI, Section 2:

This Constitution, and the Laws of the United States which shall be made in Pursuance thereof; and all Treaties made, or which shall be made, under the

Answer frame 2¹⁷

1. True. The Bill of Rights was clearly understood to impose restrictions on the national government.
2. False. Federalism describes the situation where there is a division of power between the national government and the various state governments.
3. False. They are not specifically listed. They are often referred to as *residual* or reserved powers.
4. True. The charge that the powers of the states have been diminished to enhance the authority of the power-mad centralists in Washington is a gross exaggeration.

If you missed any of the above, you should reread Frame 2¹⁷ before turning to Frame 3¹⁷ on page 115.

Frame 3¹⁷ continued

Authority of the United States, shall be the supreme Law of the Land; and the Judges in every State shall be bound thereby, anything in the Constitution of Laws of any State to the Contrary notwithstanding.

The Supreme Court in 1819 affirmed the doctrine of national supremacy in the famous *McCulloch* v. *Maryland* case. The question of the supremacy of a national law had been challenged by the legislature of the state of Maryland. The Congress had authorized the creation of the second Bank of the United States. A branch of this bank was located in Baltimore, Maryland. This establishment was in direct competition with banks chartered by the state, and was regarded as a threat to their very existence. The state of Maryland passed a law designed to reduce the national bank to impotence. This law required that the national bank pay taxes on the basis of its deposits. The second Bank of the United States refused, and the basis for *McCulloch* v. *Maryland* was laid. When the case came before the Supreme Court, the court decided against the state of Maryland. Inherent in the power to tax, affirmed Chief Justice Marshall, is the power to destroy. If Maryland has the right to tax a creation of the national government, she also possesses the power to destroy it. There is, Marshall observed, an obvious conflict between national law and state law. When the national law meets the test of constitutionality, the national law is supreme, and the state law is null and void.

Judicial Review

The doctrine of judicial review, the right of the federal judiciary—particularly the Supreme Court—to determine the constitutionality of national measures was first asserted in the case of *Marbury* v. *Madison* (1803). You will note from our previous citation of the supremacy clause that not all laws passed by Congress are "the supreme law of the land." Only those laws that are made in pursuance of the Constitution have that sanctity. You will also note that nowhere in the supremacy clause or elsewhere in the Constitution does it spell out precisely what body shall determine when any measure—a law passed by Congress, an executive proclamation—is or is not in accord with the Constitution. The significance of the *Marbury* v. *Madison* decision is that in this landmark adjudication, the Supreme Court asserted its authority as the final arbiter of constitutionality. *Marbury* v. *Madison* originated in the aftermath of the election of 1800, when the party of John Adams, the Federalists, suffered an irreparable defeat. Having lost the presidency and the Congress, the Federalists attempted to strengthen their hold on the federal judiciary. In pursuit of this end, the Federalist lame-duck Congress created several new federal judgeships and 42 justices of the peace for the District of Columbia. To fill these vacancies, John Adams appointed members of his own party, who were duly confirmed by the Senate. When the new Congress assembled in

March of 1801, several of the commissions had not yet been delivered. Thomas Jefferson, the new President, ordered his Secretary of State, James Madison, not to deliver the remaining commissions.

The Federal Judiciary Act of 1789, which created the federal court system, granted to the Supreme Court the right to issue writs of mandamus. Such writs are court orders directing public officers to perform certain duties required by law. William Marbury, one of the justices of the peace who had not received his commission, applied to the Supreme Court for a writ of mandamus ordering Madison to deliver his commission. The new Chief Justice (and formerly Adams' Secretary of State) John Marshall, speaking for the whole court, ruled that such a writ could not be issued because Congress had gone beyond the Constitution in granting the Supreme Court this jurisdiction.

Separation of Powers

Since the Watergate exposures no constitutional principle has been more widely debated than the concept of separation of powers. Many people assume it to be a very simple concept: We have three branches of government—the executive, headed by the President; a legislative, consisting of the two houses of Congress; and a judicial, composed of the entire federal judiciary. The executive branch enforces the laws, the legislative branch makes the laws, and the judicial branch interprets the laws. Simple? Yes! But, unfortunately, very inaccurate.

The American principle of *separation of powers* does not mean that we have a total separation of governmental powers, as a casual reading of the Constitution will demonstrate. While it is true that the executive branch is charged with faithfully executing the laws, it is also true that the executive branch plays a large role in *making* laws as well. The President is vested with the power of veto. If the President chooses, he can withhold his signature from acts passed by Congress and thus prohibit those acts from becoming law. Even the threat of veto is often sufficient to insure that a President will get the kind of legislation from Congress that is acceptable to him. Further, the President is constitu-

tionally obligated to appear before Congress from time to time to inform it of the state of the Union. In his annual State of the Union messages the President outlines for Congress the kind of legislation that he feels should be enacted. Usually such messages are given full coverage by all of the major TV and radio networks. The President speaks to the Congress with the full knowledge that he and he alone has a nationwide constituency. Viewers or listeners know whom to goad when they agree with the President and Congress is reluctant to act.

As the world becomes more complex, so do our legislative needs. Expertise in highly specialized areas is more at the command of the President than of the Congress. He does, after all, preside over the administrative arm of government. When a president determines that a new agricultural program is needed, he can draw on the expertise of the Department of Agriculture; when he decides to increase or decrease military expenditures, he has available the expertise of the Department of Defense; and should he decide on an enlarged involvement of the national government in education, he has the expertise of the Department of Health, Education, and Welfare.

The authority of the president to issue proclamations is a significant lawmaking tool. It was under presidential proclamation that slaves were freed; that Japanese-Americans were interned in World War II; that wages and prices were controlled in 1971.

In fact, so vast are the legislative powers of the President that Clinton Rossiter designates him as the Chief Legislator.

While the Congress is *primarily* legislative, it does exercise some executive authority as well. The President, and the President alone, may negotiate treaties with foreign powers, certainly an executive function, but under our constitutional system such treaties must meet with the approval of two thirds of the Senate of the United States. Cabinet officers and other major presidential appointees, men who are to share in the administration of government, must likewise be approved by two thirds of the Senate.

Perhaps a more significant impingement on executive powers held by Congress is its control of governmental purse strings. The President is Commander-in-Chief of the American military, but what he can do with the military depends to a large extent on whether or not the Congress is willing to appropriate sufficient funds to support his decisions. What is true for the military is also true for all other executive departments.

To insure that the laws of the land are faithfully executed, the Congress of the United States acts as a watchdog on the executive branch of government. Through congressional debate and action, any President's laxity in enforcing the laws will be publicized and he—or his party —will be held accountable by the voters in the next election.

The Supreme Court and, to a lesser extent, the entire federal judiciary have been accused by some segments of our society of forsaking their rightful task of "adjudicating" and of usurping the power of legislating. Generally these critics of the court are most concerned with the kind of "legislation" the court is writing, for by its very

nature the court cannot refrain from law making. Every time the Supreme Court determines *how* the Constitution is to be interpreted, it is legislating. For example, in 1896, the Supreme Court ruled in the *Plessy* v. *Ferguson* case that "separate but equal" facilities did not violate the "equal protection of the law" clause of the 14th amendment. In 1954, in the *Brown* v. *Topeka Board of Education* case, the Supreme Court ruled that separate educational facilities could never be equal and were in fact in violation of the 14th Amendment. In both instances the Court was clarifying a constitutional point; in both instances, as it laid down the supreme law of the land, it was interpreting the same words in the Constitution.

The American concept of separation of powers does recognize three distinct branches of government, but as we have demonstrated, that separation is far from absolute. To a large extent, there is an overlap of power within the three branches of government.

True or false?

_____ 1. The doctrine of national supremacy means that the authority of the national government is unlimited.

_____ 2. Nowhere in the Constitution does it spell out precisely what body shall determine when any measure is or is not in accord with the Constitution.

_____ 3. The American principle of separation of powers means that we have a total separation of governmental powers.

_____ 4. By its very nature the Supreme Court cannot refrain from legislating.

Now turn to Answer frame 3[17] on page 120 to check your answers.

Frame 4[17]

Checks and Balances

The Constitution of the United States is replete with a system of checks and balances designed to curb any despotic tendencies likely to emerge. These checks were designed to insure that no branch of government would acquire carte blanche authority; that each branch would be subject to the scrutiny of the other two branches of government (and in some instances checks within a branch itself). These checks

include those discussed in the following paragraphs.

The Existence of the Federal System. Within this system, the states zealously preserve the autonomy granted to them by the Constitution and vigorously defend what they consider their sovereign rights. When, however, this defense of sovereignty infringes on constitutional guarantees, the national authority is asserted generally under the auspices of the federal judiciary.

A Bicameral Legislature. Through this arrangement, both houses, each jealous of its own prerogatives, serves as a check on the possible excesses of the other. The framers, no doubt, anticipated that the House of Representatives, with a younger elective age (25) and with two-year terms, would prove to be the more radical. The Senate, with a six-year term of office and higher elective age (30), would serve as the more cautious and deliberative body. While the attitudes of the two houses have not fully met the expectations of the framers, sufficient differences have developed that the end result has met expectations.

The Separation of Powers. By this arrangement the President, through his veto power, acts as a balance to possible excesses of the combined legislative branch. The legislative branch is not, however, subject to the whims of the executive. A veto may be overridden with the concurrence of a two-thirds majority in both houses. And, should the legislative and executive branches agree to an unconstitutional act, the Supreme Court through judicial review may declare such acts null and void.

The Living Constitution

Our Constitution has become a *living document* through its ability to change as the needs of our society dictate. The framers formally recognized the need for possible changes by including the fifth article, which established the amending machinery. This method, often awkward, is, however, the *least* significant factor in providing life for our Constitution. After all, we have added but 16 amendments since 1791, when the Bill of Rights was incorporated into our organic law. One of these, the 21st, repealed the 18th; and the 20th amendment, changing the inauguration day of the President and abolishing the lame-duck sessions of Congress, is purely mechanical.

Most written constitutions are *rigid* constitutions employing very *specific* language that carefully delineates the powers of government. Certainly, this is the weakness with which most of our state constitutions is afflicted. The result is that periodically the organic law has to be scrapped, and new constitutions written. The federal Constitution, on the other hand, generally avoids specifics and provides rather for broader grants of power. The language of the Constitution is such that flexibility is added to the document.

A beautiful example of the above is the "commerce clause" from Article I, Section 8. This clause gives Congress the power "To regulate commerce with foreign Nations, and among the several States, and with the Indian Tribes." Under the *commerce* clause the Congress has passed laws which include:

1. Forbidding the transport of women across state lines for immoral purposes.
2. A federal kidnapping law.
3. The creation of a number of independent regulatory agencies, including:
   a. ICC (Interstate Commerce Commission) regulating surface carriers.
   b. FCC (Federal Communications Commission) regulating the transmission of voice and image.
   c. SEC (Securities and Exchange Commission) regulating the sale of securities.
   d. FAA (Federal Aviation Authority) regulating aviation passenger and freight services.
   e. NLRB (National Labor Relations Board) whose principal job is to insure fair elections in the collective bargaining process.
4. Minimum wage and child labor laws.
5. Antidiscrimination measures such as the Public Accommodations Act of 1964.

Had the framers chosen a more precise word —such as "trade"—none of the above could have been accomplished without amending the Constitution.

Previously we discussed the "elastic" or "necessary and proper clause," the last grant of power to the Congress in Article I, Section 8. This clause has enormously enhanced the power of Congress. It is, of course, not a blanket grant of power. This clause authorizes the Congress to pass legislation "necessary and proper" in order to carry out "the foregoing Powers and any other Powers vested by this Constitution in the Government of the United States, or in any Department or Officer thereof." The Supreme Court has ruled, however, that "necessary and proper" does

Answer frame 3¹⁷

1. False. It means that, while the authority of the national government is limited, it does possess absolute supremacy in those areas in which power has been granted by the Constitution.
2. True. The significance of the *Marbury* v. *Madison* decision is that in this adjudication the Supreme Court asserted its authority as the final arbiter of constitutionality.
3. False. For example, the executive branch plays a large role in making laws as well as executing the laws, and Congress exercises some executive authority.
4. True. Every time the Supreme Court determines *how* the Constitution is to be read, it is legislating.

If you missed any of the above, you should restudy Frame 3¹⁷ before turning to Frame 4¹⁷ on page 118.

Frame 4¹⁷ continued

not mean *indispensable;* instead, it means *convenient.* Examples of congressional employment of the necessary and proper clause are as follows:

Enumerated Power	*"Necessary and Proper" Legislation*
"To . . . provide for the . . . general welfare."	Social Security and federal highways legislation.
"To borrow money on the credit of the United States."	Legislation authorizing the Treasury Department to issue U.S. Savings Bonds. Creation of Federal Reserve System.
"To regulate commerce . . ."	Laws protecting migratory birds, wage and hours legislation.

We have thus far confined our discussion of "The Living Constitution" to congressional enactment. The flexibility of the document goes considerably beyond this. Consider, for example, the continually expanding role of the American presidency.

When Washington was president (and our population was less than four million—largely rural), his Cabinet consisted of four men; one of them, the Attorney General, was actually an officer of the Supreme Court. (Incidentally, the Constitution makes no reference at all to a Presidential Cabinet.) Currently the executive branch of government consists of 11 departments, each

headed by a Cabinet officer and a myriad of executive agencies, boards, and commissions, all necessitated by the tremendous changes that have occurred since the Constitution was written. With no constitutional amendment enhancing the powers of the presidency, our chief executive had little difficulty in assuming the role of leader of the free nations following World War II.

Certainly one of the principal factors insuring "life" for our Constitution has been the federal judiciary. Through the power of judicial review, our organic law is continually reinterpreted and updated. Perhaps the best example of the role of the judiciary in the area is the Court's changing interpretation of what is meant by "equal protection of the law." In the *Plessy* v. *Ferguson* case of 1896, the Supreme Court ruled that "separate but equal" facilities did not violate this principle, thus upholding the constitutionality of segregation laws. In the decades of the 1950s and 1960s, in contrast, there was a virtual avalanche of decisions aimed at the destruction of legally maintained segregation. In the final analysis, the Constitution means largely what the Supreme Court says that it means.

Many of the quite significant changes that have occurred in our system of government have come about in rather informal ways. For example, consider the changes in the means by which a president is chosen.

The Constitution established the electoral college and permitted the states to determine how the electors should be chosen. Initially, the electors were chosen by the legislatures of the states; not until 1828 did the practice emerge of having the legislators chosen by the people. Further, in this regard, the founders had not apparently assumed the development of political parties, and their belief was that the electors would simply choose the best man. The first electors, of course, responded by unanimously choosing Washington. With the appearance of political parties, electors came to be chosen because of pledges to particular candidates. Today, on many state ballots, the names of the electors (actually the individuals elected in a presidential contest) do not even appear. In those states where the names of the electors do appear, the voter understands for whom the electors will cast their vote.

No mention of "The Living Constitution" would be complete without some reference to American political parties. Any reference to this aspect of the American political system is absent from our Constitution. Yet most political offices are filled through the medium of our political parties. It is *within* and *between* our two parties that the struggle to influence public policy is waged. In the final chapter on the political dimensions of culture, their role will be developed.

Is each of the following true or false?

_____ 1. The federal system makes despotism a constant danger.

_____ 2. The House of Representatives is more radical than the Senate.

_____ 3. Part of the dignity of our Constitution is that it cannot be changed.

_____ 4. In the final analysis, the Constitution means largely what the Supreme Court says that it means.

Now turn to Answer frame 4¹⁷ on page 122 to check your answers.

Answer frame 4¹⁷ ———————————————————————————————

1. False. The existence of the federal system is one of several checks and balances designed to curb any despotic tendencies.
2. False. Although the framers of the Constitution possibly anticipated this, the attitudes of the two houses have not met these expectations.
3. False. Our Constitution has become a *living document* through its ability to change as the needs of our society dictate.
4. True. Through the power of judicial review, our organic law is continually reinterpreted and updated.

If you missed any of the above, you should review Frame 4¹⁷ before beginning Chapter 18.

chapter 18

THE AMERICAN PARTY SYSTEM

Frame 1¹⁸ ———————————————————————————————

In a democracy, governmental authority changes hands peaceably through contested elections. Securing candidates, defining the issues, and waging the battle for votes is the responsibility of political parties. How many parties exist, how they are structured, and what kind of discipline they impose on their membership are questions that each society answers in terms of its own culture and tradition. The focal point in this chapter is on American political parties, with occasional references to those of other nation-states.

Origins of the Party System

One can search the U.S. Constitution in vain for any reference to political parties. They are extraconstitutional but are certainly part of what we refer to as "The Living Constitution." Perhaps the best explanation for omission of mention of political parties lies in the temper of the period that brought forth our Constitution. It had been but four short years since George III had recognized the independence of his wayward subjects. British troops still occupied significant portions of the American West. Internal disorder was rampant throughout the land. States were levying restrictions against the goods of other states; Maryland and Virginia had recently barely averted bloodshed over navigation rights on the Potomac; and rebellion against duly constituted authority had just been suppressed in Massachusetts. The Congress, under the Articles of Confederation, was unable to enforce the laws it passed or to collect taxes from the states that made up the American union.

No wonder, then, that the founders' greatest desire was to achieve a sense of national unity. Partisan politics were regarded as inherently disruptive. James Madison warned his colleagues and the American people through the *Federalist Papers* of "the dangerous vice of faction." Other delegates at the convention argued that political parties were more in harmony with European politics than our own.

Hardly had the ink dried on the Constitution when the struggle for ratification began. Within that struggle were the seeds of the American republic's first political parties. The supporters of the Constitution became known as Federalists after the *Federalist Papers* penned by Madison, Hamilton, and Jay in 1787–88. Those opposed to the ratification of the document were called Anti-Federalists. After ratification, the battle centered around the extent of authority vested in the new national government. The "Loose Constructionists," those who liberally interpreted the "necessary and proper" clause to enhance the power of the national government were called "Federalists." They were, after all, the same group that had fought so bitterly to secure the Constitution's ratification. The "States' Righters," those who believed in a "strict interpretation" of the Constitution, were the "Anti-Federalists." Later the Anti-Federalists were to rally under the banner of Thomas Jefferson's Democratic-Republican party.

As history continued to unfold, the Federalist party vanished from the American scene. By 1820, we were (for a short period) a one-party state, however the disputed election of 1824 led to factionalism within the Democratic-Republican party and resulted in the birth of the National Republicans (later called Whigs) and the Democrats. During the turbulent 1850s, a bitter sectionalism led to the demise of the Whig party. Southern Whigs became Democrats and northern Whigs affiliated with the fledgling Republican party. Since 1860, when the Republicans captured the presidency, the Democratic and Republican parties have monopolized American government.

While American political parties began life struggling over ideological issues, doctrine plays an insignificant role in our contemporary two-party system. Since the close of the American Civil War, our two parties have been parties of compromise, or what some writers call "brokerage" parties. In a "brokerage" party, conflicting perspectives and interests are compromised in order that the party can put forth a united effort to elect its candidates to public office or to secure passage of desired legislation. Within the ranks of America's two major parties, one can find a host of competing interest groups—religious, ethnic, economic—and a wide variety of views. Within both parties there are "states' righters" and "centralists"; "free-traders" and "protectionists"; "nationalists" and "internationalists"; "liberals" and "conservatives."

The diversity of representation within our parties is the result of the openness of their membership. One becomes a Republican or a Democrat by the simple expedient of registering as one. Rarely do "purges" take place within our brokerage parties. Occasionally a President will become angry with members of his own party and lend the support of his office to the defeat of "undesirables." Franklin D. Roosevelt and William Howard Taft both engaged in primary fights to defeat enemies of the administration, and both had their efforts soundly repudiated by the electorate. Of more recent date, former Vice President Agnew campaigned against Charles Goodell, also a Republican, in a New York senatorial contest and helped insure his defeat. In 1964 the conservative wing of the Republican party gained control of the national convention and believing that the American people would respond to an opportunity to register a clear choice between the "liberal Democrats" and their conservative philosophy, nominated Barry Goldwater for president. Speakers from the more liberal wing were booed and heckled as they attempted to speak. They were told, in effect, that their help was not needed in the forthcoming campaign. With the brokerage philosophy repudiated and with the electorate faced with a clear ideological choice, the Republicans went down to ignominious defeat. American voters demonstrated in this election their commitment to parties of compromise.

Indicate whether each of the following statements is true or false by writing "T" or "F" in the space provided.

———— 1. The number, nature, and functioning of political parties is relatively constant with little variation across societies.

———— 2. Our Constitution spells out the limits of our political parties.

———— 3. It has been only in the 20th century that American government has been monopolized by two parties.

———— 4. Ideology or doctrine governs the identity of our political parties.

Now turn to Answer frame 1[18] on page 126 to check your responses.

Frame 2[18]

Parties of Doctrine or Ideology

Foreign observers and some domestic critics of American parties contend that our system makes elections less meaningful—that the American voter is offered a choice of "Tweedledee" and "Tweedledum." They say that the voter is not offered meaningful alternatives and that parties of compromise fail to sharpen issues for the electorate. To some extent these criticisms are valid; however, parties of compromise possess other merits which parties of doctrine lack.

In most European states, parties of doctrine predominate. Such parties appear to work reasonably well when there are not more than two or three major factions competing for the allegiance of the electorate. As the number grows, however, political chaos often develops. Certainly the proliferation of political parties was one of the principal causes for the death of the Fourth French Republic, as well as a significant factor in Hitler's assumption of power in Germany.

Doctrinal or ideological parties flourish most widely in states that have a parliamentary system. Under such a system, the executive branch of government is chosen by the legislative. When no party is able to secure a majority membership in the legislative branch, it is necessary to seek alliances among other ideological groups. By the very nature of ideological commitment, such alliances are frequently short-lived. It is for this reason that more than 40 different governments have governed Italy since World War II.

In the American system, the chief executive is chosen technically by the electoral college but actually by the voters. To secure the nomination, the candidate must not alienate the members of his own party. Candidates of the two major parties are therefore men capable of occupying the center position in their own parties. Compromise having been achieved *within* the party, compromise *between* the parties ruffles few ideological feathers. Thus, when governmental responsibility is divided (as it was in the Eisenhower and Nixon administrations, with the Democrats controlling Congress and the Republicans the presidency), we face no crisis of the magnitude that has afflicted postwar France and Italy.

In spite of the dominance of our presidential democracy and two-party tradition, parties of ideology have appeared on the American scene. Most of these parties have no concept of ever winning the presidency but are desirous of carrying their message to the American people. Occasionally, a third party appears that has as its avowed hope denying the candidates of the two major parties a majority of the electoral vote, thus throwing the decision into the House of Representatives. When the election is decided by the House, the third party feels it will be in a better bargaining position. This was certainly the goal of the Dixiecrat party of 1948, and the American Independent party of 1968.

When third parties do appear with salable programs and amass significant popular support, they literally sign their own death warrants. Such was the case of the Populist party, formed in 1891.

The Populist or People's party began as an agrarian protest. In 1892, the party offered national and local candidates and a platform that for its day was considered extremely radical. Among other planks, the platform called for election of senators by direct popular vote, a graduated income tax, adoption of the secret ballot, free coinage of silver and a more flexible currency, abolition of national banks, and an eight-hour working day. The appeal of the party was such that it polled 10 percent of the vote and secured 22 electoral votes in the 1892 election. When the Democrats assembled at their national convention four years later, they incorporated the Populists' demands for free silver, and nominated William Jennings Bryan for president. Although the Populists repudiated the Democrats and tried to remain independent, the silver-tongued Bryan drew most of the Populist votes to the Democrats in the 1896 election. The Republican, William McKinley, won the election, but the stealing of the Populists' thunder by the Democrats foreshadowed the demise of their party.

But Populist demands that in 1892 had appeared radical were met in 1913 by ratification of the 16th amendment giving Congress power to enact income taxes and in the same year by the 17th amendment providing that senators be elected by direct popular vote. Further legislation at the state and national levels has enacted into law other once-radical Populist proposals.

In some regions of the United States, minor parties have played a significant role, even when unsuccessful on the national scene. Of particular note in this connection is the now-defunct Progressive party, which unsuccessfully ran Robert M. LaFollette for president in 1924 but provided the major opposition to the Republican party in Wisconsin throughout the decade of the 1930s. The Farmer-Labor party, formed in 1920, ran poorly in the national election of that year, but it dominated the politics of Minnesota, until Franklin D. Roosevelt's New Deal incorporated many of the reforms it advocated and it then became virtually an adjunct of the Democratic party.

The Conservative party in New York through active support of the Republican administration succeeded in defeating both the Democrat and the Republican nominees for the Senate in 1970. The Liberal party, operating at its peak strength in New York City, has been a significant factor in elections in that city. The Dixiecrat or States' Rights party of 1948 and the American Independent party of 1968 both had considerable regional strength but neither has made any strong showing nationally.

Without the multiplicity of parties, the American system remains extraordinarily sensitive to "factional" voices. Such voices are articulated through pressure groups and an alert mass media.

Label each of the following statements as true or false.

_____ 1. Doctrinal or ideological parties flourish most widely in states that have a parliamentary system.

_____ 2. Third parties are usually more interested in carrying a message to the American people than winning the presidency.

_____ 3. The major political parties survive by destroying opposition from third parties.

_____ 4. Minor parties have had more influence regionally than nationally.

Now turn to Answer frame 2[18] on page 126 to check your answers.

Frame 3[18]

Pressure Groups

A pressure group is defined as a combination of persons sharing common interests who attempt to influence public policy in a way favorable to those interests. Pressure groups, contrary to the views of many Americans, are *not* inherently evil. It was through the efforts of the NAACP that the case of *Brown* v. *Topeka Board of Education* was brought before the Supreme

Answer frame 1[18]

1. False. How many parties exist, how they are structured, and what kind of discipline they impose on their membership are questions that each society answers in terms of its own culture.
2. False. There are no references to political parties in the Constitution. They are extraconstitutional.
3. False. Since 1860, when the Republicans captured the Presidency, the Democratic and Republican parties have monopolized American government.
4. False. Doctrine plays an insignificant role in our contemporary two-party system. One becomes a Republican or a Democrat by the simple expedient of registering as one.

If you missed any of the above, you should restudy Frame 1[18] before turning to Frame 2[18] on page 124.

Answer frame 2[18]

1. True. When no party is able to secure a majority membership in the legislative branch, it is necessary to seek alliances among other ideological groups.
2. True. The hope of the major third parties is to deny the candidates of the two major parties a majority of the electoral vote.
3. False. The major parties survive by incorporating elements of the third-party doctrine—or demands—and thus "stealing their thunder."
4. True. Two good examples are the Progressive party and the Dixiecrat party.

If you missed any of the above, you should reread Frame 2[18] before turning to Frame 3[18] on page 125.

Frame 3[18] continued

Court; it was through the efforts of the various women's liberation groups that Congress sent to the states the proposed 27th Amendment (equal rights under the law regardless of sex); it has been purely through the efforts of organized senior citizens that Congress has awarded increases in social security benefits.

Pressure groups attempt to influence public opinion by demonstrations, by securing time on television, by running advertisements in newspapers, and through educational programs. Generally, they attempt to persuade the public of the justice of their cause. Many pressure groups maintain paid representatives in Washington, D.C., and in many state capitals. Lobbyists, as they are called, are often persons who have previously served in the national or state legislative halls, and thus know their way through the legislative thicket. Frequently, because of the expertise they have acquired in the interests they represent, they are called upon to offer testimony on bills affecting their clients. So influential are 20th-century lobbyists that some political scientists refer to them as the "Third House of Congress."

Lobbyists are not sinister men attempting to secure their ends by such nefarious means as bribery (though this quite obviously exists). They often enlist the support of members of the legislative body who were beneficiaries of campaign contributions or who can ill afford to ignore the needs of the group represented. But the justice of a cause is its most effective promoting influence and frequently, groups with small budgets are capable of surpassing the efforts of much wealthier pressure groups. Certainly, one of the best-heeled lobbying groups in Washington is the American Medical Association, but all of their wealth was incapable of thwarting the Medicare program enacted by the Congress.

Proportional Representation

Some nation-states have resorted to a system of proportional representation to enlarge the voices to which the government must give heed. Under proportional representation, as employed in Italy today and in France under the Fourth Republic, political parties are awarded legislative seats proportionate to their share of the vote. Under such a system, minor parties tend to proliferate, and governmental instability is enhanced.

Under our political system proportionate representation cannot constitutionally exist; it is denied by the very nature of the American federal system. Under this system, all representatives to the Senate are chosen on a statewide basis, and all members of the House represent specific districts.

The American federal system is reflected in the structure of our two major political parties. Both parties have a national committee and a national chairman, while at the same time each state has its own near-autonomous state committee and state chairman. Frequently, there are pronounced differences of opinion between the various levels of party organization. The national convention, which assembles every four years for the purpose of nominating national standard bearers, is usually the arena where these differences manifest themselves. These differences, on occasion, have resulted in state delegations "walking out," and of some state committees actually designating someone other than the convention choice as the presidential candidate.

The Nonpartisan Attitude

Among the multitude of reference groups with which Americans identify, few are more lightly esteemed than are political parties. Part of this reason is the low esteem generally accorded to politicians and to politics in general; part of the reason may well be that both of our major political parties generally agree on goals for America. For whatever reason, partisan fervor in the United States is exceedingly mild when compared to that in other democratic states. Comments such as: "I *never* vote for the party. I *always* vote for the best man"; or "I may be a Democrat (or Republican), but I always vote independent"; are common among the American electorate.

Throughout American history, partisans in quest of electoral victories have catered to our basic nonpartisan attitude. Frequently, candidates with minimum party identification have been selected to head national tickets. In 1940, the Republicans chose as their standard-bearer Wendell L. Willkie, who had been a Democrat four years previous to his nomination. Dwight David Eisenhower could easily have secured the 1948 Democratic nomination (and with the blessing of Democratic president Harry S. Truman) had he desired it. In 1957, he chose the Republican ticket, defeating Robert A. Taft (popularly known as Mr. Republican) on the first ballot. The popularity of Eisenhower was great enough to bring in the second Republican Congress in three decades.

In spite of the great similarities of the two parties, there are some marginal differences. While the New Deal measures of Frankin D. Roosevelt have been thoroughly institutionalized, the proponents for further extension are more numerous among the Democrats. Republicans talk more generally of tax cuts to stimulate the economy; Democrats to help the little man. Republicans tend to support "protectionist" measures (higher tariffs), while Democrats lean more toward freer trade. Republicans place greater emphasis on "fiscal responsibility," while Democrats more generally advocate greater appropriations as a means for coping with social ills.

Perhaps the greatest single difference in the two parties however is in their support. The Republican party has seldom faced a severe problem of financing campaigns. Industrialists, bankers, and men of commerce have insured the financial integrity of the party. The Democrats have drawn their chief financial backing from American labor groups. The Republican party exerts the greater influence among old-line Americans, the white Anglo-Saxon Protestants; while the appeal of the Democratic party is to Catholics, Jews, blacks, and what politicians refer to as the "ethnic" population. Central cities are generally written off to the Democrats, while suburbia tends to vote Republican. While less so today, the South is still predominantly Democratic; New England, Republican. Democrats, once the traditional "out" party in the northern plains, are now much stronger in that region. The far West is neither party's territory.

True or false?

_____ 1. Pressure groups are inherently evil.

_____ 2. Lobbyists are generally regarded as uninfluential.

_____ 3. Political parties are major, highly esteemed, reference groups for the American people.

_____ 4. The greatest single difference in the two major parties is their sources of financial support.

Now turn to Answer frame 3[18] on page 130 to check your answers.

chapter 19

EDUCATION

Frame 1[19]

The simplest societies had no educational institutions. The child learned all he needed to know by watching and sharing in whatever was happening around him. Any formal instruction in primitive societies was assigned to some member of the family, and was thus a part of the familial institutions. The earliest specialized jobs, probably as medicine men, arrow makers, or canoe builders, were normally passed on within the family, with training given within the family.

Educational institutions—schools—first arose when it became necessary to train specialized workers who could not easily be trained within the family. The first schools probably trained either priests or bureaucrats (tax collectors, scribes, bookkeepers). Thus educational institutions arose from increasing cultural complexity since it was developments in either religious or political institutions that made schools necessary. As culture grows ever more complex and work more highly specialized, practically *everyone* needs training which cannot easily be handled by the family, so school attendance becomes universal in modern societies.

Structure of Educational Institutions

Whether the first schools arose to teach writing or priestly lore is not known; neither of these can easily be learned within the family by the "watch-and-help" method. Systematic, concentrated instruction must be given. Schools probably started with a man systematically instructing his son or nephew; then one or more additional children joined to receive the instruction and the class grew until regularly scheduled schools had developed.

Ancient schools educated only the few who had need of such training. The masses had neither the need nor the means to attend school. But education did not necessarily denote wealth or high status. The host of minor bureaucrats in ancient societies had an intermediate social status, while many a Roman patrician had a Greek slave who was far more learned than his master, and who served as business manager, accountant, adviser, and perhaps tutor to his children. During the Middle Ages the Roman Catholic Church assumed most of the responsibility for education in Western societies in order to train members for the priesthood. There was little change until the decline of feudalism and the rise of mercantilism and capitalism, which created a need for secular education among merchants, shopkeepers, and tradesmen. The first schools in the United States were also operated by churches, which were often the only suitable buildings in frontier communities, while the minister, often the only educated man, could double as teacher.

The industrial revolution created a need for many unskilled and semiskilled workers, who could quickly pick up whatever skills they needed on the job. Highly skilled labor continued to be trained mainly through the apprenticeship system. Elementary education was far from universal, and limited to the "three Rs," heavily laden with moralistic preachment in support of the conventional norms and values. Higher education was an ornamental luxury for the prosperous, with a heavy emphasis upon classical literature and languages, aimed at developing "cultured" gentlemen. Well-born young ladies might dabble delicately in music and the classics.

Recent developments in technology have brought the cybernetic revolution, with automation and computer-controlled machines rapidly shrinking the market for unskilled and semiskilled labor. Meanwhile the demand for professionals, semiprofessionals, and technicians of many kinds multiplies. The present American goal is high school graduation for everyone, while some form of education beyond high school is rapidly becoming the normal expectation.

Manifest and Latent Functions of American Educational Institutions

The most obvious of the manifest functions of our educational institutions is to *prepare for occupational role performance.* This includes basic general education and specific skill training. Today a considerable amount of technical training is being contracted out to commercial enterprises known as the "knowledge industry." Also, a growing fraction of technical training is adult education, seeking to train school dropouts and job transferees. Technological change makes job retraining necessary today for the majority of adults at least once during their lifetimes. Consequently, general education (theoretically) seeks to prepare children to *learn how to learn,* so that at some later date they can easily prepare for jobs that have not yet been created.

A second manifest function is to *preserve and transmit the culture.* Although family and peer group precede the school in a person's socialization, the school transmits selected portions of our accumulated knowledge, reinforces the dominant values, and cultivates the expected ethnocentrism. A third manifest function in our society is to *provide for upward social mobility.* A fourth is to *encourage democratic participation,* developing the person's capacity to think rationally and independently, and share in intelligent democratic decision making. A fifth is *"life enrichment,"* inspiring a person to expand his intellectual and esthetic horizons and enjoy the "finer things of life." How effectively schools fulfill these functions is a matter of debate.

The latent functions of our educational institutions are more important than is generally recognized. One is to *prolong adolescence* and delay assumption of adult roles. Older students, who are physically adult but denied adult status and adult responsibilities, have historically been a somewhat restless, disorderly crew. "Town and gown" clashes are legendary in every old university town. For the first time in history, *most* of our youth are in this equivocal status for a number of years. Students today may be no

Answer frame 3¹⁸

1. False. Pressure groups are combinations of persons sharing common interests who attempt to influence public policy in a way favorable to those interests. They are not necessarily evil.
2. False. So influential are 20th-century lobbyists that some political scientists refer to them as the "Third House of Congress."
3. False. Among the multitude of reference groups with which Americans identify (religious, ethnic, racial, class, etc.), few are more lightly esteemed than are political parties.
4. True. The Republican party gets support primarily from the industrial business community, and the Democratic party gets support primarily from American labor groups.

If you missed any of the above, you should restudy Frame 3¹⁸ before beginning Chapter 19 on page 128.

Frame 1¹⁹ continued

more disorderly than at many earlier moments in history, but their greater numbers make student disorders more serious.

A second latent function is to *transfer socialization functions from family to school and peer group.* Parental influence over later socialization has weakened. When a family comes into conflict with the school, the school generally wins. While peer groups exist in all societies, the school provides a far more favorable setting for the peer group than the world of work offered to young people. In the schools, a peer culture (subculture) has developed with great influence upon student norms and even upon school operation and control.

A third latent function of educational institutions in our society is to *promote social discontent and dissent.* One way is through overeducating some people. There is evidence that high school graduates are less happy and productive in routine, relatively unskilled jobs than are the school dropouts; yet many jobs carry educational qualifications which are not necessary for successful job performance. This has the ironic result of excluding people who would be happy in the job and hiring only those who are likely to be discontented. Another form of overeducation is preparing too many people for high-status positions. At present, after years of acute shortage, it suddenly appears that we are graduating more school teachers and more Ph.D.s than the market can absorb. Unless education and occupational training are realistically geared to the job market, we create disappointment and frustration. This has been a conspicuous product of the government and missionary schools in some of the former colonies of Asia and Africa. Another way education promotes discontent is by encouraging the habits of critical analysis and (supposedly) independent thinking. The "independent thinking" of most people may, in fact, be no more than the uncritical acceptance of deviant authorities in place of an uncritical acceptance of the conventional authorities; but it nonetheless undermines the conventional authorities.

Totalitarian governments rigidly control the content of education in an attempt to insure loyalty and preclude social criticism, but are only partly successful in this. Our ideology of dissent makes social criticism an inevitable product of education, with the probable result of accelerating changes in our norms and values. Whether this is a desirable or destructive function is a matter of values.

Changing Educational Institutions

Educational services are expanding and will continue to do so. The normal school year is being lengthened at both ends, while a growing proportion of adults are in need of periodic job retraining. Educational financing responsibility is shifting away from the local community to state and federal levels, and this trend will continue.

Our present, very limited, shift of education away from formal schools to on-the-job training, to contract training by the knowledge industry, and to television instruction are possible trends which it is difficult to forecast. The only prediction that can be made with confidence is that tomorrow's educational institutions will differ substantially from today's.

Indicate whether each of the following statements is true or false by writing "T" or "F" in the space provided.

_____ 1.   All societies, even the simplest, have had educational institutions.

_____ 2.   Since the middle ages, education has been a major function of religion.

_____ 3.   In modern societies general education primarily seeks to prepare students for occupational role performance.

_____ 4.   A function of educational institutions in modern societies is to promote discontent and dissent.

_____ 5.   Tomorrow's educational institutions will differ substantially from today's.

Now turn to Answer frame 1[19] on page 132 to check your responses.

Answer frame 1[19]

1. False. The simplest societies had no educational institutions. These arose when it became necessary to train specialized workers who could not easily be trained within the family.

2. True. During the Middle Ages the Roman Catholic Church assumed most of the responsibility for education in Western societies in order to train members for the priesthood. The first schools in the United States were operated by churches.

3. False. Preparation for occupational roles is one manifest function of education, but rapid technological change eliminates jobs. General education seeks to prepare children to learn how to learn so that they can later prepare for jobs that do not yet exist.

4. True. These are latent functions. Discontent is created when people are over-educated for relatively unskilled jobs. Dissent is created when people develop the habits of critical analysis and independent thinking.

5. True. It is very likely that tomorrow's educational institutions will be different than today's, although it is difficult to predict precisely how they will differ.

If you missed any of the above, you should restudy Frame 1[19] before beginning Chapter 20.

chapter 20

RELIGION

Frame 1[20]

It is difficult to define religion in a way which will include all varieties of religious experience. A minimum definition of religion might be *people's institutionalized beliefs and practices concerning the supernatural.* Some would object that this definition excludes a number of small religious groups and persons who are clearly religious in attitude, feelings, and purpose, but who reject supernaturalism in favor of humanistic beliefs. *Humanism* maintains that man has within himself capacities for altruism and good which need only to be unleashed, encouraged,

and directed. Despite humanistic exceptions, most religions are deeply concerned with the supernatural. Many religions, but not all, include a body of moral and ethical ideals which the practice of the religion reinforces. Most religions include elements of *magic, a set of rituals for manipulating supernatural powers,* whereas *prayer is a request addressed to the supernatural powers.* Magic operates mechanically and automatically. Recite the magic words or perform the magic ritual and the result will follow. The effectiveness of magic depends upon the exactness and perfection of the incantation or ritual, not upon the personal purity or moral character of the worker of magic. Prayer, on the other hand, is not mechanical and automatic; answers to prayer depend upon the will of the supernatural powers and upon one's personal relationship to these powers. Personal purity and moral perfection is therefore a prime factor in the efficacy of prayer. A great many different religious beliefs and practices are found among the world's peoples.

Origin of Religious Institutions

Man has entertained supernatural beliefs for hundreds of thousands of years. Prehistoric excavations show burial arrangements which indicate a belief in a life after death. We can only speculate upon just how and when the first beliefs originated. The "dream theory" notes that dreams might easily be interpreted to mean that a person has a spirit apart from the body, with sleep being a temporary departure and death a permanent departure of the spirit from the body. The anthropologist, Malinowski, noted that the Trobriand Islanders conducted magical ceremonies only at moments of emotional stress or danger, and that these rituals relieved anxiety and fear. This suggests that religious beliefs may have originated in man's desire for reassurance and emotional security. Some religions (Christianity) claim that their truths were directly revealed by God to man. This claim cannot be examined or evaluated by science, for scientists have no way of studying supernatural phenomena.

Structure of Religious Institutions

Perhaps no other set of institutions varies so greatly among societies as religious institutions. Unlike many other institutions, the complexity of religious institutions bears no relationship to the complexity of the culture. At any level of cultural complexity, we may find either a very simple set of religious beliefs and practices, or a very

elaborate system of beliefs with extensive and complicated rituals and ceremonies. Many religions have a professionalized clergy; some (Quakers, Mormons) have clerical functions performed by lay members; some have no clerical functions at all, but consist purely of individual or family observances.

Among major religions today, four forms predominate: *ecclesia, denomination, sect,* and *cult.* The *ecclesia* is found where practically all members of a society are, at least nominally, followers of the same faith as embodied in a single organized church. The church is often supported by the state, and is in harmony with the ethos of the culture. The *denomination* is found where several organized churches coexist within a society, with none claiming total membership or state support. Denominations are generally in harmony with most elements of the ethos of the culture, and usually compete vigorously for membership. The *sect* is relatively small, is passionately dedicated to a doctrine which deviates somewhat from the orthodox doctrines, and insistent that members adhere strictly to a rigorous moral code. The sect emphatically rejects important elements of the dominant ethos and institutionalized religion of the culture. It is generally born in a theological dispute, but behind these theological arguments, there often lurk clashing class interests, nationalistic impulses, or other secular motives. If they are successful in surviving and growing, sects tend to grow less critical of the dominant cultural ethos and of other religious bodies, and eventually become denominations (as have the Methodists and Baptists). The *cult* is also a small group which rejects conventional religion and conventional society. It is primarily interested in ecstatic personal experience, and is relatively uninterested in problems of personal morality or public life. It is unlikely to grow large, to make peace with conventional religions, or to become a denomination. Accordingly, cults find members mainly among the uprooted, the alienated, and somewhat anomic people who have no secure place in the mainstream of society.

Indicate whether each of the following statements is true or false by writing "T" or "F" in the space provided.

———— 1. There is no essential difference between magic and prayer.

———— 2. The claim of Christians that their truths were directly revealed by God to man cannot be examined or evaluated by science.

———— 3. There is a direct relationship between the complexity of culture and the complexity of its religious system.

———— 4. If *sects* survive and grow, they tend to become *denominations*.

Now turn to Answer frame 1[20] on page 136 to check your responses.

Frame 2[20]

Manifest and Latent Functions of the Religious Institutions

One of the manifest functions of most religions is to provide answers for man's perplexities. Questions about the meaning and purpose of life, the meaning of death and what comes after death—these are questions which science has not answered and cannot answer.

Another manifest function of religious institutions is to provide comfort, assurance, and release from anxiety. The promise "All things work together for good, unto them that love the Lord," if firmly believed, will sustain one in any crisis. Another manifest function of most (not all) religions is to reinforce the mores and help maintain social control. A belief that gods or spirits are constantly watching us, ever alert to reward good behavior and to punish our misdeeds, is a powerful control. The natives of Madagascar believed that the spirits of their ancestors were hovering around, constantly watching, and that every misfortune, accident, injury, or illness was a punishment for an infraction. Such societies had little difficulty in enforcing the mores!

Prominent among the latent functions of religious institutions is the preservation of the culture. At most times, religion is a powerful conservative force. Some faiths and denominations are so preoccupied with the next world that they encourage an unconcern for the present. Consequently, most revolutionists, before and after Marx, saw religion as the enemy of the revolution. At some times, however, religion has

become a revolutionary force. The Protestant Reformation was a political and economic, as well as a religious, revolution. The missionary schools, quite unwittingly, hastened the end of colonial rule in Africa and Asia. But churches more often support than undermine the existing social system. Even the social reforms which churches sometimes support can be interpreted as enlightened devices for preserving the existing social system.

Another latent function of religious institutions is to influence the development of the other institutions of a society. Education in Catholic and Protestant countries shows significant differences. Family life and religion are closely intertwined. Religion profoundly affects political and economic developments. Max Weber claimed that the Protestant emphasis upon work and individual responsibility provided the drive behind modern capitalism. While the cause-and-effect relationships are not all one-way, in that other institutions also affect religious developments, it remains true that religious institutions have important latent consequences for all the institutions of a society.

A third latent function of religious institutions in many societies, particularly in the U.S., is the sociability and entertainment function. Churches provide opportunities for companionship and "wholesome" recreation to their members, and courtship opportunities and education in leadership to their youth. In some societies, religion provides many holidays and festivals, with elaborate pagentry and spectacle. In many primitive societies, religious festivals include a relaxation of taboos, with heavy drinking and some degree of sexual license adding up to a highly enjoyable orgy. Sometimes it appears that the sociability and entertainment functions are the primary functions of some religions.

The Future of Religion

Communism dismisses religion as the "opiate of the people," and a bourgeois anachronism to be exorcized. Science has now answered many questions which used to be provided by religion.

Who needs religion today? A great many people, it seems. Orthodox religion survives in the Soviet Union after half a century of attempted suppression, and despite the fact that communism itself is a competing religion. Communism (like Christianity) has its body of eternal truths which must be absolutely believed, its concern with heresy and unbelief, its sacred writings, its martyrs and saints, and its demand for primary loyalty of the individual. Communists are not irreligious; communism is their religion.

Now that science has replaced many religious answers with scientific ones, dependence upon supernatural explanations for natural phenomena has declined. Faith in traditional religion has weakened, but this does not mean that people have been growing irreligious. Instead, other forms of mysticism have grown. Believers in astrology are at an all-time high. Eastern mysticism in many varieties is fashionable, and cults of many kinds are flourishing. The followers are not confined to the ignorant and unsophisticated; these movements also thrive on the campus and at the country club.

Apparently man has emotional needs which secular science and efficient technology do not fulfill. Faiths and creeds may change, and particular belief systems and church organizations may die, but religious institutions will not disappear.

True or false?
_____ 1. The functions of religion are latent rather than manifest.
_____ 2. Religion always supports the "establishment" and is the enemy of reform and revolution.
_____ 3. Communism is a religion in competition with Christianity.
_____ 4. We should not expect religion to disappear.

Now turn to Answer frame 2²⁰ on page 136 to check your answers.

Answer frame 1[20]

1. False. Magic *manipulates* supernatural powers but prayer *involves* and *addresses* *requests to* supernatural powers. Magic is mechanical and automatic but prayer is not.
2. True. Science has no way to study supernatural phenomena. Science is limited to explaining observable phenomena.
3. False. At any level of cultural complexity, we may find either a very simple set of religious beliefs and practices, or a very elaborate system of belief with extensive and complicated rituals and ceremonies.
4. True. If the sect survives, increases in size, and tends to be less critical of the dominant cultural ethos and of other religious bodies, then it generally takes on the characteristics of a denomination.

If you missed any of the above, you should restudy Frame 1[20] before turning to Frame 2[20] on page 134.

Answer frame 2[20]

1. False. At least two manifest functions can be identified, i.e., providing answers to questions of ultimates, and providing comfort and release from anxiety.
2. False. Religion has been and continues to be a source of societal change. Examples are the Protestant Reformation and the development of modern capitalism.
3. True. Communism has a sacred belief system, sacred writings, martyrs, and saints. It competes with Christianity (and other religions) for primary loyalty of the individual.
4. True. Man has needs that religion alone can fulfill. Belief systems will change and many religious associations will die, but religion, as a social institution, will not disappear.

If you missed any of the above, you should restudy Frame 2[20] before beginning Chapter 21.

chapter 21

THE FAMILY

Frame 1[21]

A recent press release of a marriage reform bill proposed in Tanzania describes the confusion resulting from political, religious, and social changes. The problem was how many wives a Tanzanian husband might have. The Christians demanded one wife per husband, the Moslems held out for four, the tribalists wanted twenty, while some members of the National Women's Organization asserted women's rights to more than one husband.

Like all institutions, the family is a system of interrelated norms and values that fulfill a set of purposes. Families developed from the need for stable and defined relationships for raising children and assigning the work necessary for their survival. Like all institutions, the family developed gradually from the process of social living. At no time did men assemble and gravely proclaim, "Let us devise a set of familial institutions to meet our need for regularized sex relations and the birth and care of children." Instead, people simply acted in ways which seemed natural and necessary to them, in the course of which certain workable practices became customary, and eventually were institutionalized.

Marriage and the family are found in all societies. The *family* is *a kinship group which provides for the raising of children and for certain other needs.* This definition sounds rather imprecise, because these "other needs" vary from society to society. In very simple societies, the family is the only social institution. They have no schools, for children can learn all they need to know through their family activity; they have no separate religious institutions, for religious ob-

servances are simply a part of family life; no economic institutions, for all work is organized within the family. *Marriage* is defined as *the approved pattern for establishing a family.*

Although there is great variation in family forms and functions, a few norms and values are common to all societies. One is the *principle of legitimacy* mentioned by Malinowski that each child's existence must be legitimated by socially recognized parents. This means that someone must be socially designated as responsible for each child (although not necessarily the biological parent of the child). A second universal characteristic is the *incest taboo,* prohibiting sexual intercourse within certain degrees of relationship. The persons prohibited from sexual access to each other are defined differently in different societies. Parent-child and brother-sister sex relations are forbidden in practically all societies, and the taboo is generally extended to certain other relatives. This taboo, in addition to being genetically desirable, encourages the development of linkages or relationships with other families in the community and helps knit the community together. It prevents sexual competition and jealousies within the family and serves to maintain family unity and stability.

Structure of the Family

There are many ways that family structure can be delineated: by family form, authority patterns, kinship relationships, marriage forms, lines of descent, etc. Most important, perhaps, is family form, nuclear or consanguine. The *nu-*

clear family, also called the conjugal family, consists of one married couple and their children. The consanguine family is based upon the blood relationship rather than the marriage relationship, and consists of the extended clan of blood relatives together with their mates and their children.

In our society, the nuclear family is the only very important family unit. The consanguine family may gather for occasional ceremonials, but all the important duties and responsibilities are assigned to the nuclear family. In many societies, the consanguine family is the important unit, and the nuclear family hardly identifiable. Responsibility for child care may be widely shared, with a woman having much the same duties and feelings toward her nephews and nieces as toward her own children. In the consanguine family as it exists in many societies, a man's responsibilities are toward his sisters' children, while his own children are the responsibility of his wife's brothers. In other words, his responsibilities and his emotional ties are to the family in which he was raised, rather than the family into which he has married. Stated differently, the nuclear family consists of a couple and their children, with a fringe of other relatives, while the consanguine family consists of a set of brothers and sisters and the children of these sisters, with a fringe of spouses. (The children of the brothers belong to their wives' families.)

This seems very odd to us, for, like all peoples, we are ethnocentric. Either pattern "works" satisfactorily within a setting of appropriate supporting norms and values (illustrating the concept of cultural relativity). All that is essential is that the society have a dependable pattern for tagging some male with responsibility for each child. We normally rely upon biological paternity for this; some other societies rely upon blood relationship (between the mother and her male relatives). Of the two, the blood relationship is the more dependable basis for assigning parental responsibilities, for it is permanent and indissoluble, whereas the marital relationship between biological parents may be severed, leaving the child's parental linkages less secure.

Marriage shows a similar variation. The American ideal of romantic love leading to blissful marriage forever after is so ingrained in the Western way of life that anything less we scorn with appropriately ethnocentric disdain. While the love basis for marriage is becoming more widespread, marriage in much of the world is generally based upon pragmatic considerations of suitability, family linkage, property, etc.

All societies impose limitations upon whom one may marry. One set of requirements is called exogamy and endogamy. Exogamy is the requirement that one may marry only outside some prohibited degree of relationship. All societies require that one's mate be from outside the nuclear family, and many societies extend this to include persons from the same clan, village, or perhaps with the same surname. Disregard of the rules of exogamy would be incest. Endogamy requires that marriage must be within certain specified categories, such as clan, village, tribe, religion, race, class, nationality. Every society has both exogamous and endogamous requirements for mate selection. The United States is exogamous in forbidding marriage within several degrees of blood relationship (varying somewhat between states), and endogamous in encouraging (by social pressure but not legal compulsion) marriage within the same race, religion, class, and ethnic group.

Another variation in marriage form is in the number of mates. Our value of monogamy (one wife to one husband) is so thoroughly ingrained that it is enforced by law. However, most societies have historically permitted polygamy, a plurality of mates. The Greenland Eskimo of the last century practiced both forms of polygamy: polygyny, or several wives to one husband, and polyandry, with several husbands to one wife, according to the hunting talents of the men. Only the most successful hunters could provide for a cluster of wives, who served as symbols of his success, while several inept hunters had to share a single wife.

Each of the other features of family structure listed earlier also varies between societies, but space forbids their description. Each is a practical expedient for meeting certain problems (tracing descent, deciding where to live, defining duties to relatives) within a particular culture.

Indicate whether each of the following statements is true or false by writing "T" or "F" in the space provided.

_____ 1.   In very simple societies, the family is the only social institution.

_____ 2.   There is such great variation in family forms and functions that no norms and values are common to all societies.

_____ 3.   In our society, the consanguine family is the most important family unit.

_____ 4.   Mate selection in the United States is limited by requirements of exogamy and endogamy.

Now turn to Answer frame 1²¹ on page 140 to check your responses.

Frame 2²¹

Functions of the Family

The first and most obvious function of the family is *reproduction*. In all societies, children are typically produced and raised by families. A related function is the *regulation of sexual activity*. Marriage provides legal and social legitimation for children and attaches responsibility for bearing children. (The fact that a number of societies have no word for the "illegitimate" child, and readily accept into the family any children born before marriage, does not alter the fact that most children are born and raised within families.) No society in history has permitted unstructured and unrestrained sexual relations for very long; irresponsible sex is too disruptive. Although many societies allow structured forms of premarital or extramarital relations, and are more or less tolerant of violations of the sex mores, there is no known society that gives complete license for promiscuous behavior.

Another major function of the family is *socialization*. The first few years of a child's life are spent almost entirely within the family, where the foundations of personality are laid before he begins to encounter other influences. All the basic perspectives, values, and norms are presented in this intimate atmosphere. The powerful effects of this early socialization generally prevent one from seriously questioning the political, religious, and moral values of his parents until he is an adult and has left the family setting (and sometimes not even then). While most adolescents go through a partial and temporary rejection of parental values, they generally retain more of their parents' values than they realize.

In this socialization process, parents function as role models for their children to copy. Some parents present poor role models as they themselves are ineffective in their family roles or in meeting the demands of social life. Their children have little opportunity to observe closely successful role models, and they repeat the cycle of ineffective life adjustment.

Another function is *status ascription*. The statement that one can choose his friends but not his family is trite but true. Children born to poor parents tend to perpetuate the pattern of poverty because of the limited opportunities that lower status parents can provide, and because of the limited expectations that others hold for the children of the poor. Children of high-status parents not only have greater opportunities, they also have a different pattern of expectations to live up to.

Other functions include the *affectional* function, meeting people's need for affection, intimacy, and someone to care about them. The *protective* function fills the need for physical, social, and psychological insulation from the threats to survival. The *economic* function provides for the assigning of work, the holding of possessions, and the distribution of goods necessary for survival of the family.

The Changing American Family

The nation's billboards proclaim that "the family that plays together stays together." This

Answer frame 1²¹

1. True. They have no schools, no separate religious associations, and no separate economic associations.
2. False. In spite of great variation in form and function, families in all societies recognize the norms of *legitimacy* and *incest taboo*.
3. False. The consanguine family may gather for occasional ceremonials, but all the important duties and responsibilities are assigned to the nuclear family.
4. True. The United States is exogamous in forbidding marriage within several degrees of blood relationship and endogamous in encouraging marriage within the same race, religion, class, and ethnic group.

If you missed any of the above, you should restudy Frame 1²¹ before turning to Frame 2²¹ on page 139.

Frame 2²¹ continued

slogan indicates how family life has changed. Concern over the "generation gap" and the "parental establishment" shows that both parents and children are aware of the needs of a changing society.

The American family used to be united by shared work under the watchful eye and patriarchal control of the father. Marriage was basically a working partnership and incidentally, if at all, a romantic adventure. Marriage was an economic necessity, for a man could not easily manage a farm by himself. A good husband was a "good provider," and a good wife was strong, fertile, frugal, and dutiful. Children were an economic asset and a form of social security. Family unity was an economic and social necessity, for each member had a contribution to make.

Industrialization and urbanization have transformed the family. Farm population fell, and the farm family no longer provides the norm for family life. Urban employment took the father away from the home, and often the mother as well. With greater legal, economic, and social equality, all roles within the family have changed. Families have become less authoritarian and patriarchal, and more democratic and equalitarian. Family size decreased as children ceased to be an economic asset. Institutions are arrangements for meeting human needs, and as the needs change, the institutions change accordingly.

Not only the structure, but also the functions of the family have changed. The reproductive and sexual regulation functions continue, as most sexual intercourse remains marital and most children are born and raised within families. The socialization function remains important, with the family still the primary socializing agency. The affectional and companionship functions are more important than ever. Our high rate of mobility and the decline of neighborhood and extended family ties makes us more dependent upon the immediate family for human response. The status ascription function is somewhat less important than formerly, as facilities for upward mobility have been expanded; yet family background remains the most reliable predictor of one's adult social status. The protective functions have declined, as other institutions have absorbed much of the family's responsibility for care of the sick, the aged, the impoverished, and the handicapped. The economic functions have shown the greatest change. Only a few families today form an economic producing unit, and the economically self-sufficient family of the past is gone. The family is no longer united by shared work, but by shared affection and companionship.

Divorce has become common and respectable. Premarital sex relations have become somewhat more common, and greatly more visible and unconcealed. Some see these changes as signs of family "decay," while others see them as adaptations of the family to changing needs and values.

Label each of the following statements as true or false.

——————1. The family, like most major social institutions, has only one major function.

——————2. Once young people leave the family house, they generally lose their parents' values.

——————3. Both the structure and the functions of the American family have changed.

——————4. Most sociologists agree that the American family is in a period of "decay."

Now turn to Answer frame 2[21] on page 142 to check your answers.

chapter 22

MINORITY/MAJORITY RELATIONS

Frame 1[22]

Definition and Classification of Races

No fully satisfactory definition of the term "race" is possible because of the overlapping of the criteria. The usual definition is biological, defining a *race* as *a category of people sharing a particular combination of inherited physical traits.* But there are, in fact, no collections of people, *all* of whom share a particular combination of physical traits, and which are shared by nobody except this particular people. To illustrate, suppose that all people on earth were either tall, slender, and light, or short, stocky, and dark. Then there would be two separate and distinct races. But each of a dozen or more physical traits (skin color, height, body build, hair color, hair texture, and several others) varies by infinite degrees through a wide range. A further difficulty is that these traits rarely come in dependable combinations. Thus, a tall people may be light or dark; a light-skinned people may have light or dark hair. A third difficulty is that, even with a particular people, there may be wide individual variations. The "Nordic type" is tall, blonde, and blue-eyed; but only a minority of Nordics have all these traits. Consequently, classifying people into races according to physical traits entails a lot of overlapping, and many arbitrary assignments.

A few sociologists have abandoned biological definitions of race. Noting the difficulties above, they suggest that race is, in practice, whatever people say it is. They contend that "race" is not a biological reality but is a socially significant

Answer frame 2²¹

1. False. There are several major functions of the family. Among these are reproduction, socialization, and status ascription.
2. False. While most sons and daughters go through a partial and temporary rejection of their parents' values, they generally retain more of their parents' values than they realize.
3. True. Families have become less patriarchal and more democratic. Also, some traditional functions, e.g., protection, have declined as other institutions have assumed them.
4. False. Sociologists try not to make moral judgments. Some people see increasing divorce rates and premarital sex relations as signs of "decay," while others see them as changes.

If you missed any of the above, you should reread Frame 2²¹ before beginning Chapter 22 on page 141.

Frame 1²² continued

myth. These sociologists would define a *race* as *any category of people who are generally defined and treated as a race*. By this definition, the Jews, who are biologically quite mixed, would nonetheless be a race because people think they are. In other words, the social designation of any particular assortment of people as a race, and treatment of them as a race, makes them a race. A race is, then, a number of people who are lumped together as a race. This concept of race is less common than the traditional biological concept, but is occasionally found in the literature.

Most classifications of races pose three major racial stocks—Caucasoid, Mongoloid, and Negroid—with a number of subdivisions of each, plus several independent and marginal categories, for a total of fifteen or eighteen. Racially mixed persons are variously classified. In the U.S. and South Africa, all Caucasoid-Negroid mixtures, regardless of proportion, are classed as Negroid if there is any trace of Negroid features at all, showing that social definition takes precedence over biological inheritance.

Ethnic Groups

While races are identified by their physical or biological differences, ethnic groups are based upon a shared cultural tradition. (The term "group" is technically incorrect here, and "category" would be more correct, but "ethnic group" is the common sociological usage.) Literally, an ethnic group shares a common *ethos*. Most ethnic groups are nationality groups—Germans, Poles, Puerto Ricans—but a few ethnic groups, such as Jews or Hindus, are based upon religion.

The U.S. has an abundance of ethnic groups. The immigrating Germans, Irish, Italians, Poles, and Slavs tended to settle in compact colonies, clustering for economic and emotional support, preserving much of the native culture. Within relatively few generations, they become assimilated and integrated into the larger society. Yet their ethnic identity remains, along with some attitudinal and behavior differences, most visible at election time as candidates bid for the "ethnic vote."

In some countries, far greater ethnic group differences have persisted for hundreds of years, even threatening the political unity and stability of the state. Examples would include the Basques in Spain, the Serbs and Croats in Yugoslavia, and the Flemings and Walloons in Belgium. In some others, such as Switzerland, two or more ethnic groups live in relative national unity and harmony.

Scientific Facts about Race Differences

Races obviously differ in their inheritance of physical characteristics—color, size and shape of body, facial features, etc. There is no substantial evidence that any of these physical features is linked with any inherited difference in learning potential, personality inclination, or behavior predisposition. The most bigoted racist, interestingly, does not maintain that differences in skin color or hair texture *within* his own race are indicative of superiority or inferiority! Many people firmly believe in innate race differences in ability, but no convincing scientific evidence of such a difference has yet been presented, so scientists doubt that there is any difference. Great differences in the *current behavior* of different races can easily be observed, but there is no evidence that these are due to any innate or inherited differences, and a great deal of evidence that they are learned. Therefore, unless and until convincing scientific evidence is presented, virtually all scientists agree in assuming that all race differences in behavior—in personality and achievement (except purely physical behavior) —are a product of differences in group history, opportunity, and reward.

In the above sentence, the word "assumed" is used. It is extremely difficult to *prove* anything conclusive about comparative racial abilities. In any scientific comparison, effects of one variable can be measured only when all other variables are held constant. The variable of a possible racial inequality in learning capacity (or

anything else) can be measured only when all other variables—tradition, motivation, opportunity, reward—are held constant. Only when two races have lived and worked under conditions of equal opportunity and reward for a long time can we draw any scientific conclusions about their comparative levels of innate capacity. In the absence of evidence of innate race differences in capacity, scientists assume that all races have equal intellectual or learning capacity.

Most popular thought about race differences has been little more than a rationalization of wishes and interests. To cite a single example, before about 1940 the exclusion of blacks from major league professional baseball was "explained" by the assumption that blacks lack the fine coordination necessary. Considerable medical and physiological evidence was offered in support of this claim. After the first handful of black players were signed by a few clubs, and other managers discovered that black players worked harder and cheaper than whites, the problem of black coordination somehow disappeared. Black athletes today are disproportionately numerous in professional baseball and football, but relatively rare in golf, tennis, and polo. Do you think the reasons are biological or cultural?

Indicate whether each of the following statements is true or false by writing "T" or "F" in the space provided.

_____ 1. No fully satisfactory definition of the term *race* is possible.
_____ 2. Ethnic groups are based upon a shared cultural tradition.
_____ 3. The observed differences in behavior of different races are due to inherited biological differences.
_____ 4. The reason there are so few black athletes in sports like golf and tennis is that blacks have less natural aptitude for these sports.

Now turn to Answer frame 1²² on page 144 to check your responses.

Frame 2²²

Historical Background of Racism

The ancient world was not race conscious. Religion and nationality were important as a basis for treatment of persons, but race, as a biological category of people, had not occurred to

them. The Bible makes no mention of "race" in the modern sense of a biological classification of people. Many ancient peoples felt themselves superior to all others, but this had nothing to do with race. Ancient and medieval slavery was not based upon race or color, and carried no imputa-

Answer frame 1²²

1. True. The usual biological definition of race entails a lot of overlapping and many arbitrary assignments. In addition, social definition takes precedence over biological inheritance.
2. True. While racial categories are identified by their physical differences, ethnic groups are based upon a shared—national or religious—culture.
3. False. There is no evidence that these are due to any innate or inherited differences. There is a great deal of evidence that these observed differences are learned.
4. False. The reasons are cultural, i.e., these are traditionally upper-middle and upper-class nonteam sports, played primarily in private clubs. Also, the number of available positions is few.

If you missed any of the above, you should restudy Frame 1²² before turning to Frame 2²² on page 143.

Frame 2²² continued

tion of natural inferiority. Instead, slavery was a misfortune which might happen to anyone, through losing a war or going bankrupt.

The concept of race, and notions of race superiority and inferiority, developed when the European colonial expansion created a need for a rationale to legitimate the acts of colonial powers. By defining the simple primitives as inferior, the colonial powers were "doing a service" to the primitive tribes by managing their affairs, meanwhile relieving them of their natural resources and conducting an immensely profitable slave trade, and giving them Christianity as compensation for any minor inconveniences. The technological superiority of the whites only confirmed the natural inferiority of the natives, while their illiteracy proved their inability to learn.

In order to maintain the myth of the ignorant jungle savage, it was necessary to suppress the history of the impressive African kingdoms, and only within the past few years has their history been rediscovered. Early social research, along with Biblical interpretation, conveniently supported the assumptions of racial inferiority. More recent, more objective research has shown the theory of racial superiority to be scientifically insupportable. An occasional scientist (Shuey in 1958 and Jensen in 1969) creates a momentary stir by publishing a warmed-over defense of innate race differences. Without exception, they ignore or minimize the subtle effects of social and cultural influences upon learning; conse-

quently, they fail to convince their fellow scientists.

Theories of Race Prejudice

A *race prejudice* is a *tendency to attribute certain characteristics to a person or group because of racial identity*, instead of discovering his characteristics through observing him as a person. Prejudice literally means to pre-judge—to make a judgment without observing the factual reality. Prejudice is expressed, for example, in attributing either special musical talent or inferior intellectual capacity to a person because he is black.

It is difficult to find many places in the world where different races live together in harmony. Either hatred and conflict or an uncomfortable accommodation are normal. There are a number of theories of why race (or ethnic) prejudice arises. Space permits only a brief outline (adapted from Brewton Berry, *Race and Ethnic Relations*).

A. *Economic Theories.*
   1. The economic competition theory: Whenever racial or ethnic groups compete, prejudice and hostility develop.
   2. The economic exploitation theory: Prejudice arises as a justification for economic exploitation.
B. *Symbolic Theories.* A number of theories, some of them fantastic, see prejudice as aris-

ing when we perceive in other groups certain traits which we fear, hate, or envy. The group comes to symbolize what we hate, fear, or envy, so we come to hate that group.

C. *Psychological Theories.*
   1. The *scapegoat* theory: We shift the blame for our failures and troubles upon a racial or ethnic out-group.
   2. The *frustration-aggression theory:* Frustration creates aggressive impulses which are released against racial or ethnic out-groups.
   3. The *Social neurosis* theory: Prejudice is a symptom of a maladjusted, neurotic personality; the secure, well-adjusted personality is more tolerant.

Each one of these theories has some evidence to support it, and each probably explains the development of prejudice among some persons or in some circumstances. It is likely that prejudice is a reaction which arises in any of a variety of situations.

Patterns of Racial or Ethnic Relations

The arrangements worked out between racial or ethnic groups fall into two classifications: (1) racist patterns, based upon the assumption that innate differences or irreconcilable conflicts make harmonious contact impossible, and (2) equalitarian patterns, which assume the possibility of harmonious interaction as equals.

Racist Patterns of Relationship. ANNIHILATION. There have been many efforts to exterminate another racial or ethnic group. Examples would include early Hebrews and Canaanites, Lutherans and Mennonites, American settlers and Indians, Hitler and the Jews, and many others. A few peoples were totally exterminated, such as the native population of Tasmania, whom the whites hunted as sport or for dogmeat. But total annihilation is seldom successful because, as with the Hebrews, American settlers, or modern Germans, some of the exterminator groups develop sympathies for the victims, or some of the victims manage to escape, or exhaustion ends the massacre before it is complete. The legal term for attempted annihilation is *genocide.*

EXPULSION OR PARTITION. A common way of handling a racial or ethnic minority is to expel them. History provides many examples—the expulsion of the Moors from Spain, of Catholics from England to Ireland, removal of American Indians to reservations, post–World War II removal of Germans from Slavic countries, and many others. Expulsion not only removes an unwelcome people but permits seizure of their lands and property.

Partition divides a country between its racial or ethnic groups, with a mutual exchange of populations to solve the minority problem. Examples include the division of colonial India into India and Pakistan, the partition of Northern from Southern Ireland, the *apartheid* program in South Africa, the United Nations' proposed boundaries for Israel (rejected by the Arab states and revised by warfare), and the proposed partition of Crete. The black nationalists in the U.S. are proposing partition, asking that a few of the United States be given over to black occupation and self-rule. Partition is seldom fully successful, for boundaries are disputed, many individuals usually suffer property losses, and the exchange of populations is rarely completed, leaving some minority members stranded among hostile neighbors. While partition may sometimes be the only practical alternative to endless warfare, the failures of partition are revealed by the troubles in all of the above areas.

SEGREGATION AND DISCRIMINATION. Segregation means that the racial or ethnic groups inhabit the same localities, but live, work, play, worship, and go to school separately with a minimum of social interaction with each other. While it is theoretically possible for two equal-status groups to segregate themselves from each other, segregation is virtually always accompanied by discrimination and inequality of status. *Discrimination* consists of unequal access to opportunities and rewards. It is sometimes defined as "the unequal treatment of equals." Occasionally there is *self-segregation,* such as the medieval Jews banding together in the ghetto for mutual protection, or the pleasant compounds which Western diplomats and managers established in non-Western countries for their own comfort and convenience. But segregation and discrimination are normally imposed upon one racial or ethnic group by another, generally for the purpose of economic exploitation and prestige satisfactions for the dominant people.

The rationale for segregation is that it will reduce conflict by reducing contacts between the races or ethnic groups. But segregation never prevents *all* contacts; it generally maintains exploitative contacts while preventing equality contacts, thus perpetuating prejudices, misconceptions, and conflict.

Is each of the following true or false?
_____ 1. The ancient world was intensely race conscious.
_____ 2. The theory of racial superiority was an ideological development of European colonists.
_____ 3. Relations among races in the world are characterized more by cooperation and assimilation than by conflict.
_____ 4. The causes of race prejudice are purely economic.
_____ 5. Segregation is very seldom accompanied by discrimination and inequality of status.

Now turn to Answer frame 2[22] on page 148 to check your answers.

Frame 3[22]

Equalitarian Patterns of Race and Ethnic Relationship. CULTURAL PLURALISM. In cultural pluralism, each racial or ethnic group maintains some degree of autonomy, retaining its own customs, language, and religion. Yet all are a part of the society, without segregation or discrimination. Switzerland is the classic example, with its French, German, and Italian populations living quite harmoniously within the Swiss Confederation. The United States is pluralistic in religion and ethnic groups, but has not followed racial pluralism (except possibly in Hawaii).

INTEGRATION. Whereas cultural pluralism seeks harmonious cooperation between groups preserving different subcultures, and segregation has different groups participating unequally in the same culture, integration seeks to have all races and ethnic groups participate equally in the same culture. Integration implies equality of opportunity and reward; equal access to jobs, housing, schools, and political and economic power; equal pay for equal work; and no discrimination based upon race or ethnic identity. Successful examples are hard to find, with Hawaii one of the best.

AMALGAMATION. Amalgamation refers to the interbreeding of racial and ethnic groups until they eventually disappear as identifiable groups. (Where racial intermixture is infrequent or disapproved, the more value-laden term, *miscegenation,* is likely to be used.) In Hawaii, amalgamation has almost eliminated the pure Polynesian, while in the continental U.S. most blacks have some white ancestry and more whites than is generally realized have some black ancestry. The Portuguese population has thoroughly absorbed a substantial Negro infusion. Theoretically, amalgamation could end all separate races by a thorough intermixture into one common human race, but such a development is most improbable, and in any event would take thousands of years to complete.

Adjustment to Prejudice and Discrimination

Racial or ethnic groups which are the victims of prejudice and discrimination must make some sort of response to this treatment. Scholars have prepared several lists of responses which differ slightly in wording but which generally describe the following responses.

Emotional Acceptance. Some people have been so successfully socialized for their inferior role and status that they accept their "place" as proper and right. They honestly believe themselves to be what the dominant group has proclaimed them to be, and accept their treatment as just and benevolent. These persons are probably the most happy and contented members of their race or ethnic group. But a self-fulfilling prophecy is set in operation. When a group is described as lazy and shiftless, and treated as lazy and shiftless, and denied opportunity and reward for ambition, many members of that group will actually become lazy, shiftless, and unambitious. These traits are intelligent, functionally useful adjustments to lack of opportunity.

Some sociologists consider this to be the most important single insight to be found in the study of race relations. It can be stated in several ways: (1) a racial or ethnic group tends to become whatever the dominant group says it is; (2) laziness and shiftlessness are intelligent adjustments to a lack of equal opportunity and reward; (3) whatever a suppressed group has become, it has become as a result of the conditions of life forced upon it over the generations by the dominant group.

Avoidance or Withdrawal. Those who suffer prejudice and discrimination sometimes withdraw from all but the unavoidable contacts with the dominant group. Self-segregation is an avoidance technique.

Submissive Adaptation or Manipulation. Many are resentful of the discrimination they suffer, yet attempt to manipulate "the system" to their advantage. They show an outward deference to the demands and vanities of the dominant group, and work hard and behave as the dominant group approves in order to "get ahead."

Aggression. Many are emotionally unable to practice any of the three forms of accommodation listed above. Their anger bursts out in aggressions against someone—against each other,

against another oppressed group, or against the dominant group in the form of insults ("honkie"), assaults, riots, and various attacks upon the persons and properties of the dominant group.

The *oppression psychosis* is an exaggerated sensitivity to oppression, which develops among some of those who experience oppression. A psychosis is a mental disorder which prevents one from accurately perceiving reality. One who has developed the oppression psychosis will interpret everything unpleasant that happens to him as an act of oppression. His perception of reality is distorted in that he imagines discrimination even when it is not present.

Organized Protest. When the aggression is not a spontaneous outburst of anger but is part of an organized, calculated campaign to change things, it falls under organized protest. This includes all organized, systematic efforts to promote changes, including voter registration drives, pressure for legislative enactments, prosecution of court litigation, economic boycotts, strikes, demonstrations, confrontations, and planned riots, disorders, and acts of terrorism. (Note that many of the above acts can be simply spontaneous acts of aggression, unplanned and usually unproductive; or they can be part of a carefully planned campaign of action.) A continuing debate rages over which forms of organized protest are effective, and under what conditions and for what goals, and which forms are self-defeating.

This brief chapter barely lays a foundation for beginning to study the problem of race relations and the resolutions of racial conflicts. That problem is another entire course of study.

Label each of the following statements as true or false.
_____ 1. "Cultural pluralism" is easier to achieve in religion and ethnicity than it is in race.
_____ 2. The dominant social group can create a "lazy, shiftless, and unambitious" minority group by denying the minority group opportunity to achieve and reward for ambition.
_____ 3. Self-segregation is an avoidance technique.
_____ 4. The civil rights movement clearly proved that planned riots were the most effective form of organized protest.

Now turn to Answer frame 3²² on page 148 to check your answers.

Answer frame 2²²

1. False. The ancient world was not race conscious. Religion and nationality were important as a basis for treatment of persons, but race, as a biological category, had not occurred to them.
2. True. By defining the natives as inferior, the colonial powers justified their economic exploitation and missionary enterprises.
3. False. It is difficult to find many places in the world where different races live together in harmony. Either conflict or an uncomfortable accommodation is typical.
4. False. Each theory has some evidence to support it, and no theory is completely adequate to explain all prejudices.
5. False. Segregation and discrimination are typical and are normally imposed upon one racial or ethnic group by another. Generally, this is done for the purpose of economic exploitation and political power.

If you missed any of the above, you should review Frame 2²² before turning to Frame 3²² on page 146.

Answer frame 3²²

1. True. In cultural pluralism all groups are a part of the society, without segregation or discrimination. The U.S. is pluralistic in religion and ethnicity, but has not followed racial pluralism.
2. True. This is a "self-fulfilling prophecy." The minority has been so successfully socialized into their inferior roles that they accept their identity as proper and right.
3. True. Those who suffer prejudice and discrimination sometimes withdraw from all but the unavoidable contacts with the dominant group. Self-segregation becomes an adjustment to prejudice and discrimination.
4. False. Urban riots were not a part of the civil rights movement. Which forms of organized protest are effective is a subject of continuing debate.

If you missed any of the above, you should reread Frame 3²² before beginning Chapter 23 on page 149.

chapter 23

COLLECTIVE BEHAVIOR

Frame 1[23]

How can a group of respectable citizens be transformed into a bloodthirsty mob? Why may workers burn down the factory which provides their jobs? Why may a peaceful neighborhood be suddenly transformed into an inferno of hate and destruction? Why do ladies' hemlines go up, down, up, down? What explains the popularity of pop art, long hair, and "rock" music?

Nature of Collective Behavior

Under the heading of *collective behavior* we study the *temporary behavior of groups and publics*. Although it occurs often enough to observe frequently, collective behavior is not a regular routine of daily life. Collective behavior is *unstructured and spontaneous* in that there are no set rules or procedures to follow. What makes the behavior unique is that it is *irrational and unpredictable*. It is not reason that impels the audience to tear down the goalposts at the homecoming game, nor is it entirely predictable. Whether the posts topple depends upon the climate or atmosphere of the game, the mood of the audience, the emergence of leadership, and perhaps still other variables.

The spontaneous and unpredictable aspects of collective behavior make it difficult to study scientifically, but not impossible. To be sure, collective behavior cannot be easily duplicated in the controlled conditions of the laboratory. A social scientist cannot sink a cruise ship or burn a theater to observe how people react to a disaster, but by careful *ex post facto* observation (collecting eyewitness accounts) and by dili-

gently reconstructing the sequence of events, he can identify and formulate patterns of reaction. In this fashion, past observations can be used to test predictions. After collective behavior is over, the participants can be located, interviewed, and compared with control groups to see wherein the participants differ from other people. Occasionally, a social scientist is present, so the sequence of events can be recorded by a trained observer. Because of the complex nature of collective behavior, the theoretical formulations are not entirely satisfactory. Neil Smelser (*Theory of Collective Behavior*) gives a series of requisites.

His first requirement is *structural conduciveness* of the society. Complex urbanized societies are more prone to mass behavior because of their masses of people. By definition, collective behavior requires a collectivity of people. Scattered rural populations with very little geographic mobility are difficult, although not impossible, to assemble and arouse to mass action. The highly anonymous, transient, urban life of Western societies is more conducive to extreme collective actions.

Structural strain is a second requirement. A group may harbor fears of repression, anxieties about the future, and a feeling that they have no control of the situation. The sense of injustice, whether imagined or genuine, creates resentments and hostilities. Thus the minority groups smarting under discrimination, the angry poor and the fearful rich, those suffering downward class mobility or status anxiety—all these are candidates for extreme action.

The *belief that extreme action may alleviate*

the sources of strain justifies the action. The action may be realistically directed at the source of strain, as when a hated group is attacked or massacred; or the action may be directed at persons or objects unrelated to the source of the strain, as in aimless window smashing.

Some *precipitating events* are generally necessary to give direction to the action. Our urban ghettos are often described as "riots waiting to happen" as soon as some igniting spark falls upon the tinder.

Mobilization for action follows quickly upon the heels of the precipitating events. Crowds gather, rumors spread, spontaneous leadership arises, and action begins.

The *operation of social controls* may halt collective behavior at any of the above points. Short-run measures such as effective police action, or long-run measures such as changes in social policy, may prevent action.

Crowd Behavior

Whereas most other groups have a more permanent structure, a crowd is a *temporary collection of people acting together.* A crowd is more than a collectivity or an aggregation; the members of a crowd have a common focal interest that they pursue collectively. The crowd is characterized by *anonymity,* as individual identity merges into the collectivity, so that it is not Joe Green throwing a bottle—it is the crowd acting collectively. The size of the group and the temporary nature of its existence remove the sense of individuality from the members. The usual restraints upon personal behavior are relaxed and his behavior is less likely to be censured. Anonymity transfers personal responsibility from the individual to the crowd. People in crowds are capable of highly irresponsible actions because they do not feel accountable as individuals and probably will not be held to account as individuals.

Crowd behavior is *impersonal,* like all group interaction. The crowd may have nothing against Joe Green, a police officer; but they will pelt any police officer within throwing distance. Thus in riots, killing and looting is indiscriminate. A friend of the author's who is on the riot squad of a police agency reports that during lulls in a riot at a major university, he frequently engaged in a friendly exchange of dirty stories with the rioters; then when the action resumed, he again received verbal and physical abuse. During lulls in the confrontation, people interacted as individuals, but when the crowd action resumed, they again became impersonal antagonists.

The unstructured nature of crowds makes for a high degree of *suggestibility.* Any action suggested by a self-appointed leader may be uncritically followed. *Social contagion* refers to the escalation of excitement as crowd members stimulate and respond to one another. These characteristics of crowd behavior—anonymity, impersonality, suggestibility, and social contagion—all work together to produce excesses of violence and cruelty from which many crowd members, individually, would recoil in horror and disbelief.

There is also a degree of selectivity in the membership of crowds. Crowds tend to attract and hold those who have resentments and hostilities to express. The lonely, the bored, and the alienated seek crowds as a refuge. The excesses of crowd behavior reflect the emotions of its members, protected by the cloak of anonymity. Thus the frustrated, the irresponsible, and the embittered and hate-filled can use the crowd to unload their suppressed antagonisms.

Indicate whether each of the following statements is true or false by writing "T" or "F" in the space provided.

   _____ 1. The scientific study of collective behavior is made difficult because such behavior involves large numbers of people.

   _____ 2. The theoretical explanations of collective behavior are not entirely satisfactory.

   _____ 3. The reduction (or loss) of external social controls enables collective behavior to occur.

   _____ 4. Individual responsibility is increased in crowd behavior.

_____5.   The membership of violent crowds is usually representative of the larger community.

Now turn to Answer frame 1²³ on page 152 to check your responses.

Frame 2²³

Limitations upon Crowd Behavior. This discussion should not suggest that crowds are totally uncontrolled, for there are several limitations upon crowd behavior. One is found in the *mores of the culture.* Crowds commit only those acts which carry some degree of cultural support, even though the acts may also carry some condemnation. But without some support in the mores, the acts do not happen. Lynchings took place only where many of the people approved of lynchings as a means of presumably justified punishment. Mobs in our society may loot, burn, and even kill; but they never eat their victims. The mores of the culture set the limits of crowd behavior.

The *leadership* that emerges within crowds often determines whether they will remain orderly, become only mildly disorderly, or turn into a frenzy of destruction. Leadership in crowds is situational and unstructured, and is "up for grabs." Crowds will generally follow anyone whose own characteristics enable him to establish rapport, provide clear direction, and offer suggestions reasonably in accord with any of their several behavior inclinations. Often the most excitable member seizes leadership as he arouses the greatest emotional response. Leaders gain support by first building emotional tension by a recital of grievances, and then suggesting action to relieve the tension. Crowd leadership seldom lasts long, for it is situational and seldom transferable to stable long-term leadership positions.

Police control of crowd behavior is growing more professional. Many police agencies are now using the technical knowledge of the social sciences in seeking to control crowd behavior. Most of the fatal shootings in recent confrontations have been committed not by police with riot training, but by police and National Guardsmen with no special training in the handling of crowds.

Some Forms of Crowd Behavior

The *audience* is a group to which stimuli are directed. The stimuli are mainly one-way, but at times considerable interaction can develop. There is some degree of communication between members and emotion can be socially contagious, but audience reaction is generally directed and controlled. If reaction gets out of control the audience becomes a mob. "Rock" music festivals often become so disorderly that it is difficult to find a community which will tolerate them.

A *mob* is a highly emotional crowd taking aggressive action. Their actions are generally uncontrolled, or controlled by rapidly shifting leadership, and directed against any convenient symbol of their resentment.

A *riot* is a mob engaged in violent conflict or destruction. The behavior expresses hostility against a hated group, or against the status quo, and is intended to disrupt the routine of events. Behavior is extreme and violent but it may not be entirely irrational. While often spontaneous, riots are sometimes staged for the purpose of dramatizing grievances and arousing corrective action. In recent urban ghetto riots, the burned buildings seldom included those agencies which ghetto residents perceived as helpful to them.

A *panic* is a collective flight based upon hysterical fear. Panics occur when people perceive a danger, with inadequate escape routes. Decisive leadership with clear directions for orderly action can often avert a panic, if delivered before panic begins.

A *rumor* is a widely distributed report unsubstantiated by fact. People tend to accept rumors uncritically if they fit in with their prejudices and confirm their hostilities, and to reject, equally uncritically, all rumors which do not confirm their prejudices and antipathies. In short, people believe rumors because they want to believe them.

The *fad* is a trivial, short-lived variation in

Answer frame 1[23]

1. False. It is the spontaneous and irrational aspects of collective behavior that make it difficult to study scientifically.
2. True. Because of the complex nature of collective behavior, the theoretical formulations are not entirely satisfactory. There are several competing "theories" of collective behavior.
3. True. The operation of social controls may halt collective behavior at any of the points Smelser lists. Short-run measures such as effective police action or long-run measures such as changes in social policy may prevent collective action.
4. False. Anonymity transfers personal responsibility from the individual to the crowd. People in crowds are capable of highly irresponsible actions because they do not feel accountable as individuals and probably will not be held to account as individuals.
5. False. Violent crowds tend to attract and hold those who have resentments and hostilities to express. The lonely, the bored, and the alienated seek crowds as a refuge.

If you missed any of the above, you should restudy Frame 1[23] before turning to Frame 2[23] on page 151.

Frame 2[23] continued

behavior. Fads include catch words and phrases, "snappy" retorts, decorative details of dress, and other noticeable trivialities. Fads develop and spread from the desire to attract attention and be different, but cannot be too greatly different lest they bring not status but ridicule. Once the fad has diffused throughout the population, it confers no status and quickly dies. A current popular song that begins, "What's the use of being different now when it's different now that looks alike," is an apt illustration.

Fashions are less trivial and more expensive than fads, and therefore somewhat longer-lived. Each skirt length or furniture style has a life of a few years. Most fashion changes today arise through deliberate promotion by manufacturers and retailers. Some, however, like long hair, beards, and old clothes among American youth, arise spontaneously.

The *craze* is a fad which becomes an obsession, dominating the follower's life for a time. Crazes may be recreational (hula hoops), economic (speculative booms), political (bandwagons), religious (revivals), or any other obsession which spreads rapidly and dies out quickly.

Mass hysteria is irrational, compulsive behavior that quickly spreads among people. Although sometimes born of monotony and boredom (Salem witchcraft hysteria), it is usually born of fear. The mass hysteria spread by Orson Welles' famous "Invasion from Mars" broadcast stimulated a number of suicides and mass confusion lasting for days.

Publics and Public Opinion

A *public* is *a scattered number of people who share a common interest in the same topic.* Thus we have a baseball public, a theater public, a religious public, etc. The term "the public" is used to refer to everyone in the society. While these two usages are inconsistent, both usages are very common.

Public opinion refers to the opinions most widely held among a population. Today, public opinion polls are a highly sophisticated measure of the varieties of opinion held by the people. Propaganda is a deliberate attempt to modify the opinions of the public, or of a part of the public. Like all forms of collective behavior, public opinion is subject to unpredicted changes, irrational shifts, and even to fads and fashions.

Any opinion has at least three dimensions: *direction, intensity,* and *integration.* Direction refers to what is approved or disapproved. Intensity refers to the strength of an opinion, whether mildly or violently held. Integration refers to its tie-in with a person's entire belief and value system. An opinion which is a logical expression of one's value system is less easily changed than an "independent" opinion with no such ideological foundation. For example, one man supports amnesty for draft evaders because he is a pacifist, opposed to all military force; another man supports amnesty because his church favors it. Opinions which are deeply rooted in one's basic beliefs and values are the most resistant to change.

Is each of the following true or false?

_____ 1. The *mores* place limitations on crowd behavior.

_____ 2. There is only one form of crowd behavior.

_____ 3. The term *public* can refer to both a scattered number of people who share a common interest in the same topic, and everyone in the society.

_____ 4. Opinions that are deeply rooted in one's basic beliefs and values are the least resistant to change.

Now turn to Answer frame 2²³ on page 154 to check your answers.

chapter 24

DEVIANCE

Frame 1²⁴

Social control refers to *all the ways in which people are made to act the way they are supposed to act.*

Means of Social Control

Control through Socialization. An orderly society is possible only if most people are trained so that they will *want* to do what it is socially necessary for them to do. Social control is achieved mainly by socializing people so that their wishes and their internalized restraints will lead them to do voluntarily what the society needs to have them do. Wherever socialization is highly successful, with few failures in socialization, there is comparatively little misconduct.

A vital part of socialization consists of *internalizing the mores* of one's society. When the mores have been fully internalized, they make it psychologically almost impossible for one to violate them. There are very few students whom any kind of reward could persuade to shoot their parents or to eat their baby sister. But, whereas our mores forbidding parricide, infanticide, and cannibalism are unanimously supported, our mores on premarital sexual intercourse or drug

Answer frame 2²³

1. True. One limitation on crowd behavior is the culture's *mores*. Crowds commit only those acts which carry some degree of cultural support, even though the acts may also carry some condemnation.

2. False. At least *nine* forms of crowd behavior are identifiable. Some examples of these are as follows: audiences, riots, rumors, fashions, and mass hysteria.

3. True. While these two usages are slightly inconsistent, they are very common. The inconsistency is reduced when the term is used to describe *opinion*—viz. "public opinion."

4. False. An opinion that is a logical extension of one's value system is less easily changed than an "independent" opinion with no such ideological foundation.

If you missed any of the above, you should review Frame 2²³ before beginning Chapter 24 on page 153.

Frame 1²⁴ continued

use are undermined by debate and uncertainty. Only when support is unanimous and unquestioning are the mores fully effective as controls.

Control through Group Sanctions. Socialization develops internal controls, operating through one's conscience. *Group sanctions* bring the pressure of the group to bear upon the individual. The sanctions may be *positive* (approving and rewarding certain behavior), or *negative* (disapproving and punishing certain behavior). In small informal groups, the rewards consist of acceptance, fellowship, respect, and prestige within the group. In formally organized groups, the rewards may be expanded to include access to occupations, income, prizes, medals, and other recognitions. The punishments in small informal groups are loss of status, denial of fellowship, ridicule, and ostracism; in formally organized groups, punishments are extended to include fines, suspension or expulsion, and perhaps even imprisonment or death.

The power of the group to control the individual is most impressive. In primitive tribal societies, where groups are small and there are few secrets, misconduct is rare. One cannot move to another village and begin anew; he must live with the reputation he makes. The penalty of loss of status, ridicule, and exclusion from the fellowship of the group is too great to be endured. In more complex societies such as ours, variation in behavior attracts less attention, and informal group sanctions are less compelling. Complex societies must resort to regulations,

laws, police agencies, and formal punishments in an only partly successful attempt to compel people to conform.

In summary, the goal of social control is first to socialize the person to the norms and values of society and then through group sanctions and pressures to encourage the person to act as expected. Ideally, the character and conscience we develop will make us want to behave as expected, but in reality this is not always so.

Situational Determinants of Behavior

Behavior in any situation is partly a product of the habits, values, and moral standards one brings to the situation, and partly a product of the pressures inherent within that situation. For example, when students feel that the examinations are satisfactory and the grading is fair, only a few will cheat; but if the professor is careless and cheating becomes so widespread that one cannot pass without cheating, most students will cheat. This is what is meant by *situational determinants of behavior—factors within the behavior situation which strongly encourage a particular response.*

Are most people honest? Yes and no! Most people are honest in not cheating the blind newspaperman (to cheat this poor, unfortunate man would do more than ten cents' damage to our self-image). Most people are dishonest when they dent another car in a parking lot, or have an opportunity to "pad" their insurance claim a little. In every war, atrocities are committed by both sides; the pressures of the war situation make them inevitable.

Isn't moral principle important? Most people have a long series of "principles" and justifications for behavior. In any behavior situation, it is not hard to dredge up a suitable "principle" to justify the action which the behavior situation inspires. One's perception of the situation determines which of his storehouse of norms is applicable. Thus, many young men apply one set of norms in their treatment of "nice girls," and another for treatment of "pick-ups." Much behavior control takes the form of manipulating the behavior situation so that the desired behavior will be encouraged.

Social Deviation

The mechanisms of social control are not equally effective upon all people. Even in the most rigid, simple societies, some deviation appears. *Deviation* (or deviance) is defined as *behavior that is contrary to the generally accepted norms of the society*. In our society, nudists, revolutionists, and hippies are deviants.

Not all deviance is culturally disapproved. Spectacular achievement, total dedication to a respected goal, and remarkable creativity are deviations from normal behavior. Most such deviation in the direction of extraordinary achievement is culturally approved and nonproblematic. It is the disapproved forms of deviation which concern the society.

Individual and Group Deviation. Individual deviation occurs when an individual, acting alone, deviates from the conventional norms. Such deviants, however, tend to find other deviants like themselves and to form a group, and

eventually perhaps a deviant subculture. The delinquent gang, youth riots, and hippie culture are examples of group deviance, wherein the individual is supported by the group in his deviation. The concepts of individual and group deviation are distinct, although in practice there are no clear boundaries.

A particular deviant may, therefore, be (*a*) a deviant member of a conforming subculture (the delinquent from a "good" family and neighborhood), or (*b*) a conforming member of a deviant subculture (a delinquent gang member from an area where delinquent behavior is a normal youth experience). This distinction is important for analysis and therapy. The individual deviant is presumably a product of an unsuccessful socialization in that he failed to internalize the conventional norms by which he was surrounded. Therapy consists of seeking to resolve the emotional blocks or psychological problems which led him to reject the norms of his cultural world. The group delinquent—a conforming member of a deviant subculture—represents no such failure in socialization, for he *has* internalized the norms of *his* cultural world. Individualized therapy is not often successful in reforming him; only through changing the subculture is he likely to be reformed.

In practice, many deviant subcultures (hippies, sex deviants) are shared by persons who joined the deviant group only after they had become deviant from the conventional norms. Once again, the two categories—individual and group deviants—overlap. The distinction lies in whether the deviant has largely withdrawn from conventional society and is now finding companionship and group support for his deviation from a deviant group, or remains in conventional society while deviant from some of its major norms.

Indicate whether each of the following statements is true or false by writing "T" or "F" in the space provided.

———— 1. There is a definite relationship between the success of socialization and the amount of misconduct.

———— 2. Socialization and group sanctions are both important ingredients for achieving social control.

———— 3. Behavior in any situation is solely a product of the habits, values, and moral standards one brings to the situation.

———— 4. The therapy is the same for a deviant member of a conforming subculture and a conforming member of a deviant subculture.

Now turn to Answer frame 1²⁴ on page 158 to check your responses.

Frame 2²⁴

Norms of Evasion. When a deviant pattern of behavior has become so widely tolerated and practiced among otherwise conforming people that it becomes the expected behavior, a *norm of evasion* has developed. Padding the expense account, "fudging" a bit on one's income tax, and driving a little above the speed limit are examples. Gambling, underage drinking, use of marijuana, and premarital sexual intercourse are normal for some groups. Norms of evasion are a means of handling the discrepancy between real and ideal cultures. They permit people to enjoy the "respectability" of supporting the ideal culture without giving up the indulgences of the real culture, meanwhile preserving a relatively clear conscience.

Cultural Factors in Deviance. The amount of deviant behavior in a society is affected by the ways in which the culture encourages or discourages deviance. As stated earlier, simple, stable tribal societies have little deviance, while in large, complex, rapidly changing societies, deviance is more common. Why?

Complex, rapidly changing societies are in a state of *social disorganization.* Different parts of the culture are changing, but not necessarily in the same direction or at the same rate of speed. Since a culture is integrated, cultural change upsets this integration, and the various parts of the culture become imperfectly harmonized with one another. For example, parental chaperonage of courtship became ineffective as people moved from hamlet to city and the automobile replaced the horse. Social disorganization describes *the undermining of traditional norms, values, and controls by social and cultural changes which render them unworkable.* But outworn controls are not immediately replaced by new ones. It takes time to develop new controls which are really binding, and meanwhile the control machinery is weakened. Since change is continuous today, disorganization and reorganization are continuous, and the control system continuously weakened and uncertain.

A stable society shows a value agreement and normative consensus. Agreement is virtually unanimous upon life goals, standards of right and wrong, and proper behavior. A complex, changing society has a lot of *value conflict* and *normative dissensus* (lack of agreement upon values and norms). A complex society develops many subcultures, and the values and norms of these subcultures often clash. With rapid change, not all persons and groups change their ideas at the same rate or in the same direction. It is very difficult for one to reject a norm or value which is firmly endorsed by everyone he knows or even hears about; to reject such a norm is to isolate oneself from humanity. But it is far easier to reject a norm which some revere but others disparage. Parents and preachers may say "Don't," but their warnings lose power when many of one's peers say "Why not?" and supply convincing arguments and group support for rejection of this norm. Is a girl most likely to wind up happily married by guarding her chastity all the way to the altar, or by a judiciously timed surrender? Victorian society had a firm, positive answer; today's answer is hotly debated. Such value conflicts and normative dissensus make it less likely that the individual will internalize a firm, unyielding set of inner controls, and easier for him to deviate from traditional norms.

Theories of Individual Deviance. *Physical type theories* attempt to find an association between certain physical characteristics and certain personality traits. Lombroso a century ago maintained that deviants are by birth a distinct type, and the physical features of the body identify the "criminal type." He based this on studies of prison inmates, without comparing them with a control group of the general population. More recently, Sheldon sought to link physical type with personality, but methodological errors led him to claim an association which more careful studies failed to substantiate. Currently, the double-Y chromosome is being studied as a possible explanation for violent crime, but so far, no valid associations between physical type and personality or behavior characteristics have been established.

Freud's psychoanalytic theory saw deviance arising when the impulse drives of the id achieved victory over the ego and superego and ruled the person. Through psychoanalysis, the rationality of the ego might be strengthened so that it could regain control over the person. Freud's concepts of the id, ego, and superego are difficult either to verify or to disprove through empirical research, and his theories remain sharply debated among behavior scientists. Psychoanalytic theories of deviance today see most deviance as a result of inner emotional conflicts.

The *deviant subculture* approach sees deviance becoming common among people where there is a deviant subculture for them to absorb. The Gluecks, Albert Cohen, and others have shown how the seriously delinquent boys associate mainly with other delinquent boys within a subculture which provides status, rewards, and group support for deviant behavior.

The *achievement barrier* theories see deviance arising from the frustration and anger of those who are blocked from attaining the rewards which the culture has encouraged them to desire. Our culture encourages everyone to strive for advancement, status, and success, but it is impossible for everyone to be "on top." For there to be winners, there must be losers. Merton claims that much deviation develops when the losers "break the rules" in seeking success, or turn to unapproved activities in the search for identity and status. Cloward and Ohlin see delinquent gangs as a "retreatist" reaction to the lack of opportunity for underprivileged youth. High Negro crime rates are interpreted, in part, as their angry response to inequality of opportunity and reward.

Anomie and deviation are seen as related to each other. *Anomie is a condition in which the individual has no firm sense of belonging to anything dependable* because traditional norms are not applicable to the behavior situation and there are no clear guidelines. In an "anomic society" there is no definite and binding moral code, no fully accepted norms to follow. An anomic individual has internalized no binding set of norms and values, and so suffers feelings of normlessness, helplessness, confusion, lack of purpose in life, and a feeling that he cannot count on anyone to help him or care about him. All complex, changing societies are in some degree anomic, and individual feelings of anomie are widespread. Merton suggests that anomie results when one accepts the goals of his culture but is unable to attain the means to achieve those goals.

Learning theory provides insights into how a person learns deviant behavior. Sutherland developed a "differential association theory" suggesting that criminal behavior is learned the same as any other behavior. The criminal is exposed to criminal patterns of behavior more often and more attractively than to conventional patterns of behavior, while the noncriminal is more often and more attractively exposed to noncriminal patterns of behavior. The criminal deviant learns both the criminal skills and the supporting values and norms that justify a criminal career. Becker in *Becoming a Marijuana User* has shown that the techniques of marijuana smoking have to be learned, interpreted pleasurably, and encouraged by group support. The process is no different than learning socially approved behavior; only in the definition of the behavior as deviant does the situation differ from any other learning situation.

Labeling theory helps to explain the process

Answer frame 1²⁴

1. True. Wherever socialization is highly successful there is comparatively little misconduct. People will *want* to do what it is socially necessary for them to do.
2. True. Social control is achieved by (1) socializing the person to the norms and values of society, and (2) encouraging the person to act as expected through group sanctions and pressures.
3. False. It also depends on the pressures within that situation. In any behavior situation, it is not hard to dredge up a suitable "principle" to justify the action which the situation inspires (e.g., cheating in a class where many other students are cheating).
4. False. The individual deviant is probably a product of unsuccessful socialization; therapy consists of seeking to resolve the emotional blocks or psychological problems which led him to reject the norms of his culture. The group deviant would not be helped in this way since he *has* internalized the norms of *his* cultural world; only through changing the subculture is he likely to be reformed.

If you missed any of the above, you should restudy Frame 1²⁴ before turning to Frame 2²⁴ on page 156.

Frame 2²⁴ continued

whereby deviant behavior patterns are confirmed and reinforced. One may be *secretly* a drug user, homosexual, or embezzler, yet remain accepted in conventional society. But a *public definition* of one's behavior as deviant often carries legal and social penalties which tend to exclude one from conforming society, and cast one into the company of fellow deviants. Many of the social influences toward conformity are thus replaced by influences toward further deviation. For this reason, the public labeling of one as deviant is often the "point of no return" in the development of a deviant life organization.

Lemert originated and Becker elaborated upon the concept of *secondary deviation*. This is *that further deviation which arises from the definition and treatment of one as deviant.* For example, the definition of drug addiction as a crime rather than an illness has made (illegal) narcotics so expensive that addicts often engage in prostitution, thievery, and other crimes in order to finance their habit. There is no intrinsic reason why long hair should be associated with deviant behavior; but youths with long hair may be defined and treated in ways which alienate them from conforming society and encourage deviant behavior. Primary and secondary deviation are not always easy to distinguish. It is not known, for example, whether some observed accompaniments of marijuana use (falling grades, loss of ambition) are due to the marijuana itself, or to the consequences of our having labeled marijuana use as deviant.

These several interpretations of deviation are not mutually exclusive, nor does any one explain all types of deviation. Deviant behavior has as many explanations as any other kind of behavior.

Deviation and Social Stability.   Although deviance is generally viewed as disruptive and a threat to the stability of society, it serves some positive purposes as well. Individual deviance is a reflection of strain and stress in society. Group deviance reflects the changing norms of the culture. Deviance can and does serve as a safety valve to relieve pressures of social conflict, and is a process whereby new norms arise and gain acceptance. In a changing society, some kinds of deviation are a necessary part of the adaptive process whereby a changing society maintains some degree of cultural integration.

True or false?

———— 1. "Everyone is doing it" is an example of trying to explain away deviant behavior as a norm of evasion.

———— 2. Deviance is more common in primitive, stable societies than it is in our society.

_____ 3. Each of the various theories of individual deviance is entirely separate from all of the others and there is one that explains all types of deviation.

_____ 4. Deviant behavior can gain status, rewards, and group support.

Now turn to Answer frame 2^{24} on page 160 to check your answers.

Answer frame 2²⁴

1. True. When a deviant pattern of behavior has become so widely tolerated and practiced among otherwise conforming people that it becomes the expected behavior (e.g., drinking alcoholic beverages during prohibition), a *norm of evasion* has developed. It is a means of handling the discrepancy between real and ideal cultures while preserving a relatively clear conscience.

2. False. Our society (as a complex, rapidly changing society) is in a state of social disorganization (where social and cultural changes render traditional norms, values, and controls unworkable). Thus, the control system is weakened and uncertain and deviance is more common. The primitive culture has little normative dissensus (lack of agreement upon values and norms) and thus relatively little deviance.

3. False. The several theories are *not* mutually exclusive, nor does any one explain all types of deviation. The double-Y chromosome theory is being studied as a possible explanation of violent crime but has not been completely accepted as of this writing. Lombroso's and Sheldon's theories have been largely discredited due to methodological errors. Freud's theories remain sharply debated among behavior scientists.

4. True. A deviant subculture can supply status, rewards, and group support. Learning theory suggests that deviant behavior can be learned just like socially approved behavior; it can be interpreted pleasurably and encouraged by group support.

If you missed any of the above, you should restudy Frame 2²⁴.

appendix

THE CONSTITUTION
OF THE UNITED STATES*

Preamble—WE THE PEOPLE of the United States, in Order to form a more perfect Union, establish Justice, insure domestic Tranquility, provide for the common defence, promote the general Welfare, and secure the Blessings of Liberty to ourselves and our Posterity, do ordain and establish this Constitution for the United States of America.

ARTICLE I

SECTION 1

Legislative powers vested in Congress—All legislative Powers herein granted shall be vested in a Congress of the United States, which shall consist of a Senate and House of Representatives.

SECTION 2

Composition of the House of Representatives—1. The House of Representatives shall be composed of Members chosen every second Year by the People of the several States, and the Electors in each State shall have the Qualifications requisite for Electors of the most numerous Branch of the State Legislature.

Qualifications of Representatives—2. No Person shall be a Representative who shall not have attained to the Age of twenty-five Years, and been seven Years a Citizen of the United States, and who shall not, when elected, be an Inhabitant of that State in which he shall be chosen.

Apportionment of Representatives and census—†3. [Representatives and direct Taxes shall be apportioned among the several States which may be included within this Union, according to their respective Numbers, which shall be determined by adding to the whole Number of free Persons, including those bound to Service for a term of Years and excluding Indians not taxed, three fifths of all other persons.] The actual Enumeration shall be made within three Years after the first Meeting of the Congress of the United States, and within every subsequent Term of ten Years, in such Manner as they shall by Law direct. The Number of Representatives shall not exceed one for every thirty thousand, but each State shall have at Least one

---

*Subject headings, which do not appear in the original document, are modifications of those to be found in *State of New Hampshire Manual for the General Court* (Concord, N.H., 1969), pp. 15–42.

†The clause included in brackets is amended by the Fourteenth Amendment.

161

Representative; and until such enumeration shall be made, the State of New Hampshire shall be entitled to chuse three, Massachusetts eight, Rhode-Island and Providence Plantations one, Connecticut five, New York six, New Jersey four, Pennsylvania eight, Delaware one, Maryland six, Virginia ten, North Carolina five, South Carolina five, and Georgia three.

Vacancies—4. When vacancies happen in the Representation from any State, the Executive Authority thereof shall issue Writs of Election to fill such Vacancies.

Selection of officers; impeachment—5. The House of Representatives shall chuse their Speaker and other Officers; and shall have the sole Power of Impeachment.

*SECTION 3

The Senate—[1. The Senate of the United States shall be composed of two Senators from each State, chosen by the Legislature thereof, for six Years; and each Senator shall have one Vote.]

Classification of Senators; vacancies—2. Immediately after they shall be assembled in Consequence of the first Election, they shall be divided as equally as may be into three Classes. The Seats of the Senators of the first Class shall be vacated at the Expiration of the second Year, of the second Class at the Expiration of the fourth Year, and of the third Class at the Expiration of the sixth Year, so that one-third may be chosen every second Year; and if Vacancies happen by Resignation, or otherwise, during the Recess of the Legislature of any State, the Executive thereof may make temporary Appointments [until the next Meeting of the Legislature, which shall then fill such Vacancies.]

Qualification of Senators—3. No person shall be a Senator who shall not have attained to the Age of thirty Years, and been nine Years a Citizen of the United States, and who shall not, when elected, be an Inhabitant of that State for which he shall be chosen.

Vice President—4. The Vice-President of the United States shall be President of the Senate, but shall have no Vote, unless they be equally divided.

Senate Officers; President pro tempore—5. The Senate, shall chuse their other Officers, and also a President pro tempore, in the absence of the Vice-President, or when he shall exercise the Office of President of the United States.

Senate to try impeachment—6. The Senate shall have the sole Power to try all Impeachments. When sitting for that Purpose, they shall be on Oath or Affirmation. When the President of the United States is tried, the Chief Justice shall preside: And no Person shall be convicted without the Concurrence of two thirds of the Members present.

Judgment in case of impeachment—7. Judgment in Cases of Impeachment shall not extend further than to removal from Office, and disqualification to hold and enjoy any Office of honor, Trust, or Profit under the United States: but the Party convicted shall nevertheless be liable and subject to Indictment, Trial, Judgment and Punishment, according to Law.

---

*The first paragraph of section three of Article I of the Constitution of the United States, and so much of paragraph two of the same section as relates to filling vacancies are amended by the Seventeenth Amendment to the Constitution.

SECTION 4

Control of Congressional elections–1. The Times, Places and Manner of holding Elections for Senators and Representatives, shall be prescribed in each State by the Legislature thereof; but the Congress may at any time by Law make or alter such Regulations, except as to the Places of chusing Senators.

*Time for assembling of Congress–2. The Congress shall assemble at least one in every Year, and such Meeting shall be on the first Monday in December, unless they shall by Law appoint a different day.

SECTION 5

Election and qualifications of members; quorum–1. Each House shall be the Judge of the Elections, Returns and Qualifications of its own Members, and a Majority of each shall constitute a Quorum to do Business; but a smaller Number may adjourn from day to day, and may be authorized to compel the Attendance of absent Members, in such Manner, and under such Penalties as each House may provide.

Each House to determine its own rules–2. Each House may determine the Rules of its Proceedings, punish its Members for disorderly Behavior, and, with the Concurrence of two thirds, expel a Member.

Journals and yeas and nays–3. Each House shall keep a Journal of its Proceedings, and from time to time publish the same, excepting such Parts as may in their judgment require Secrecy; and the Yeas and Nays of the Members of either House on any question shall, at the Desire of one fifth of those Present, be entered on the Journal.

Adjournment–4. Neither House, during the Session of Congress shall, without the Consent of the other, adjourn for more than three days, nor to any other Place than that in which the two Houses shall be sitting.

SECTION 6

Compensation and privileges of Members of Congress–1. The Senators and Representatives shall receive a Compensation for their Services, to be ascertained by Law, and paid out of the Treasury of the United States. They shall in all Cases, except Treason, Felony and Breach of the Peace, be privileged from Arrest during their Attendance at the Session of their respective Houses, and in going to and returning from the same; and for any Speech or Debate in either House, they shall not be questioned in any other place.

Incompatible offices–2. No Senator or Representative shall, during the Time for which he was elected, be appointed to any civil Office under the Authority of the United States, which shall have been created, or the Emoluments whereof shall have been encreased during such time; and no Person holding any Office under the United States, shall be a Member of either House during his continuance in Office.

SECTION 7

Revenue bills–1. All Bills for raising Revenue shall originate in the House of Representatives; but the Senate may propose or concur with Amendments as on other Bills.

Manner of passing bills; veto power of President–2. Every Bill which shall have passed the House of Representatives and the Senate, shall

---

*Amended by Article XX, section 2, of the amendments to the Constitution.

before it becomes a Law, be presented to the President of the United States; If he approve he shall sign it, but if not he shall return it, with his Objections to that House in which it shall have originated, who shall enter the Objections at large on their Journal, and proceed to reconsider it. If after such Reconsideration two thirds of that House shall agree to pass the Bill, it shall be sent, together with the Objections, to the other House, by which it shall likewise be reconsidered, and if approved by two thirds of that House, it shall become a Law. But in all such Cases the Votes of both Houses shall be determined by Yeas and Nays, and the Names of the Persons voting for and against the Bill shall be entered on the Journal of each House respectively. If any Bill shall not be returned by the President within ten days (Sundays excepted) after it shall have been presented to him, the Same shall be a Law, in like Manner as if he had signed it, unless the Congress by their Adjournment prevent its Return, in which Case it shall not be a Law.

Concurrent orders or resolutions—3. Every Order, Resolution, or Vote to which the Concurrence of the Senate and House of Representatives may be necessary (except on a question of adjournment) shall be presented to the President of the United States; and before the Same shall take Effect, shall be approved by him, or being disapproved by him, shall be repassed by two thirds of the Senate and House of Representatives, according to the Rules and Limitations prescribed in the Case of a Bill.

SECTION 8

The Congress shall have Power: Taxes—1. To lay and collect Taxes, Duties, Imposts and Excises, to pay the Debts and provide for the common Defence and general Welfare of the United States; but all Duties, Imposts and Excises shall be uniform throughout the United States.

Borrowing—2. To borrow money on the credit of the United States.

Regulation of commerce—3. To regulate Commerce with foreign Nations, and among the several States, and with the Indian tribes.

Naturalization and bankruptcy—4. To establish an uniform Rule of Naturalization, and uniform Laws on the subject of Bankruptcies throughout the United States.

Money, weights and measures—5. To coin Money, regulate the Value thereof, and of foreign Coin, and fix the Standard of Weights and Measures.

Counterfeiting—6. To provide for the Punishment of counterfeiting the Securities and current Coin of the United States.

Post offices—7. To establish Post Offices and post roads.

Patents and copyrights—8. To promote the Progress of Science and useful Arts, by securing for limited Times to Authors and Inventors the exclusive Right to their respective Writings and Discoveries.

Inferior courts—9. To constitute Tribunals inferior to the supreme Court.

Piracies and felonies—10. To define and punish Piracies and Felonies committed on the high Seas, and Offenses against the Law of Nations.

War—11. To declare war, grant Letters of Marque and Reprisal, and make Rules concerning Captures on Land and Water.

Armies—12. To raise and support Armies, but no Appropriation of Money to that Use shall be for a longer Term than two Years.

Navy—13. To provide and maintain a Navy.

Land and naval forces – 14. To make Rules for the Government and Regulation of the land and naval Forces.

Calling out militia – 15. To provide for calling forth the Militia to execute the Laws of the Union, suppress Insurrections and repel Invasions.

Organizing, arming and disciplining militia – 16. To provide for organizing, arming, and disciplining the Militia, and for governing such Part of them as may be employed in the Service of the United States, reserving to the States, repectively, the Appointment of the Officers, and the Authority of training the Militia according to the discipline prescribed by Congress.

District of Columbia – 17. To exercise exclusive Legislation in all Cases whatsoever, over such District (not exceeding ten Miles square) as may, by Cession of particular States, and the acceptance of Congress, become the Seat of the Government of the United States, and to exercise like Authority over all Places purchased by the Consent of the Legislature of the State in which the Same shall be, for the Erection of Forts, Magazines, Arsenals, dock-Yards, and other needful Buildings; – and

To enact laws necessary to enforce Constitution – 18. To make all Laws which shall be necessary and proper for carrying into Execution the foregoing Powers, and all other Powers vested by this Constitution in the Government of the United States, or in any department or Office thereof.

Section 9

Slave trade – 1. The Migration or Importation of such Persons as any of the States now existing shall think proper to admit shall not be prohibited by the Congress prior to the Year one thousand eight hundred and eight, but a tax or duty may be imposed on such Importation, not exceeding ten dollars for each Person.

Writ of habeas corpus – 2. The privilege of the Writ of Habeas Corpus shall not be suspended, unless when in Cases of Rebellion or Invasion the public Safety may require it.

Bills of attainder and ex post facto laws prohibited – 3. No Bill of Attainder or ex post facto Law shall be passed.

Capitation and other direct taxes – 4. No capitation, or other direct tax shall be laid, unless in Proportion to the Census of Enumeration herein before directed to be taken.

Exports not to be taxed – 5. No Tax or Duty shall be laid on Articles exported from any State.

Shipping – 6. No Preference shall be given by any Regulation of Commerce or Revenue to the Ports of one State over those of another; nor shall Vessels bound to, or from, one State, be obliged to enter, clear, or pay Duties in another.

Appropriations; reports – 7. No Money shall be drawn from the Treasury, but in Consequence of Appropriations made by Law; and a regular Statement and Account of the Receipts and Expenditures of all public Money shall be published from time to time.

Titles of nobility; favors from foreign powers – 8. No Title of Nobility shall be granted by the United States: And no Person holding any office of Profit or Trust under them, shall without the Consent of the Congress, accept of any present, Emolument, Office, or Title, of any kind whatever, from any King, Prince, or foreign State.

SECTION 10

Limitations of the powers of the several States–1. No State shall enter into any Treaty, Alliance, or Confederation; grant Letters of Marque and Reprisal; coin Money; emit Bills of Credit; make any Thing but gold and silver Coin a Tender in Payment of Debts; pass any Bill of Attainder, ex post facto Law, or Law impairing the Obligation of Contracts or grant any Title of Nobility.

State imposts and duties– 2. No State shall, without the Consent of the Congress, lay any Imposts or Duties on Imports or Exports, except what may be absolutely necessary for executing its inspection Laws; and the net Produce of all Duties and Imposts, laid by any State on Imports or Exports, shall be for the Use of the Treasury of the United States; and all such Laws shall be subject to the Revision and Control of the Congress.

Further restrictions on powers of States– 3. No State shall, without the consent of Congress, lay any duty of Tonnage, keep Troops, or Ships of War in time of Peace, enter into any Agreement or Compact with another State, or with a foreign Power, or engage in War, unless actually invaded, or in such imminent Danger as will not admit of delay.

ARTICLE II

SECTION I

The President; the executive power– 1. The executive Power shall be vested in a President of the United States of America. He shall hold his Office during the Term of four Years, and, together with the Vice-President, chosen for the same Term, be elected, as follows:

Appointment and qualifications of presidential electors– 2. Each State shall appoint, in such Manner as the Legislature thereof may direct, a Number of Electors, equal to the whole Number of Senators and Representatives to which the State may be entitled in the Congress; but no Senator or Representative or Person holding an Office of Trust or Profit under the United States, shall be appointed an Elector.

Original method of electing the President and Vice-President– 3. *[The Electors shall meet in their respective States, and vote by Ballot for two persons, of whom one at least shall not be an Inhabitant of the same State with themselves. And they shall make a List of all the Persons voted for, and of the Number of Votes for each; which List they shall sign and certify, and transmit sealed to the Seat of the Government of the United States, directed to the President of the Senate. The President of the Senate shall, in the Presence of the Senate and House of Representatives, open all the Certificates, and the Votes shall then be counted. The Person having the greatest Number of Votes shall be the President, if such Number be a Majority of the whole Number of Electors appointed; and if there be more than one who have such Majority, and have an equal Number of Votes, then the House of Representatives shall immediately chuse by Ballot one of them for President; and if no Person have a Majority, then from the five highest on the list the said House shall in like Manner chuse the President. But in chusing the President, the Votes shall be taken by States, the Representation from each State having one Vote; A quorum for this Purpose shall consist of a Member or Members from two thirds of the States, and a Majority of all the States shall be necessary to a Choice. In every case, after the Choice of the

---

*This clause has been superseded by the Twelfth Amendment.

President, the Person having the greatest Number of Votes of the Electors shall be the Vice-President. But if there should remain two or more who have equal Votes, the Senate shall chuse from them by Ballot the Vice-President.]

Electors—4. The Congress may determine the Time of chusing the Electors, and the Day on which they shall give their Votes; which Day shall be the same throughout the United States.

*Qualifications for President—5. No person except a natural born Citizen, or a Citizen of the United States, at the time of the Adoption of this Constitution, shall be eligible to the Office of President; neither shall any Person be eligible to that office who shall not have attained to the Age of thirty-five Years, and been fourteen Years a Resident within the United States.

†Filling vacancy in the office of President—6. In Case of the Removal of the President from Office, or of his Death, Resignation, or Inability to discharge the Powers and Duties of the said Office, the same shall devolve on the Vice-President, and the Congress may by Law provide for the Case of Removal, Death, Resignation or Inability, both of the President and Vice-President, declaring what Officer shall then act as President, and such Officer shall act accordingly, until the Disability be removed, or a President shall be elected.

Compensation of the President—7. The President shall, at stated Times, receive for his Services, a Compensation, which shall neither be encreased nor diminished during the Period for which he shall have been elected, and he shall not receive within that Period any other Emolument from the United States, or any of them.

Oath to be taken by the President—8. Before he enter on the Execution of his Office, he shall take the following Oath or Affirmation:—"I do solemnly swear (or affirm) that I will faithfully execute the Office of President of the United States, and will to the best of my Ability, preserve, protect and defend the Constitution of the United States."

SECTION 2

The President to be commander-in-chief and head of executive department; reprieves and pardons—1. The President shall be Commander-in-Chief of the Army and Navy of the United States, and of the Militia of the several States, when called into the actual Service of the United States; he may require the Opinion, in writing, of the principal Officer in each of the executive Departments, upon any subject relating to the Duties of their respective Offices, and he shall have Power to grant Reprieves and Pardons for Offenses against the United States, except in Cases of Impeachment.

Treaties; ambassadors; inferior officers—2. He shall have Power, by and with the Advice and Consent of the Senate to make Treaties, provided two thirds of the Senators present concur; and he shall nominate, and by and with the Advice and Consent of the Senate, shall appoint Ambassadors, other public Ministers and Consuls, Judges of the Supreme Court, and all other Officers of the United States, whose Appointments are not herein otherwise provided for, and which shall be established by Law; but the Congress may by Law vest the Appointment of such inferior Officers, as they

*For qualifications of the Vice-President, see Article XII of the Amendments.

†Amended by Articles XX and XXV of the Amendments to the Constitution.

think proper, in the President alone, in the Courts of Law, or in the Heads of Departments.

President may fill vacancies in office during recess of Senate—3. The President shall have Power to fill all Vacancies that may happen during the Recess of the Senate, by granting Commissions which shall expire at the End of their next Session.

Section 3

President to give advice to Congress; may convene or adjourn it on certain occasions; to receive ambassadors, etc.; have laws executed and commission all officers—He shall from time to time give to the Congress Information of the State of the Union, and recommend to their Consideration such Measures as he shall judge necessary and expedient; he may, on extraordinary Occasions, convene both Houses, or either of them, and in Case of Disagreement between them, with Respect to the Time of Adjournment, he may adjourn them to such Time as he shall think proper; he shall receive Ambassadors and other public Ministers; he shall take Care that the Laws be faithfully executed, and shall Commission all the Officers of the United States.

Section 4

All civil officers removable by impeachment—The President, Vice-President and all civil Officers of the United States, shall be removed from Office on Impeachment for, and Conviction of, Treason, Bribery, or other high crimes and Misdemeanors.

ARTICLE III

Section 1

Judicial power; term of office and compensation of judges—The judicial Power of the United States, shall be vested in one supreme Court, and in such inferior Courts as the Congress may from time to time ordain and establish. The Judges, both of the supreme and inferior Courts, shall hold their offices during good Behaviour, and shall, at stated Times, receive for their Services a Compensation which shall not be diminished during their Continuance in office.

Section 2

*Jurisdiction of Federal courts—1. The judicial Power shall extend to all Cases, in Law and Equity, arising under this Constitution, the Laws of the United States, and Treaties made, or which shall be made, under their Authority;—to all Cases affecting Ambassadors, other public Ministers and consuls;—to all Cases of Admiralty and maritime Jurisdiction;—to Controversies to which the United States shall be a Party;—to Controversies between two or more States;—between a State and Citizens of another State; —between Citizens of different States; between Citizens of the same States claiming Lands under Grants of different States, and between a State, or the Citizens thereof, and foreign States, Citizens or Subjects.

Original and appellate jurisdiction of Supreme Court—2. In all cases affecting Ambassadors, other public Ministers and Consuls, and those in which a State shall be Party, the Supreme Court shall have original Jurisdiction. In all the other Cases before mentioned, the Supreme Court shall

---

*This section is abridged by Article XI of the Amendments.

have appellate Jurisdiction, both as to Law and Fact, with such Exceptions, and under such Regulations as the Congress shall make.

Trial of all crimes, except impeachment, to be by jury—3. The trial of all Crimes, except in Cases of Impeachment, shall be by Jury; and such Trial shall be held in the State where the said Crimes shall have been committed; but when not committed within any State, the trial shall be at such Place or Places as the Congress may by Law have directed.

Section 3

Treason defined; conviction of—1. Treason against the United States, shall consist only in levying War against them, or, in adhering to their Enemies, giving them Aid and Comfort. No Person shall be convicted of Treason unless on the Testimony of two Witnesses to the same overt Act, or on Confession in open Court.

Congress to declare punishment for treason—2. The Congress shall have power to declare the Punishment of Treason, but no Attainder of Treason shall work Corruption of Blood, or Forfeiture except during the Life of the Person attained.

ARTICLE IV

Section 1

Each State to give full faith and credit to the public acts and records of other States—Full Faith and Credit shall be given in each State to the public Acts, Records, and judicial Proceedings of every other State. And the Congress may by general Laws prescribe the Manner in which such Acts, Records and Proceedings shall be proved, and the Effect thereof.

Section 2

Privileges of citizens—1. Citizens of each State shall be entitled to all Privileges and Immunities of Citizens in the several States.

Extradition between the several States—2. A Person charged in any State with Treason, Felony, or other Crime, who shall flee from Justice, and be found in another State, shall on demand of the executive Authority of the State from which he fled, be delivered up, to be removed to the State having Jurisdiction of the Crime.

Slaves—3. No Person held to Serve or Labour in one State under the Laws thereof, escaping into another, shall, in Consequence of any Law or Regulation therein, be discharged from such Service or Labour, but shall be delivered up on Claim of the Party to whom such Service or Labour may be due.

Section 3

New States—1. New States may be admitted by the Congress into this Union; but no new State shall be formed or erected within the Jurisdiction of any other State; nor any State be formed by Junction of two or more States, or parts of States, without the Consent of the Legislatures of the States concerned as well as of the Congress.

Regulations concerning territory—2. The Congress shall have Power to dispose of and make all needful Rules and Regulations respecting the Territory or other Property belonging to the United States; and nothing in this Constitution shall be so construed as to Prejudice any Claims of the United States, or of any particular State.

SECTION 4

Republican form of government and protection guaranteed the several States—The United States shall guarantee to every State in this Union a Republican Form of Government, and shall protect each of them against Invasion; and on Application of the Legislature, or of the Executive (when the Legislature cannot be convened) against domestic violence.

ARTICLE V

Ways in which the Constitution can be amended—The Congress, whenever two thirds of both Houses shall deem it necessary, shall propose Amendments to this Constitution, or, on the Application of the Legislatures of two thirds of the several States, shall call a Convention for proposing Amendments, which, in either Case, shall be valid to all Intents and Purposes, as part of this Constitution, when ratified by the Legislature of three fourths of the several States, or by Conventions in three fourths thereof, as the one or the other Mode of Ratification may be proposed by the Congress; Provided that no Amendment which may be made prior to the year One thousand eight hundred and eight shall in any Manner affect the first and fourth Clauses in the Ninth Section of the first Article; and that no State, without its Consent, shall be deprived of its equal Suffrage in the Senate.

ARTICLE VI

Debts contracted under the Confederation secured—1. All Debts contracted and Engagements entered into, before the Adoption of this Constitution, shall be as valid against the United States under this Constitution, as under the Confederation.

Constitution, laws and treaties of the United States to be supreme—2. This Constitution, and the Laws of the United States which shall be made in Pursuance thereof; and all Treaties made, or which shall be made, under the Authority of the United States, shall be the supreme Law of the Land; and the Judges in every State shall be bound thereby, any Thing in the Constitution or Laws of any State to the Contrary notwithstanding.

Who shall take constitutional oaths; no religious test—3. The Senators and Representatives before mentioned, and the Members of the several State Legislatures, and all executive and judicial Officers, both of the United States and of the several States, shall be bound by Oath or Affirmation, to support this Constitution; but no religious Test shall ever be required as a Qualification to any office or public Trust under the United States.

ARTICLE VII

Ratification—The Ratification of the Conventions of nine States shall be sufficient for the Establishment of this Constitution between the States so ratifying the Same.

Done in Convention by the Unanimous Consent of the States present the Seventeenth Day of September in the Year of our Lord one thousand seven hundred and Eighty seven and of the Independence of the United States of America the Twelfth. In Witness whereof We have hereunto subscribed our Names.

G°. WASHINGTON
President and Deputy from Virginia

New Hampshire.

John Langdon   Nicholas Gilman

Massachusetts.

Nathaniel Gorham   Rufus King

Connecticut.

Wm Saml Johnson   Roger Sherman

New York.

Alexander Hamilton

New Jersey.

Wil: Livingston   Wm Patterson
David Brearley   Jona: Dayton

Pennsylvania.

B. Franklin   Thomas Mifflin
Robt. Morris   Geo. Clymer
Thos. Fitzsimons   Jared Ingersoll
James Wilson   Gouv Morris

Delaware.

Geo: Reed   Gunning Bedford Jun
John Dickinson   Richard Bassett
Jaco: Broom

MARYLAND.

James McHenry   Dan: of St. Thos Jenifer
Danl Carroll

VIRGINIA.

John Blair—   James Madison Jr.

NORTH CAROLINA.

Wm Blount   Richd Dobbs Spaight
Hu Williamson

SOUTH CAROLINA.

J. Rutledge   Charles Cotesworth Pinckney
Charles Pinckney   Pierce Butler

GEORGIA.

William Few   Abr Baldwin

Attest: WILLIAM JACKSON, *Secretary*. . .

AMENDMENTS TO THE CONSTITUTION OF THE UNITED STATES

The first ten Amendments were proposed on 25 September 1789 and were ratified on 15 December 1791.

ARTICLE I

Freedom of religion, of speech, of the press, and right of petition— Congress shall make no law respecting an establishment of religion, or prohibiting the free exercise thereof; or abridging the freedom of speech, or of the press; or the right of the people peaceably to assemble, and to petition the Government for a redress of grievances.

ARTICLE II

Right of people to bear arms not to be infringed—A well regulated Militia, being necessary to the security of a free State, the right of the people to keep and bear Arms, shall not be infringed.

ARTICLE III

Quartering of troops—No Soldier shall, in time of peace be quartered in any house, without the consent of the Owner, nor in time of war, but in a manner to be prescribed by law.

ARTICLE IV

Searches and seizures – The right of the people to be secure in their persons, houses, papers, and effects against unreasonable searches and seizures, shall not be violated, and no Warrants shall issue, but upon probable cause, supported by Oath or affirmation, and particularly describing the place to be searched, and the persons or things to be seized.

ARTICLE V

Trials for crimes; just compensation for private property taken for public use – No person shall be held to answer for a capital, or otherwise infamous crime, unless on a presentment or indictment of a Grand Jury, except in cases arising in the land or naval forces, or in the Militia, when in actual service in time of War or public danger; nor shall any person be subject for the same offense to be twice put in jeopardy of life or limb; nor shall be compelled in any criminal case to be a witness against himself, nor be deprived of life, liberty, or property, without due process of law; nor shall private property be taken for public use, without just compensation.

ARTICLE VI

Civil rights in trials for crime – In all criminal prosecutions, the accused shall enjoy the right to a speedy and public trial, by an impartial jury of the State and district wherein the crime shall have been committed, which district shall have been previously ascertained by law, and to be informed of the nature and cause of the accusation; to be confronted with the witnesses against him; to have compulsory process for obtaining witnesses in his favor, and to have the Assistance of Counsel for his defence.

ARTICLE VII

Civil rights in civil suits – In suits at common law, where the value in controversy shall exceed twenty dollars, the right of trial by jury shall be preserved, and no fact tried in a jury, shall be otherwise re-examined in any Court of the United States, than according to the rules of the common law.

ARTICLE VIII

Excessive bail, fines and punishments prohibited – Excessive bail shall not be required, nor excessive fines imposed, nor cruel and unusual punishments inflicted.

ARTICLE IX

Reserved rights of people – The enumeration in the Constitution of certain rights, shall not be construed to deny or disparage others retained by the people.

ARTICLE X

Powers not delegated, reserved to States and people – The powers not delegated to the United States by the Constitution, nor prohibited by it to the States, are reserved to the States respectively, or to the people.

Proposed 4 March 1794, ratified 7 February 1795.
ARTICLE XI

Judicial power of United States not to extend to suits against a State—The Judicial power of the United States shall not be construed to extend to any suit in law or equity, commenced or prosecuted against one of the United States by Citizens of another State, or by Citizens or Subjects of any Foreign State.

Proposed 9 December 1803, ratified 15 June 1804.
ARTICLE XII

*Present mode of electing President and Vice-President—The Electors shall meet in their respective states and vote by ballot for President and Vice-President, one of whom, at least, shall not be an inhabitant of the same state with themselves; they shall name in their ballots the person voted for as President, and in distinct ballots the person voted for as Vice-President, and they shall make distinct lists of all persons voted for as President, and of all persons voted for as Vice-President, and of the number of votes for each, which lists they shall sign and certify, and transmit sealed to the seat of the government of the United States, directed to the President of the Senate;—The President of the Senate shall, in the presence of the Senate and House of Representatives, open all the certificates and the votes shall then be counted;—The person having the greatest number of votes for President, shall be the President, if such number be a majority of the whole number of electors appointed; and if no person have such majority, then from the persons having the highest numbers not exceeding three on the list of those voted for as President, the House of Representatives shall choose immediately, by ballot, the President. But in choosing the President, the votes shall be taken by states, the representation from each State having one vote; a quorum for this purpose shall consist of a member or members from two thirds of the states, and a majority of all the states shall be necessary to a choice. And if the House of Representatives shall not choose a President whenever the right of choice shall devolve upon them, before the fourth day of March next following, then the Vice-President shall act as President, as in the case of the death or other constitutional disability of the President. The Person having the greatest number of votes as Vice-President, shall be the Vice-President, if such number be a majority of the whole number of electors appointed, and if no person have a majority, then from the two highest numbers on the list, the Senate shall choose the Vice-President; a quorum for the purpose shall consist of two thirds of the whole number of Senators and a majority of the whole number shall be necessary to a choice. But no person constitutionally ineligible to the office of President shall be eligible to that of Vice-President of the United States.

---

*Amended by Articles XX and XXV of the Amendments to the Constitution.

Proposed 31 January 1865, ratified 6 December 1865.

ARTICLE XIII

SECTION 1

Slavery prohibited—Neither slavery nor involuntary servitude, except as a punishment for crime whereof the party shall have been duly convicted, shall exist within the United States, or any place subject to their jurisdiction.

SECTION 2

Congress given power to enforce this article—Congress shall have power to enforce this article by appropriate legislation.

Proposed 13 June 1866, ratified 9 July 1868.

ARTICLE XIV

SECTION 1

Citizenship defined; privileges of citizens—All persons born or naturalized in the United States, and subject to the jurisdiction thereof, are citizens of the United States and of the State wherein they reside. No State shall make or enforce any law which shall abridge the privileges or immunities of citizens of the United States; nor shall any State deprive any person of life, liberty, or property, without due process of law; nor deny to any person within its jurisdiction the equal protection of the laws.

SECTION 2

Apportionment of Representatives—Representatives shall be apportioned among the several States according to their respective numbers, counting the whole number of persons in each State, excluding Indians not taxed. But when the right to vote at any election for the choice of electors for President and Vice-President of the United States, Representatives in Congress, the Executive and Judicial officers of a State, or the members of the Legislature thereof, is denied to any of the male inhabitants of such State, being twenty-one years of age, and citizens of the United States, or in any way abridged, except for participation in rebellion, or other crime, the basis of representation therein shall be reduced in the proportion which the number of such male citizens shall bear to the whole number of male citizens twenty-one years of age in such State.

SECTION 3

Disqualification for office; removal of disability—No person shall be a Senator or Representative in Congress, or elector of President and Vice-President, or hold any office, civil or military, under the United States, or under any State, who, having previously taken an oath, as a member of Congress, or as an officer of the United States, or as a member of any State legislature, or as an executive or judicial officer of any State, to support the Constitution of the United States, shall have engaged in insurrection or rebellion against the same, or given aid or comfort to the enemies thereof. But Congress may by a vote of two-thirds of each House, remove such disability.

SECTION 4

Public debt not to be questioned; payment of debts and claims incurred in aid of rebellion forbidden—The validity of the public debt of the

United States, authorized by law, including debts incurred for payment of pensions and bounties for services in suppressing insurrection or rebellion, shall not be questioned. But neither the United States nor any State shall assume or pay any debt or obligation incurred in aid of insurrection or rebellion against the United States, or any claim for the loss or emancipation of any slave; but all such debts, obligations and claims shall be held illegal and void.

SECTION 5

Congress given power to enforce this article—The Congress shall have power to enforce, by appropriate legislation, the provisions of this article.

Proposed 28 February 1869, ratified 3 February 1870.
ARTICLE XV

SECTION 1

Right of certain citizens to vote established—The right of citizens of the United States to vote shall not be denied or abridged by the United States or by any State, on account of race, color, or previous condition of servitude.

SECTION 2

Congress given power to enforce this article—The Congress shall have power to enforce this article by appropriate legislation.

Proposed 2 July 1909, ratified 3 February 1913.
ARTICLE XVI

Taxes on incomes—The Congress shall have power to pay and collect taxes on incomes, from whatever source derived, without apportionment among the several States, and without regard to any census or enumeration.

Proposed 13 May 1912, ratified 8 April 1913.
ARTICLE XVII

Election of United States Senators; filling of vacancies; qualification of electors—1. The Senate of the United States will be composed of two Senators from each State, elected by the people thereof, for six years; and each Senator shall have one vote. The electors in each State shall have the qualifications requisite for electors of the most numerous branch of the State legislatures.

2. When vacancies happen in the representation of any State in the Senate, the executive authority of such State shall issue writs of election to fill such vacancies: Provided, that the legislature of any State may empower the executive thereof to make temporary appointment until the people fill the vacancies by election as the legislature may direct.

3. This amendment shall not be so construed as to affect the election or term of any Senator chosen before it becomes valid as part of the Constitution.

Proposed 18 December 1917, ratified 16 January 1919.

*ARTICLE XVIII

Liquors, for beverage purposes, prohibited—1. After one year from the ratification of this article the manufacture, sale, or transportation of intoxicating liquors within, the importation thereof into, or the exportation thereof from the United States and all territory subject to the jurisdiction thereof for beverage purposes is hereby prohibited.

Legislation to enforce this article—2. The Congress and the several States shall have concurrent power to enforce this article by appropriate legislation.

Ratification—3. This article shall be inoperative unless it shall have been ratified as an amendment to the Constitution by the legislatures of the several States, as provided in the Constitution within seven years from the date of the submission hereof to the States by the Congress.

Proposed 4 June 1919, ratified 18 August 1920.

ARTICLE XIX

The right of citizens to vote shall not be denied because of sex—The right of citizens of the United States to vote shall not be denied or abridged by the United States or by any State on account of sex.

Congress shall have power to enforce this article by appropriate legislation.

Proposed 2 March 1932, ratified 23 January 1933.

ARTICLE XX

SECTION 1

Terms of President, Vice-President, Senators and Representatives—The terms of the President and Vice-President shall end at noon on the 20th day of January, and the terms of Senators and Representatives at noon on the 3d day of January, of the years in which such terms would have ended if this article had not been ratified; and the terms of their successors shall then begin.

SECTION 2

Time of assembling Congress—The Congress shall assemble at least once in every year, and such meeting shall begin at noon on the 3d day of January, unless they shall by law appoint a different day.

SECTION 3

Filling vacancy in office of President—If, at the time fixed for the beginning of the term of the President, the President elect shall have died, the Vice-President elect shall become President. If a President shall not have been chosen before the time fixed for the beginning of his term, or if the President elect shall have failed to qualify, then the Vice-President elect shall act as President until a President shall have qualified; and the Congress may by law provide for the case wherein neither a President elect nor a Vice-President elect shall have qualified, declaring who shall then act as President, or the manner in which one who is to act shall be selected, and such person shall act accordingly until a President or Vice-President shall have qualified.

---

*Repealed by Article XXI, effective 5 December 1933.

Section 4

Power of Congress in Presidential succession – The Congress may by law provide for the case of the death of any of the persons from whom the House of Representatives may choose a President whenever the right of choice shall have devolved upon them, and for the case of the death of any of the persons from whom the Senate may choose a Vice-President whenever the right of choice shall have devolved upon them.

Section 5

Time of taking effect – Sections 1 and 2 shall take effect on the 15th day of October following the ratification of this article.

Section 6

Ratification – This article shall be inoperative unless it shall have been ratified as an amendment to the Constitution by the legislatures of three fourths of the several States within seven years from the date of its submission.

Proposed 20 February 1933, ratified 5 December 1933.

ARTICLE XXI

Section 1

Repeal of Prohibition Amendment – The eighteenth article of amendment to the Constitution of the United States is hereby repealed.

Section 2

Transportation of intoxicating Liquors – The transportation or importation into any State, Territory, or possession of the United States for delivery or use therein of intoxicating liquors, in violation of the laws thereof, is hereby prohibited.

Section 3

Ratification – This article shall be inoperative unless it shall have been ratified as an amendment to the Constitution by conventions in the several States, as provided in the Constitution, within seven years from the date of the submission hereof to the States by the Congress.

Proposed 24 March 1947, ratified 27 February 1951.

ARTICLE XXII

Section 1

Term of the office of President – No person shall be elected to the office of the President more than twice, and no person who has held the office of President, or acted as President, for more than two years of a term to which some other person was elected President shall be elected to the office of the President more than once. But this Article shall not apply to any person holding the office of President when this Article was proposed by the Congress, and shall not prevent any person who may be holding the office of President, or acting as President, during the term within which this Article becomes operative from holding the office of President or acting as President during the remainder of such term.

SECTION 2

Ratification—This article shall be inoperative unless it shall have been ratified as an amendment to the Constitution by the legislatures of three fourths of the several States within seven years from the date of its submission to the States by the Congress.

Proposed 16 June 1960, ratified 29 March 1961.

ARTICLE XXIII

SECTION 1

District of Columbia—The District constituting the seat of Government of the United States shall appoint in such manner as the Congress may direct:

A number of electors of President and Vice President equal to the whole number of Senators and Representatives in Congress to which the District would be entitled if it were a State, but in no event more than the least populous State; they shall be in addition to those appointed by the States, but they shall be considered, for the purposes of the election of President and Vice President, to be electors appointed by a State; and they shall meet in the District and perform such duties as provided by the twelfth article of amendment.

SECTION 2

Congress given power to enforce this article—The Congress shall have power to enforce this article by appropriate legislation.

Proposed 27 August 1962, ratified 23 January 1964.

ARTICLE XXIV

SECTION 1

Relating to the qualifications of electors—The rights of citizens of the United States to vote in any primary or other election for President or Vice President, for electors for President or Vice-President, or for Senator or Representative in Congress, shall not be denied or abridged by the United States or any State by reason of failure to pay any poll tax or other tax.

SECTION 2

Congress given power to enforce this article—The Congress shall have power to enforce this article by appropriate legislation.

Proposed 6 January 1965, ratified 23 February 1967.

ARTICLE XXV

SECTION 1

Vice-President to become President—In case of the removal of the President from office or of his death or resignation, the Vice-President shall become President.

SECTION 2

President to nominate Vice-President when vacancy in office of Vice-President—Whenever there is a vacancy in the office of the Vice-President, the President shall nominate a Vice-President who shall take office upon confirmation by a majority vote of both Houses of Congress.

SECTION 3

President unable to discharge duties; Vice-President to be Acting President – Whenever the President transmits to the President pro tempore of the Senate and the Speaker of the House of Representatives his written declaration that he is unable to discharge the powers and duties of his office, and until he transmits to them a written declaration to the contrary, such powers and duties shall be discharged by the Vice-President as Acting President.

SECTION 4

President unable to discharge duties: how determined – Whenever the Vice-President and a majority of either of the principal officers of the executive departments or of such other body as Congress may by law provide, transmit to the President pro tempore of the Senate and the Speaker of the House of Representatives their written declaration that the President is unable to discharge the powers and duties of his office, the Vice-President shall immediately assume the powers and duties of the office as Acting President.

Thereafter, when the President transmits to the President pro tempore of the Senate and the Speaker of the House of Representatives his written declaration that no inability exists, he shall resume the powers and duties of his office unless the Vice-President and a majority of either the principal officers of the executive department or of such other body as Congress may by law provide, transmit within four days to the President pro tempore of the Senate and the Speaker of the House of Representatives their written declaration that the President is unable to discharge the powers and duties of his office. Thereupon Congress shall decide the issue, assembling within forty-eight hours for that purpose if not in session. If the Congress, within twenty-one days after receipt of the latter written declaration, or, if Congress is not in session, within twenty-one days after Congress is required to assemble, determines by two-thirds vote of both Houses that the President is unable to discharge the powers and duties of his office, the Vice-President shall continue to discharge the same as Acting President; otherwise, the President shall resume the powers and duties of his office.

Proposed 23 March 1971, ratified 1 July 1971.

ARTICLE XXVI

SECTION 1

The right of citizens eighteen years of age or older to vote – The right of citizens of the United States, who are eighteen years of age or older, to vote shall not be denied or abridged by the United States or by any State on account of age.

SECTION 2

Congress given power to enforce this article – The Congress shall have power to enforce this article by appropriate legislation.

Proposed 22 March 1972, ratification pending.

ARTICLE XXVII

SECTION 1

The equality of rights under law shall not be denied because of sex—Equality of rights under law shall not be denied or abridged by the United States or any State on account of sex.

SECTION 2

Congress given power to enforce this article—The Congress shall have the power to enforce by appropriate legislation the provisions of this article.

SECTION 3

Time of taking effect—This Amendment shall take effect two years after the date of ratification.

GLOSSARY / INDEX

A

Accommodation–process of achieving temporary working agreements between parties who are in present or potential conflict, 33–35

Achieved role; *see* Role

Achieved status; *see* Status

Adams, John, 116

Age of Reason, 2, 4, 12

Aggregation–a physical gathering together of people without a shared sense of identity or interaction, 53

Agnew, Spiro, 123

Amalgamation; *see* Race

American Constitution; *see* Constitution, U.S.

American Independent Party, 124, 125

American Indians, 49

American Medical Association, 126

Annihilation–as pattern or race or ethnic relations, 145

Anomie–a condition in which the individual has no firm sense of belonging to anything dependable, 157

Anthropology–the all-embracing study of man and society, usually restricted to study of nonliterate groups, 1, 6, 7, 9

Anti-urban bias, 62–63

Aquinas, St. Thomas, 1, 13

Arbitration, 34

Archaeology, 9

Aristocracy–rule by a few elite citizens, 107

Aristotle, 11, 13, 15, 106

Articles of Confederation, 122

Asch, Solomon, 8

Ascribed role; *see* Role

Ascribed status; *see* Status

Assimilation–process whereby persons or groups become culturally similar, 35

Associations–formal organizations formed around particular interests and designed to accomplish particular goals, 51, 55–56

Audience–a group to which stimuli are directed; a

Audience–*Cont.*
group with interest focused upon a particular phenomenon, 151

Authoritarianism, 107, 115

Autistic children, 25

B

Bacon, Francis, 2, 4

Baker v. Carr, 113

Balance of trade, 96, 98

Barron v. Baltimore, 114

Becker, Howard, 157–58

Behavioral sciences–psychology, anthropology, and sociology so termed because of their interrelationships in exploring social behavior, 7, 14

Benedict, Ruth, 14

Berkeley, George, 15

Berry, Brewton, 144

Bicameral legislature–law-making body with two houses, 118–19

Bill of Rights, 107, 113, 119

Bismarck, Prince Otto von, 19

Black suffrage–the right to vote extended to the members of the black race, 108, 111

Boas, Franz, 14

Bodin, Jean, 106

Break in transportation theory of city location, 60

Brokerage party–compromise party made up of several factions, 123

Brown v. Topeka Board of Education, 118, 125

Bryan, William Jennings, 125

Burgess, Ernest W., 60

C

Calvinism, 13, 91

Capital, 76, 77

Capitalism, 95, 98–101, 104

Caste, 2, 68

Category–a classification of persons who share some common characteristic, 53

Central disciplines, 7